COACH YOUR TEAM TO SCORE MORE GOALS

Data-Driven Analysis of Europe's Elite Used to Create 16 Training Sessions

Written by
Paco Cordobés

Published by

COACH YOUR TEAM TO SCORE MORE GOALS

Data-Driven Analysis of Europe's Elite Used to Create 16 Training Sessions

First Published July 2023 by SoccerTutor.com
info@soccertutor.com | www.SoccerTutor.com

UK: 0208 1234 007 | **US:** (305) 767 4443 | **ROTW:** +44 208 1234 007
ISBN: 978-1-910491-64-5

Copyright: SoccerTutor.com Limited © 2023. All Rights Reserved.

All rights reserved. No part of this publication may be reproduced, stored in a retrieval system, or transmitted in any form or by any means, electronic, mechanical, photocopy, recording or otherwise, without prior written permission of the copyright owner. Nor can it be circulated in any form of binding or cover other than that in which it is published and without similar condition including this condition being imposed on a subsequent purchaser.

Author: Paco Cordobés

Editor: Alex Fitzgerald - SoccerTutor.com

Diagrams Design by SoccerTutor.com
All diagrams in this book have been created using Tactics Manager Software - Available from www.SoccerTutor.com

Note: While every effort has been made to ensure the technical accuracy of the content of this book, neither the author nor publishers can accept any responsibility for any injury or loss sustained as a result of the use of this material.

CONTENTS

Meet the Author: Paco Cordobés (UEFA Pro Coach) 8
Introduction 9
Champions League Group Stage Goals (2022-2023 Season) 10
How did we Compile the Statistics for this Book? 11
Statistics → Tactical Examples → Training Sessions 12
Pitch Zones: Determining Where Goals are Assisted and Scored From 13
Summary of Key Statistical Findings in Our Research 14
Diagram Key & Coaching Format 15

SET PLAY GOALS:
Breakdown of the Type of Set Play Goals Scored 16

Type of Goal: Open Play and Set Plays 17
Type of Goal: Free Kick or Corner Kick? 18
Set Play Goals: Breakdown or the Type or Set Play Goals Scored 19

Tactical Examples: 1. Corner Kicks (10.9% Of Goals) 20
Goal Example 1 (FC Barcelona) 21
Goal Example 2 (Napoli) 22

Training Session 1 for Corner Kicks 23
1. Delivery Options and Signals, Runs, and Player Roles in an Unopposed Corner Kick Practice 24
2. Corner Kick Practice in a 10v7 +GK Functional Practice with Counter Attacks 25
3. Short Corner Kick Variations in an Unopposed Corner Kick Practice 26
4. Short Corner Kick Variations in a 10v7 +GK Functional Practice with Counter Attacks 27

TYPE OF ASSIST:
Breakdown of How Goals are Created 28

Type of Assist: Breakdown of How Goals are Created 29

Tactical Examples: 2. Cut Backs (20.0% Of Goals) 30
Goal Example 1 (Real Madrid) 31
Goal Example 2 (Manchester City) 32

Training Session 2 for Cut Backs 33
1. 3v1 in Wide Area, Overlapping Full Back Run and Cut Back for Oncoming Runners to Score 34
2. Pass to Winger Out Wide for 1v1 and Cut Back for Oncoming Runners to Score 35
3. Pass to Winger for 1v1 High Up the Flank and Cut Back to Edge of the Box for Shot 36
4. Cut Backs and Finishing in a 6v6 (+2) Four Corner Area Game 37

Tactical Examples: 3. Through Passes (17.1% Of Goals) 38
Goal Example 1 (Bayern Munich) 39
Goal Example 2 (Napoli) 40

Training Session 3 for Through Passes 41
1. 4v4 Possession in Centre Circle + Through Pass to the Forward in a 1v1 (+GK) Situation 42
2. 5 (+1) v 4 in Midfield Zone + Through Pass in Behind for Forward's 1v1 vs GK 43
3. Build-up Play in Defensive Half + Through Pass into Attacking Half in a 4v4 (+2) +GKs Conditioned Game 44
4. Build-up Play in Defensive Half + Through Pass into Attacking Half in a 7v7 +GKs Conditioned Game 45

ZONE OF ASSISTS:
What Specific Pitch Zones are Assists Played from? 46
Zone of Assists: What Specific Pitch Zone are Assists Played from? 47

Tactical Examples: 4. Goals Assisted from Side of Box (18.4% Of Goals) .. 48
Goal Example 1 (FC Barcelona) 49
Goal Example 2 (Manchester City) 50

Training Session 4 for Goals Assisted from Side of Box 51
1. Double One-Two with Through Pass into Side of Box, Cut Back, and Finish in Pairs 52
2a. Wide Combination, Wing Play into Side of Box, and Cut Back for Finish in a 2v2 Situation 53
2b. Wide Combination, Midfield Run into Side of Box, and Cut Back for Finish in a 2v2 Situation .. 54
2c. Wide Combination, Third Man Run into Side of Box, and Cut Back for Finish in a 2v2 Situation 55
3. Assists from the Side of Box Areas in a 6v6 (+2) +GKs Conditioned Small Sided Game 56

Tactical Examples: 5. Goals Assisted from Wide Areas (18.4% Of Goals) .. 57
Goal Example 1A (Bayern Munich) 58
Goal Example 1B (PSG) 59
Goal Example 2A (Manchester City) 60
Goal Example 2B (Inter) 61

Training Session 5 for Goals Assisted from Wide Areas 62
1. One-Two to Receive Wide, Deep Cross into Box from Low Wide Zone, Control and Finish 63
2. One-Two, Pass Wide to Winger, Dribble into High Wide Zone, Cross and Finish 64
3. Conditioned 6v6 (+4) +GKs SSG with Diagonally Opposite Goals and Multiple Wide Zones for Assists 65
4. Assists from Wide Areas in a Conditioned 7v7 +GKs SSG with Wide Zones 66

Tactical Examples: 6. Goals Assisted from Centre Space (13.2% Of Goals) 67
Goal Example 1 (Liverpool) 68
Goal Example 2 (PSG) 69

Training Session 6 for Goals Assisted from Centre Space 70
1. Pass, Turn in Centre Space, Through Pass for Run in Behind, and Finish 71
2. Different Passing Options in the Centre Space, Turn, Through Pass in Behind, and Finish 72
3. Play Through the Centre Space in a 4v2 Situation and Finish with 2v1 in the Box 73
4. Goals Assisted from the Centre Space in a 6v6 (+2) +GKs Narrow Conditioned Game 74

Tactical Examples: 7. Goals Assisted from Half Spaces (10.9% Of Goals) . 75
Goal Example 1 (Manchester City) 76
Goal Example 2 (PSG) 77

Training Session 7 for Goals Assisted from Half Spaces 78
1. Receive in the Half Space and Deliver an Accurate Pass into the Box for a Finish 79
2. Pass Inside, then into the Half Space for a Through Pass into the Box for a Finish 80
3. Goals Assisted from the Half Space Zones in a 4v4 (+2) +GK Conditioned Small Sided Game ... 81
4. Goals Assisted from the Half Space Zones in an 8v8 +GKs Conditioned Game 82

ZONE OF GOALS:
What Specific Pitch Zones are Goals Scored from? 83
Zone of Goals: What Specific Pitch Zones are Goals Scored from? 84

Tactical Examples: 8. Goals Assisted from Centre of Box (72.7% Of Goals) 85
Goal Example 1A (AC Milan) - Front Centre of Box 86
Goal Example 1B (Bayern Munich) - Front Centre of Box 87
Goal Example 2A (FC Barcelona) - Back Centre of Box 88
Goal Example 2B (AC Milan) - Back Centre of Box 89

Training Session 8A for Goals Scored from FRONT Centre of Box (52.3% of Goals) 90
1. 3 (+1) v 1 Possession in the Centre + Play into the Front Centre of the Box for a 2v1 Finish 91
2. 4v1 Possession in the Centre, Pass Wide, and Score in the Front Centre of the Box with a 1v1 Situation 92
3. Score in the Front Centre of the Box in a Multi-Zone 4v4 (+3) +GKs SSG with Wide Crossing Zones 93
4. Score in the Front Centre of the Box and Quick Changes of Direction in a 7v7 +GKs SSG 94

Training Session 8B for Goals Scored from BACK Centre of Box (20.4% of Goals) 95
1. Attacking Pattern of Play with Finish in Back Centre of Box Zone with Assist or Individual Play 96
2. Attacking Pattern of Play with Finish in Back Centre of Box Zone with Assists from Wide Players 97
3. Score Goals from Back Centre of Box Zone in an 8v8 (+1) +GKs Game with Corner Crossing Zones 98
4. Score Goals from Back Centre of Box Zone in a Conditioned Tactical Game with Corner Zones .. 99

TACTICAL ASPECT:
What Tactics are Used to Score the Most Goals?.................100
Tactical Aspect: What Tactics are Used to Score the Most Goals?..............................101

Tactical Examples: 9. Build-up Play/Attacks (31.6% Of Goals)..............103
Goal Example 1/5 (Real Madrid) - Play Through Lines = 25 of 304 Goals Scored (8.2%)..........104
Goal Example 2/5 (Real Madrid) - Switch of Play = 21 of 304 Goals Scored (6.9%).................105
Goal Example 3/5 (Real Madrid) - Attack Wide/Crossing = 21 of 304 Goals Scored (6.9%).......106
Goal Example 4/5 (Inter) - Attack Through Centre = 15 of 304 Goals Scored (4.9%).............107
Goal Example 5/5 (Liverpool) - Long Pass = 14 of 304 Goals Scored (4.6%)......................108

Training Session 9A for Play Through Lines & Attack Through Centre (13.1% of Goals)..109
1. Play Through the Lines and Attack Through the Centre Pattern of Play 110
2. Play Through the Lines (Zones) and in Behind in a Dynamic Functional Practice................111
3. Attack Through the Centre and Play in Behind in a 5v5 (+2) +GKs Small Sided Game 112
4. Complete 5 Passes and Attack Through the Centre in a Multi-Zone Two-Direction SSG........113

Training Session 9B for Attacking Out Wide / Crossing (6.9% of Goals) 114
1. Quick Combination Play Out Wide, One-Two, Overlap Run, Cross, and Finish..................115
2. Quick Combination Play, 2v1 Out Wide with One-Two and Overlap Run, Cross, and Finish vs Defender..116
3. Crossing and Finishing in a Multi-Zone 6v6 (+1) +GKs Conditioned Small Sided Game........117
4. Crossing and Finishing in a Multi-Zone 8v8 (+2) +GKs Conditioned Small Sided Game 118

Training Session 9C for Switch of Play & Long Passes (11.5% of Goals) ... 119
1. Long Passes and Switches of Play in a Functional Practice with Cut Back and Finish 120
2. Long Pass into the Receiving Zone and Attacking Combination Play to Finish in the Final Third 121
3. Long Passes into Opposition's Half and Second Ball Attacks Across (6v3 +GK) with 2v1 Zones..122
4. Switching Play from Zone to Zone and Creating 2v1 Situations for the Second Ball in a Conditioned Game...123

Tactical Examples: 10. Attacking Combination Play in Final Third (19.0% Of Goals)..124
Example 1 (FC Barcelona) - <u>CENTRE</u> 125
Example 2 (Napoli) - <u>WIDE</u>...126

Training Session 10A for Attacking Combination Play in Final Third Centre (14.1% of Goals)..127
1. Attacking Combination Play Around the Box, Through Pass, and Finish 128
2. Combination Play and Passing in Behind Defensive Line (Edge of Box) in a Functional 6v3 +GK Practice...129
3. Attacking Combination Play Through the Centre in a 4v4 (+1) +GK 3-Zone Functional Game ..130
4. Attacking Combination Play Through the Centre in a Two-Direction 8v8 (+2) +GKs 5-Zone Game..131

Training Session 10B for Attacking Combination Play in Final Third Wide (4.9% of Goals) 132
1. Attacking Combination Play Out Wide with Give & Go, Cross, and Finish 133
2. Attacking Combination Play Out Wide in a 4v3 +GK Functional Practice 134
3. Attacking Combination Play Out Wide in a 6v6 (+1) +GKs Game with Vertically Split Zones 135
4. Attacking Combination Play Out Wide in a Conditioned Multi-Zone Game..................... 136

Tactical Examples: 11. Counter Attacks (20.7% Of Goals) 137
Goal Example 1 (Liverpool): Counter Attack from Low Zone = 14 of 304 Goals Scored (4.6%) 138
Goal Example 2 (AC Milan): Counter Attack from Middle Zone = 34 of 304 Goals Scored (11.2%) . 139
Goal Example 3 (Manchester City) High Press + Counter = 15 of 304 Goals Scored (4.9%). 140

Training Session 11A for Counter Attacks from Low or Middle Zones (15.8% of Goals) 141
1. Defending a Free Kick + Fast Counter Attack from the Low Zone 142
2. Win the Ball and Launch a Fast Counter Attack in Dynamic 4 (+1) v 3 +GKs Functional Game .. 143
3. Win the Ball in the Defensive Half and Launch a Counter Attack in a 2-Zone 8v6 +GKs Transition Game 144
4. Win the Ball in the Defensive Half and Launch a Counter Attack in a 7v7 (+2) +GKs Conditioned Game 145

Training Session 11B for High Press + Counter (4.9% of Goals) 146
1. 3v1 Pressing High Up the Pitch + Fast Transition to Attack and Score 147
2. 4v2 Pressing High Up the Pitch + Fast Transition to Attack and Score 148
3. 5v5 Pressing High Up the Pitch + Fast Transition to Attack and Score..................... 149
4. High Press + Counter in a Dynamic 2-Zone Conditioned Transition Game.................... 150

COMBINED SESSION:
Using the Data to Create Training Sessions for Goal Scoring Efficiency 151
Using the Data to Create Training Sessions for Goal Scoring Efficiency 152

Combined Training Session Example 153
1. Pass to Winger Out Wide for 1v1 and Cut Back for Oncoming Runners to Score 153
2. Wide Combination, Wing Play into Side of Box, and Cut Back for Finish in a 2v2 Situation..... 154
3. Score in the Front Centre of the Box in a Multi-Zone 4v4 (+3) +GKs SSG with Wide Crossing Zones.. 155
4. Win the Ball in the Defensive Half and Launch a Counter Attack in a 2-Zone 8v6 +GKs Transition Game 156

MEET THE AUTHOR:
PACO CORDOBÉS (UEFA PRO COACH)

- **UEFA Pro Coach**
- **Degree in Physical Education**
- **Professional Football Coach & Analyst**
- **Owner of Football Coaching Education Company (abfutbol)**
- **Editor for Coaching Books and Magazines**
- **Former Professional Football Player**

Paco Cordobés (UEFA Pro Licence) is a professional football coach, academy football coach, analyst and football coaching book and magazine editor.

This provides Paco with a unique insight into what it takes to reach the elite level and what is required for coach and player development.

Roles and Experience in Football:

- Professional football analyst at Atlético Madrid, where I participated in top signings such as Lucas and Theo Hernández, and Saúl.

- Editor and publisher of 150+ titles of football coaching books and magazines (abfutbol).

- Books include working with World Cup winner Vincente Del Bosque, Champions League winner Rafa Benitez, Europa League winners Unai Emery and Julen Lopetegui, and Premier League winner Manuel Pellegrini.

- Professional football coach at various Spanish academies (U7 to U18).

- Professional football player at A.D. Alcorcón (Spain).

- Professional football analyst at AFC United Eskilstuna in Allsveskan (Swedish top tier league).

- Runner-up in Swedish Cup (Svenska Cupen) as coach in 2019.

INTRODUCTION

This book is born from the **idea of uniting two very interesting aspects for the coach, the analysis of the real game and the training**. Coming closer to understanding that most goals at the professional level start in training, there is a lot of work behind each goal.

Spectators think that most of the goals we see are the product of the individual quality of the players, of their inspiration. Much of this statement is so, the different decisions of the player are born from his intuition, but although we do not perceive it, another large part comes from previous training work, from practice. A player's decision making can be between two, four, ten decisions, but he can only choose one and it has to be the correct one. The previous correct training work leads to a correct final decision and increases the percentage of success in his actions. **With the real match goal examples and training sessions related to these goals, we hope to inspire the creativity of coaches to design tactical solutions**.

Each way to defend or attack is chosen based on the team you have, as a coach you must use training sessions that best suit your team. A coach can play with a game system, or a style, however, if he does not have the right players, it may be more difficult to achieve a successful result. For example, if you don't have fast players in your attack and you decide to play counter attacking football, everything will be more difficult for your team.

We focus on **Manchester City, Inter, Real Madrid, AC Milan, Bayern Munich, Napoli, Liverpool, PSG,** and **FC Barcelona**.

They are among the best teams in Europe, and the world. We present goal examples for various different attack types in different sections, all followed by the work behind this attacking style.

To analyse Champions League goals is to understand what modern football is like. In this book, we introduce ourselves into small details of how the best football teams play, and we relate it to a practical part to understand how to train to play like this.

Despite Big Data, GPS and the rest of the spectacular technologies, intelligence and thinking are still the most important part to work on in training. Football is increasingly being studied, analysed, but also thought about, both from the outside with the coaches preparing their matches, and inside the training pitch, with the decision-making of the footballers, which is why the training sessions have to be creative.

We are not trying to show a magic recipe, that is not our mission. We try to make the coaches who read this book think. The **question is how the best teams and coaches in the world score their goals, and then we present ideas for how to train these methods**. In this way, I want coaches who read this book to be inspired to look for solutions for their attacking play. We must understand that goals do not come by chance, but by the way your team trains, **"How you train is how you play. That's how you play, that's how you score."**

I hope coaches enjoy this book because it is full of examples and tactical solutions, and ideas to do other original exercises.

CHAMPIONS LEAGUE GROUP STAGE GOALS (2022-2023 SEASON)

304 Goals in 96 Matches

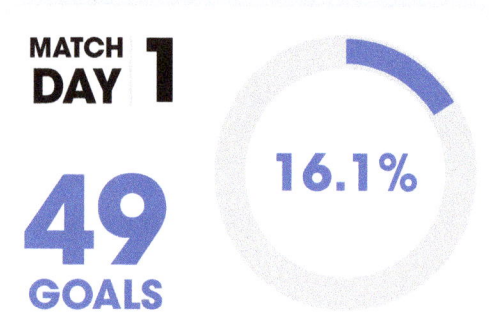

MATCH DAY 1
49 GOALS
16.1%

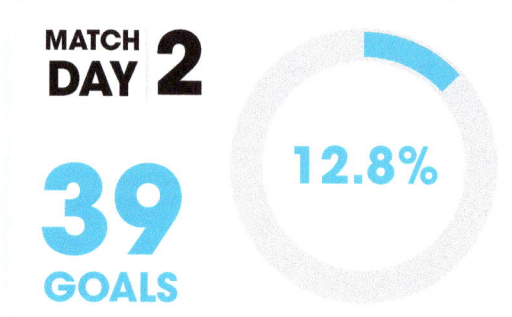

MATCH DAY 2
39 GOALS
12.8%

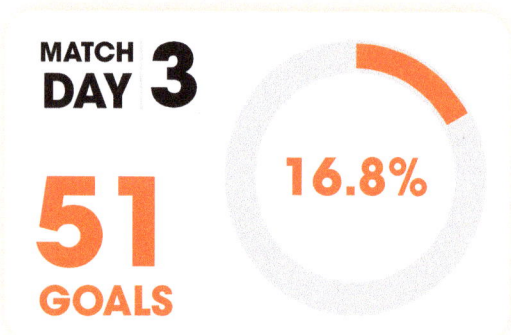

MATCH DAY 3
51 GOALS
16.8%

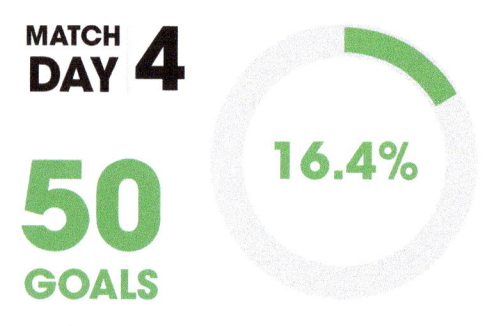

MATCH DAY 4
50 GOALS
16.4%

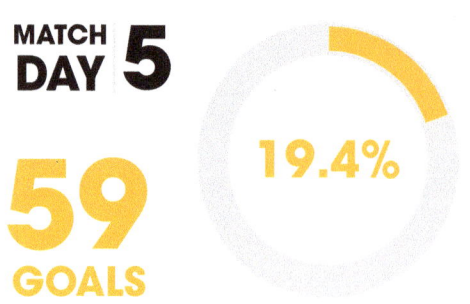

MATCH DAY 5
59 GOALS
19.4%

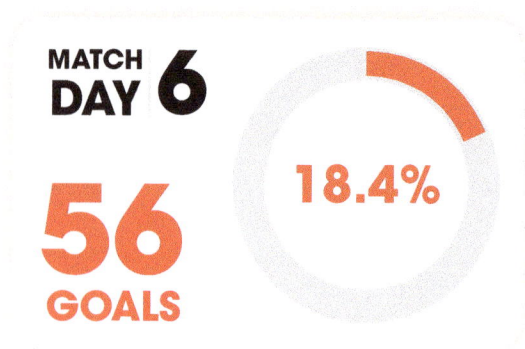

MATCH DAY 6
56 GOALS
18.4%

HOW DID WE COMPILE THE STATISTICS FOR THIS BOOK?

The data and statistics is the key to the book, with all the goals from the group stage of the 2022/23 Champions League viewed and analysed.

They were then classified based on different categories:

- **Type of Goal**
- **Type of Assist**
- **Pitch Zone of Assist**
- **Pitch Zone Goal Was Scored (Finished)**
- **Tactical Aspect for Each Goal Scored**

Based on these premises, different classifications have been made to delve deeper into the following question…

HOW ARE GOALS SCORED AT THE ELITE LEVEL?

The "goal" is the summary of everything that has happened before achieving it. By analysing the goals of some of the best teams in world football, we can discover how these teams attack and why they play like this.

From this, we enter the second large part of this book, which is the full progressive training sessions. As mentioned in the introduction, we do not seek to give magical solutions. The aim is to inspire coaches, to make them think, so that they are clear, that finding the right tasks in training will have an optimal result in the achievements of their team.

It is evident that we have focused on looking at only one major aspect of the game, the attacking phase (and counter attack). We have analysed all the goals thoroughly and classified them because we wanted to study the attacking play of the top teams in Europe, but with small details within the explanations of the tactical examples, we have also mentioned defensive errors in some cases.

Therefore, another of the functions of this book is that it serves to realise that most of the goals that occur in professional football come in part due to defensive errors that must also be worked on.

As you can imagine, watching all the goals from so many teams and then classifying them is an "exhaustive" job, but it was necessary. It is the "scientific" test to know what is happening in modern elite football. Perhaps it would be good if there were more works of this type to delve deeper into the game, and by relation, into the type of training that makes the game better. I believe that this is what we, the authors, the publishers are for - to help coaches in these aspects, to give them clues, inspire them, help them to improve their training, and indirectly improve the game of football as a whole.

STATISTICS → TACTICAL EXAMPLES → TRAINING SESSIONS

1 Statistics

- **Data source from UEFA Champions League Group Stage matches during the 2022/2023 season.** Goal statistics collected by studying each of the 304 goals scored across the 96 matches (6th September - 2nd November 2022).
- Each goal was assessed and put into various categories: Type of goal, type of assist, pitch zone of assist, pitch zone where goal was scored from, and the tactical aspect for each goal scored.

2 Tactical Examples

- **Real match examples of top UEFA Champions League teams scoring a goal** using the relevant data statistic e.g. Goals scored from through passes, or goals scored from centre of box, etc.
- Each action, pass, individual movement with or without the ball, and the positioning of each player on the pitch including their body shape, are presented, along with a full description of the goal.

3 Training Sessions

- The statistical analysis and tactical examples are then used to create full progressive training sessions to coach the specific topic described. There are **16 Training Sessions included in the book which fully outline how to create and score goals**.
- You the coach can then implement the practices into your sessions, so your team can be more efficient in training and score more goals in competitive matches.

PITCH ZONES: DETERMINING WHERE GOALS ARE ASSISTED AND SCORED FROM

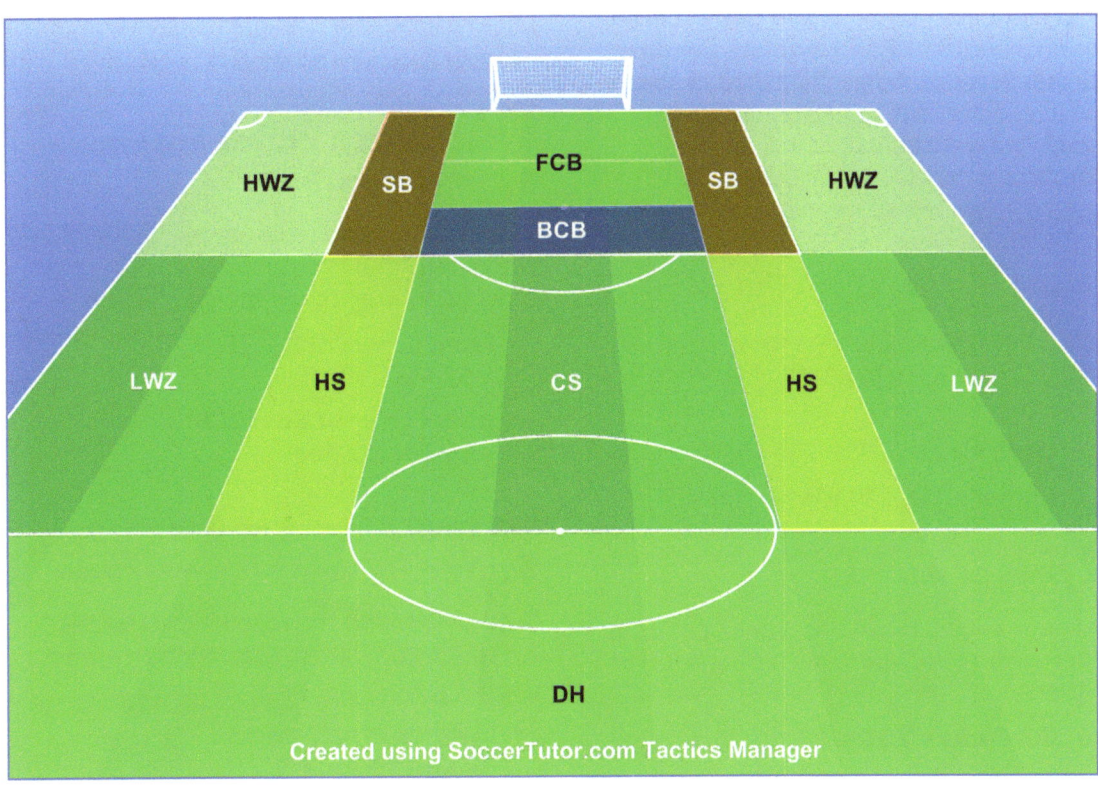

- **DH** = Defensive Half
- **LWZ** = Low Wide Zones
- **HS** = Half Spaces
- **CS** = Centre Space
- **HWZ** = High Wide Zones
- **SB** = Side of Box
- **FCB** = Front Centre of Box
- **BCB** = Back Centre of Box

This is how we divided the zones of the pitch before beginning our research.

When analysing each goal, we could then determine which zone the assist was played from, and which zone the goal was scored (finished) from.

This is valuable information because we can determine how and where most goals are created from, and where they are finished from. This can then be applied into your training so that you maximise the efficiency of your team to create chances and score goals.

SUMMARY OF KEY STATISTICAL FINDINGS IN OUR RESEARCH

From our analysis of all **304 goals scored during the 96 UEFA Champions League Group Stage matches (2022/2023 season)**, which you will see in full detail throughout book, we were able to come to many important conclusions about how the best teams in Europe score their goals.

Open Play and Set Plays

With our first simple breakdown of the goal statistics, we found the following key results:

- **Open Play = 77.3%** (235 goals)
- **Corner Kicks = 10.9%** (33 goals)

Types of Assists

After breaking down the types of assists, there were two types which clearly led all others:

- **Cut Backs = 20.0%** (61 goals)
- **Through Passes = 17.1%** (52 goals)

Which Pitch Zones are Assists Played from?

Space is very important for where goals come from and where goals are scored from, which helps you think about how you currently play, and position your players where they can give the best results.

Our statistical analysis showed the following leaders for which zone of the pitch assists were played from:

- **Side of Box = 18.4%** (56 goals)
- **Wide Areas = 18.4%** (56 goals)
- **Centre Space = 13.2%** (40 goals)
- **Half Spaces = 10.9%** (33 goals)

Which Pitch Zones are Goals Scored from?

The research showed two clear leaders when determining which zone of the pitch most goals are scored (finished) from:

- **Front Centre of Box (FCB) = 52.3%** (159 goals)
- **Back Centre of Box (BCB) = 20.4%** (62 goals)

Tactical Aspect of Each Goal Scored

Lastly, we found the following key statistics for which tactical aspects led to the most goals:

- **Build-up Play/Attacks = 31.6%** (96 goals)
- **Counter Attacks = 20.7%** (63 goals)
- **Attacking Combination Play in the Final Third = 19.1%** (58 goals)

The key statistical findings outlined here are the ones that we have then focused on for the book. We show goal examples from the top teams in the Champions League for each topic, followed by a full progressive training session for how to train your team to score more goals in that same way.

DIAGRAM KEY & COACHING FORMAT

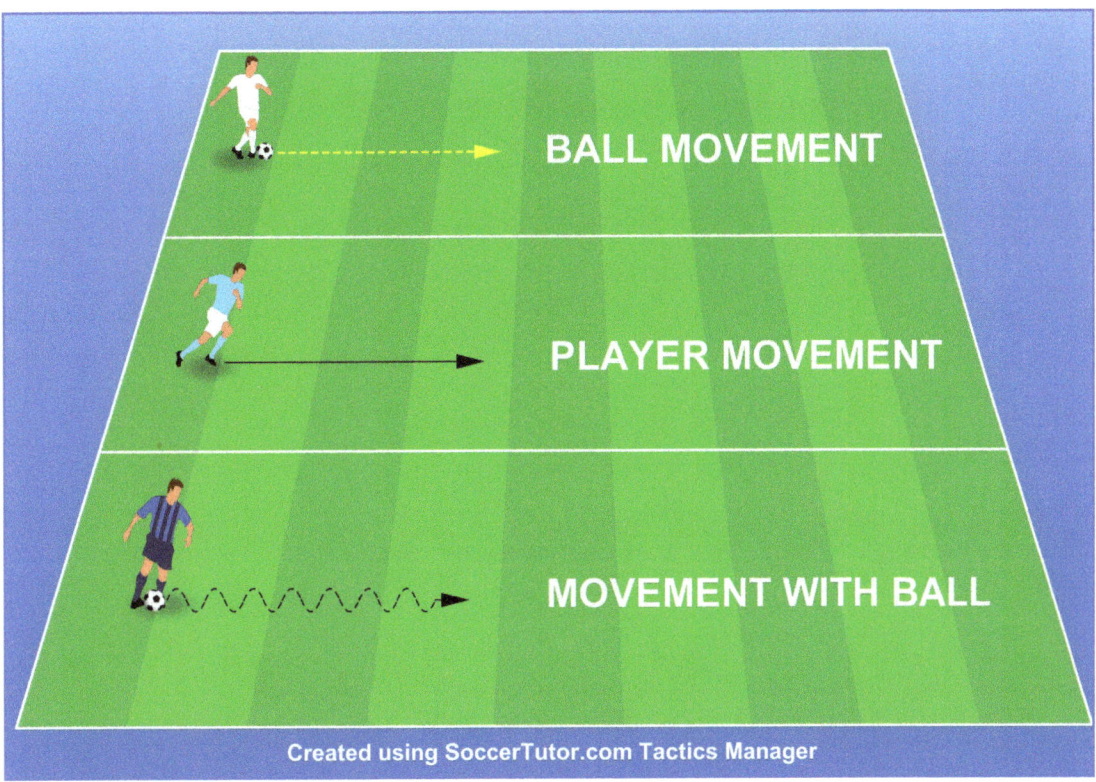

Tactical Examples

- The goal examples all come from the **UEFA Champions League Group Stage matches during the 2022/2023 season** (6th September - 2nd November 2022).
- Each action, pass, individual movement (with or without the ball) and the positioning of each player on the pitch including their body shape, are presented with a full description of the goal.

Training Sessions Based on Goal Type

- Technical and Functional Practices
- Small Sided Games
- Tactical Conditioned Games
- Name (Objective) and Full Description

SET PLAY GOALS

Breakdown of the Type of Set Play Goals Scored

Set Play Goals: Breakdown of the Type of Set Play Goals Scored

TYPE OF GOAL: OPEN PLAY AND SET PLAYS

Types of Goals Scored during the Champions League Group Stages in the 2022-2023 Season (304 Total Goals)

OPEN PLAY — 77.3% — **235 GOALS**

CORNER KICK — 10.9% — **33 GOALS**

PENALTY — 8.9% — **27 GOALS**

FREE KICK — 3.0% — **9 GOALS**

Set Play Goals: Breakdown of the Type of Set Play Goals Scored

TYPE OF GOAL: FREE KICK OR CORNER KICK?

Types of Set Play Goals Scored during the Champions League Group Stages in the 2022-2023 Season (42 Total Goals)

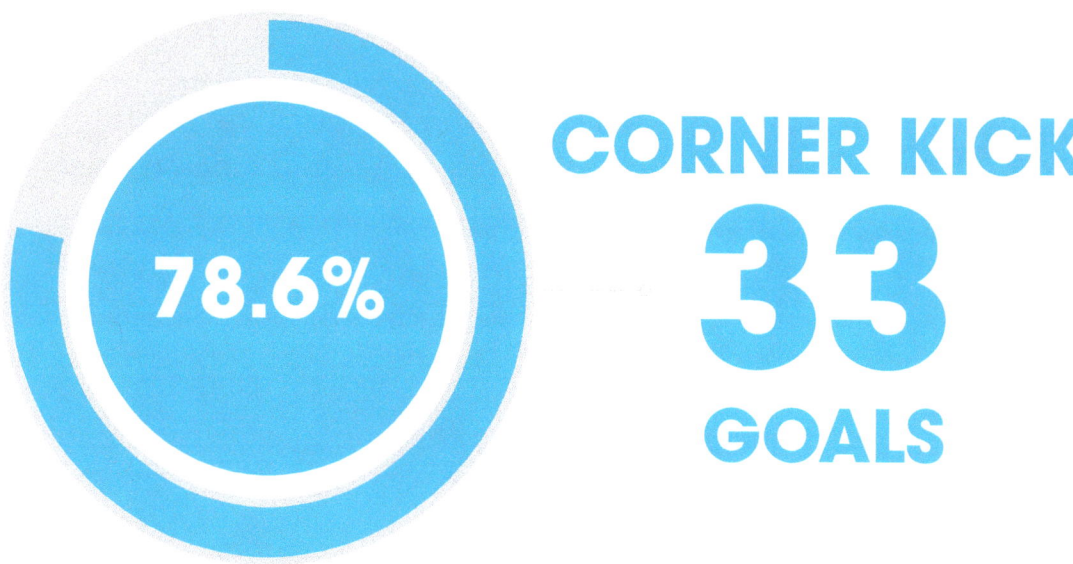

CORNER KICK
33
GOALS

78.6%

FREE KICK
9
GOALS

21.4%

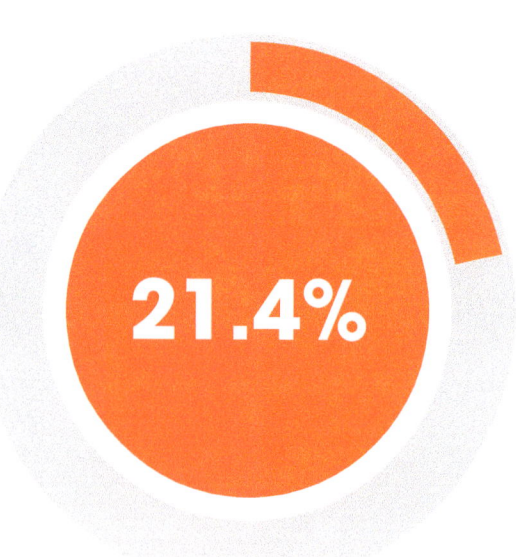

SET PLAY GOALS: BREAKDOWN OF THE TYPE OF SET PLAY GOALS SCORED

Specific Types of Set Play Goals Breakdown During the Champions League Group Stages in the 2022-2023 Season (42 Total Goals)

Direct Cross from Corner
20 GOALS — 47.6%

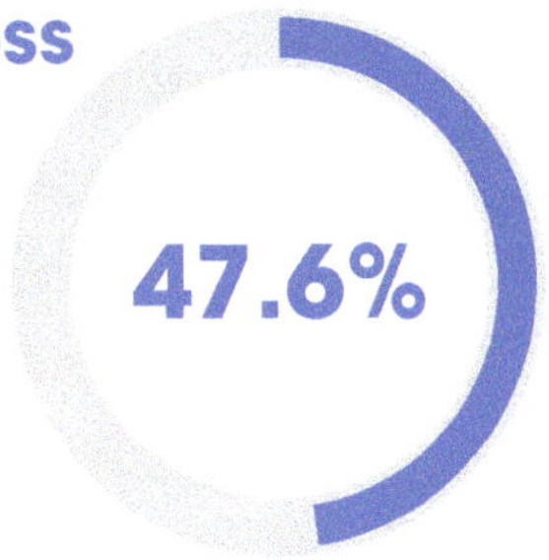

Corner (Flick-on/ 2nd Balls)
9 GOALS — 21.4%

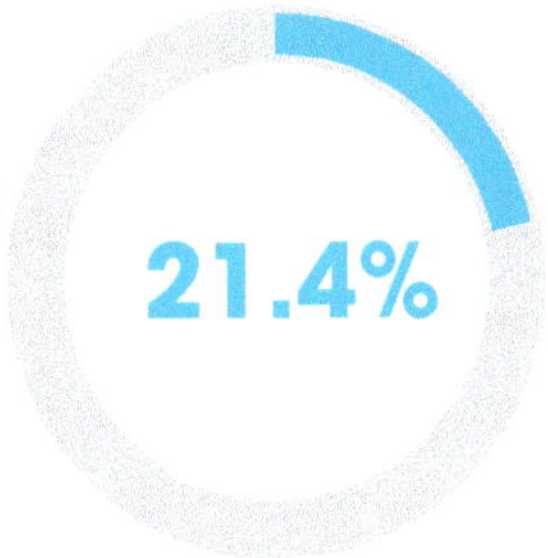

Indirect Free Kick
6 GOALS — 14.3%

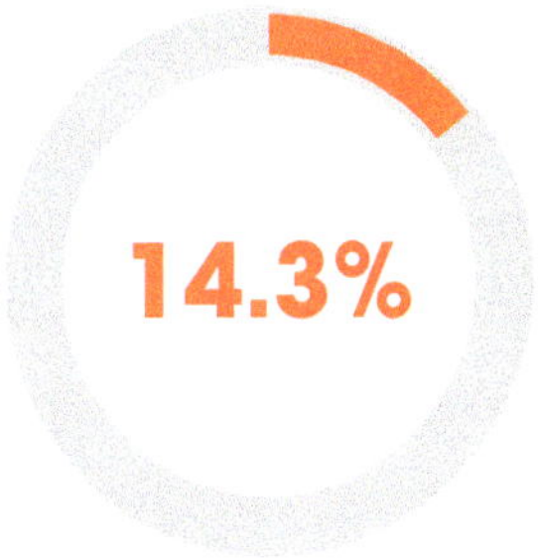

Short Corner + Cross
4 GOALS — 9.5%

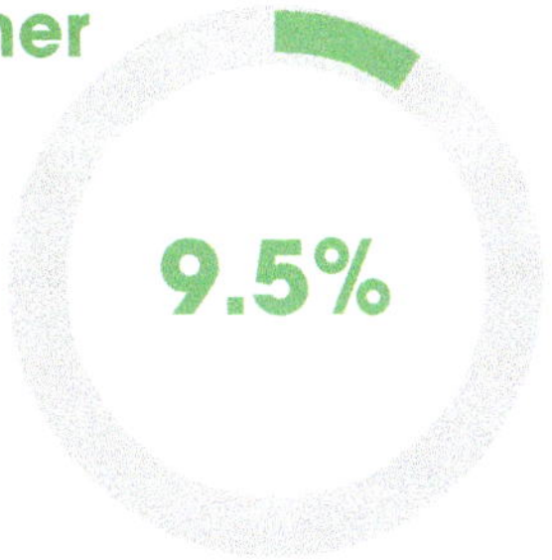

Direct Free Kick
3 GOALS — 7.1%

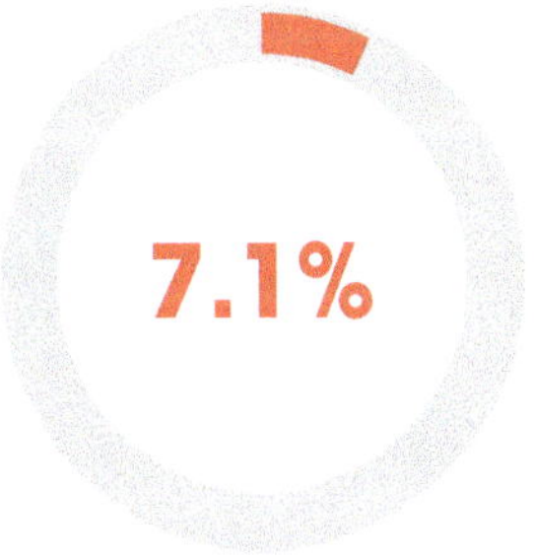

TACTICAL EXAMPLES

1. CORNER KICKS (10.9% OF GOALS)

Goals Scored from Corner Kicks

1. Corner Kicks = 10.9% of All Goals Scored

FC Barcelona 5-1 Viktoria Plzen (Kessié 13') - 07/09/2022

Goal Example 1 (FC Barcelona)

Corner Kicks = 33 of 304 Goals Scored (10.9%)

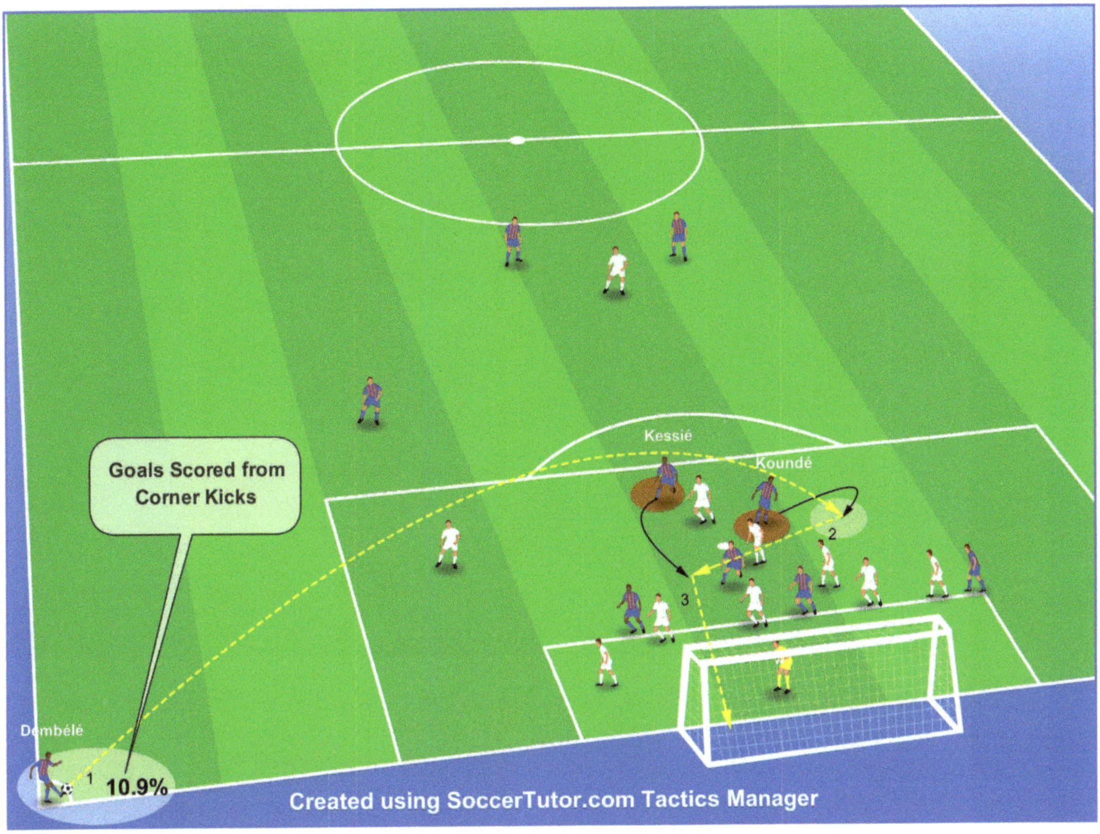

Description

Viktoria Plzen positioned 1 player in the near post zone, 4 players along the 6-yard box line, and 3 more players are man marking opponents.

FC Barcelona positioned 3 players along the 6-yard box line and 3 other players started from the penalty spot area.

Dembelé crosses the ball and the centre back **Koundé** moves back and away from it. He then attacks the cross to head it into the centre of the penalty area.

The central midfielder **Kessié** arrives with good timing and heads the ball into the bottom corner to score.

Key Aspects

1. With 3 players along the 6-yard box line, the 4 defenders' attention is occupied, leaving the penalty spot area more free.

2. Centre back **Koundé** uses good movement to win the first header.

3. As **Kessié** is moving forward and the defenders are static, he can easily win the header to score.

1. Corner Kicks = 10.9% of All Goals Scored

Ajax 1-6 Napoli (Di Lorenzo 33') - 04/10/2022

Goal Example 2 (Napoli)
Corner Kicks = 33 of 304 Goals Scored (10.9%)

Description

Napoli midfielder **Zieliński** passes to the winger **Kvaratskhelia** (short corner), who moves forward to receive and delivers a perfect cross into the centre of the box. They are able to do this before the 2 defenders can move to intercept or block the ball.

The right back **Di Lorenzo** makes a run around the back of an Ajax defender and leaps highest to win the aerial contest, heading the ball into the far top corner of the goal.

Key Aspects

1. The short corner forces 2 Ajax players to move outside of the box. Once you add the player defending the edge of the box and the forward in an advanced position for a potential counter attack, there are 4 players unable to defend the cross.

2. Of the 6 Ajax players left to defend, 3 are away from the goal defending the back post area against 3 Napoli players.

3. The winger **Kvaratskhelia** arrives from deep where there is no Ajax player (too far from box). This is an advantage to be able to receive the ball with time/space, raise his head, look up, and then deliver the perfect cross onto the head of right back **Di Lorenzo** in the centre of the box.

4. There is a 2v3 duel in the centre of the box (2 attackers vs 3 defenders). **Di Lorenzo** uses the speed from his movement to jump up above the defenders and beat them to the ball.

TRAINING SESSION 1

Corner Kicks
33 Goals

FOR CORNER KICKS (10.9% OF GOALS)

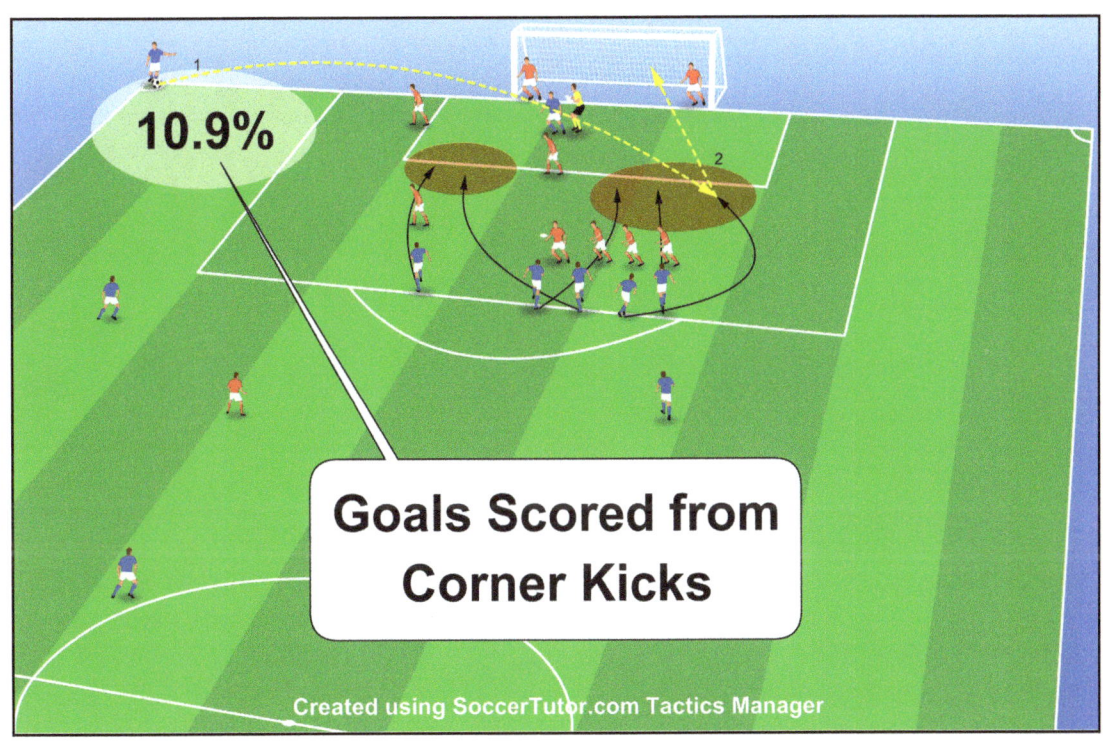

Goals Scored from Corner Kicks

Training Session 1: Corner Kicks (10.9% of All Goals Scored)

SESSION FOR THIS TACTICAL SITUATION (4 PRACTICES)

1. Delivery Options and Signals, Runs, and Player Roles in an Unopposed Corner Kick Practice

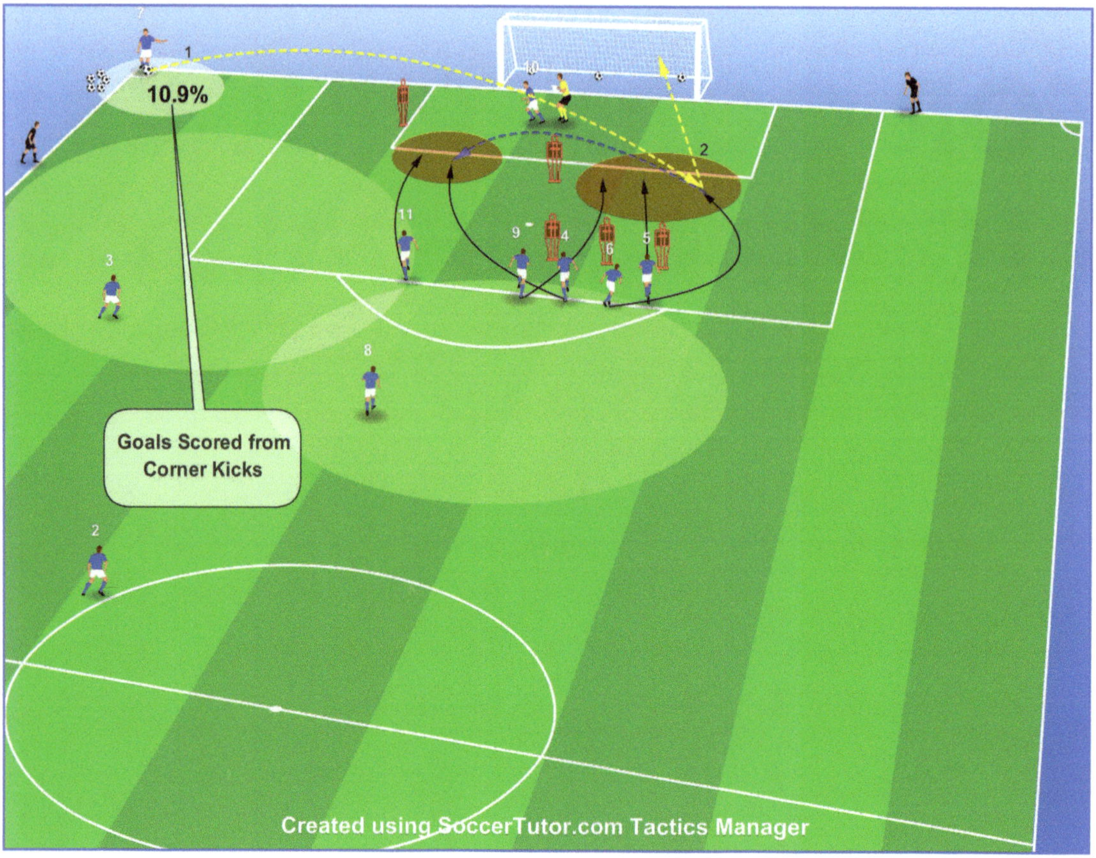

Goals Scored from Corner Kicks: 10.9%

Description

- The practice begins with a group meeting. The Coach and players establish 5 types of corners with 5 different signals. This signal is made by the player who takes the corner.

- In these signals, there must be 2 options:

  1 - Direct corner kick.
  2 - Short corner + cross.

- In both options, the player delivering the cross has 3 options, to send it to the near post, the far post, or the penalty spot.

- The players make different runs to cover all potential areas to score. The outside players are positioned for second balls.

- In this first practice, there are no active defenders. The objective is simply to practice the corner kick deliveries, the runs and to memorise the signals.

- The 5 mannequins represent the defenders and provide obstacles for the players' movements.

- Make sure to practice the corner kicks from both sides (left and right).

Training Session 1: Corner Kicks (10.9% of All Goals Scored)

PROGRESSION
2. Corner Kick Practice in a 10v7 +GK Functional Practice with Counter Attacks

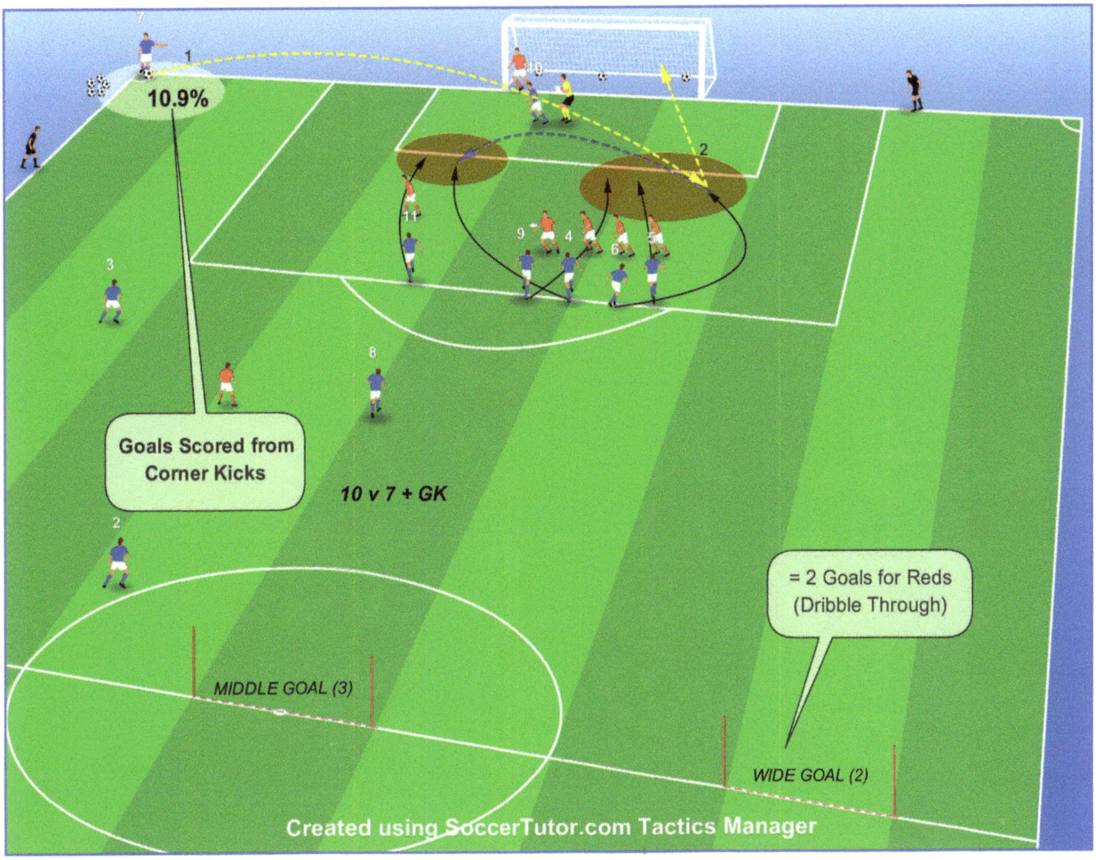

Description
- In this progression of the previous practice, we add 7 red defenders and remove the mannequins.
- The blue team can use any of the corner kicks that they have practiced in the previous practice to try and score a goal.
- The players in the box make the same runs as previously practiced. The outside players need to be prepared for any second balls from clearances. If this happens, the attack continues.
- If the reds are able to win the ball, they launch a fast counter attack.
- If they dribble through either of the 2 wide pole gates, they score 2 goals. If they dribble through the middle pole gate, they score 3 goals.

Training Session 1: Corner Kicks (10.9% of All Goals Scored)

PROGRESSION

3. Short Corner Kick Variations in an Unopposed Corner Kick Practice

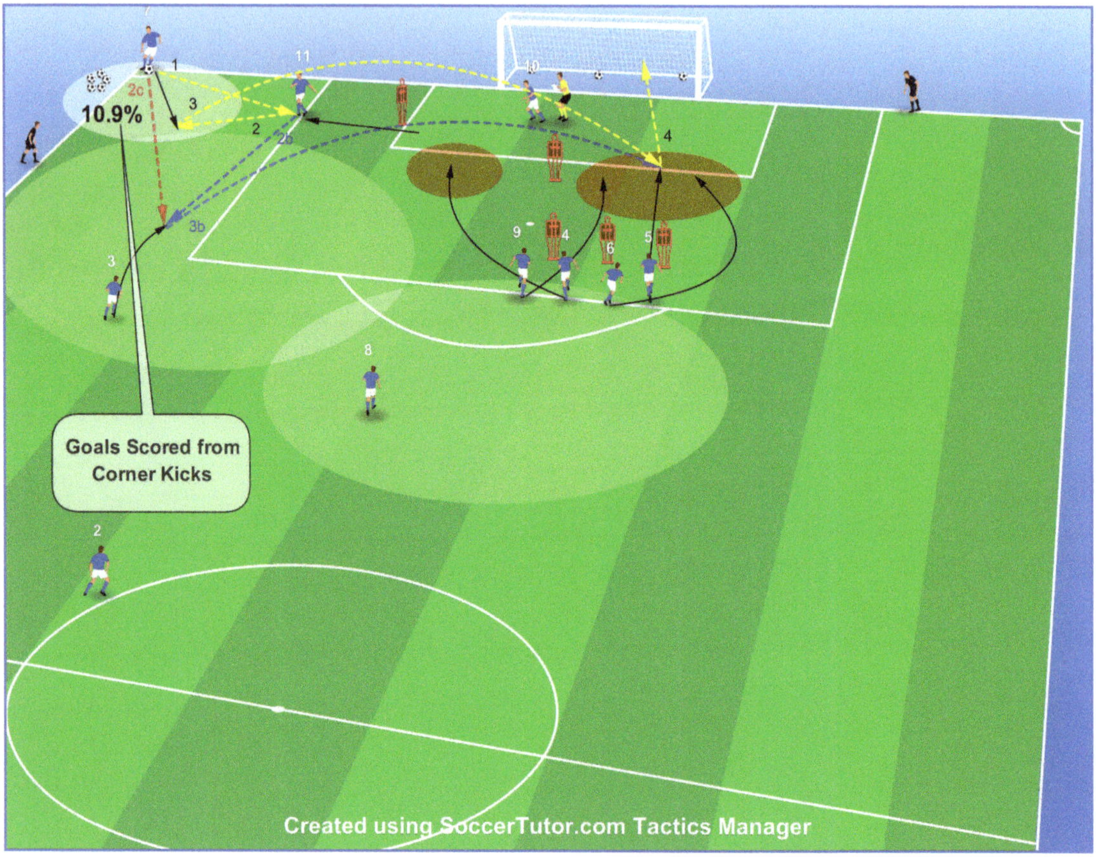

Description

- The Coach and players establish 5 types of corners with 5 different signals. This signal is made by the corner taker.
- **Example 1 (yellow arrows)** shows the corner kick taker playing a one-two and then crossing into the box.
- **Example 2 (red arrow)** shows a short corner played to the left back (3), who then delivers a cross into the box.
- **Example 3 (blue arrows)** shows the full back (3) receiving via a link player (11).
- The player crossing the ball has 3 options, to send it to the near post, the far post, or the penalty spot. The players make different runs to cover all potential areas to score. The outside players are positioned for second balls.
- In this practice, there are no active defenders. The objective is simply to practice the corner kick deliveries, the runs and to memorise the signals.
- Make sure to practice the corner kicks from both sides (left and right).

Training Session 1: Corner Kicks (10.9% of All Goals Scored)

PROGRESSION

4. Short Corner Kick Variations in a 10v7 +GK Functional Practice with Counter Attacks

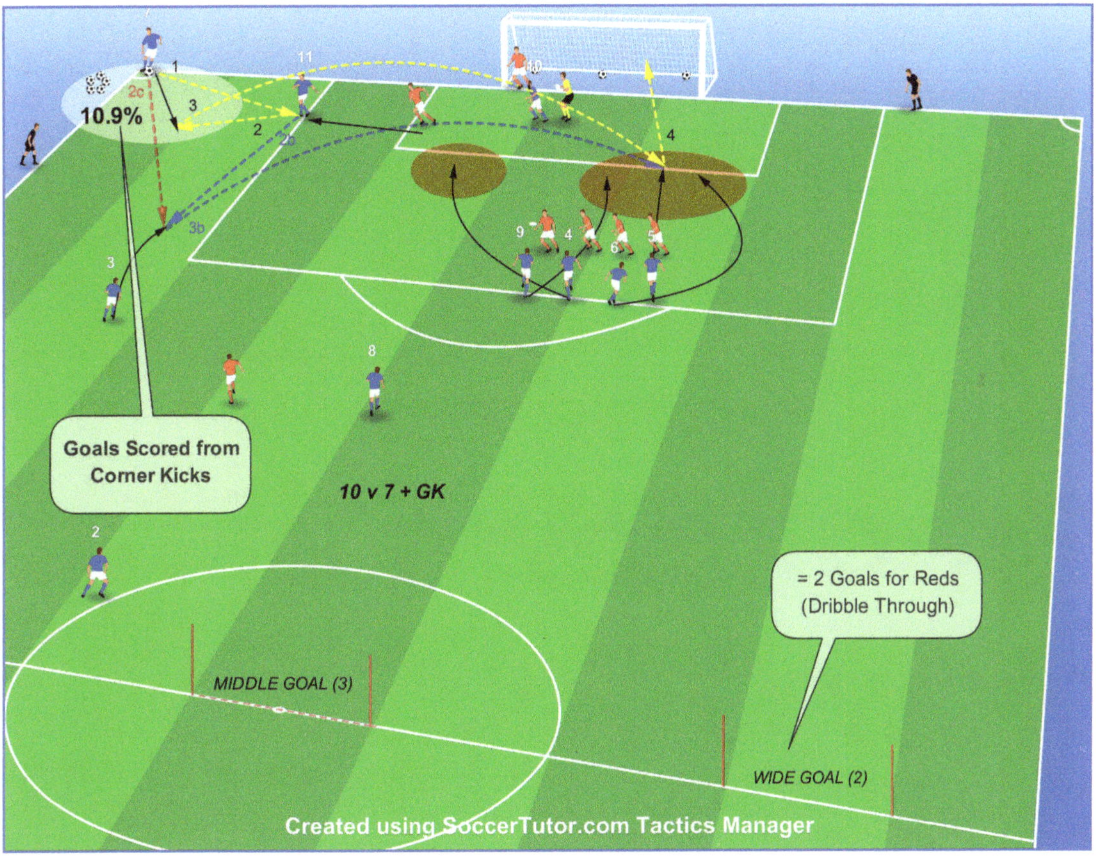

Description

- In this progression of the previous practice, we add 7 red defenders and remove the mannequins.
- The blue team can use any of the short corner kick routines that they have practiced in the previous practice to try and score a goal.
- The players in the box make the same runs as previously practiced. The outside players need to be prepared for any second balls from clearances. If this happens, the attack continues.
- If the reds are able to win the ball, they launch a fast counter attack.
- If they dribble through either of the 2 wide pole gates, they score 2 goals. If they dribble through the middle pole gate, they score 3 goals.

COACH YOUR TEAM TO SCORE MORE GOALS

TYPE OF ASSIST

Breakdown of How Goals are Created

Type of Assist: Breakdown of How Goals are Created

TYPE OF ASSIST: BREAKDOWN OF HOW GOALS ARE CREATED

Type of Assist for All Goals Scored During the Champions League Group Stages in the 2022-2023 Season (304 Total Goals)

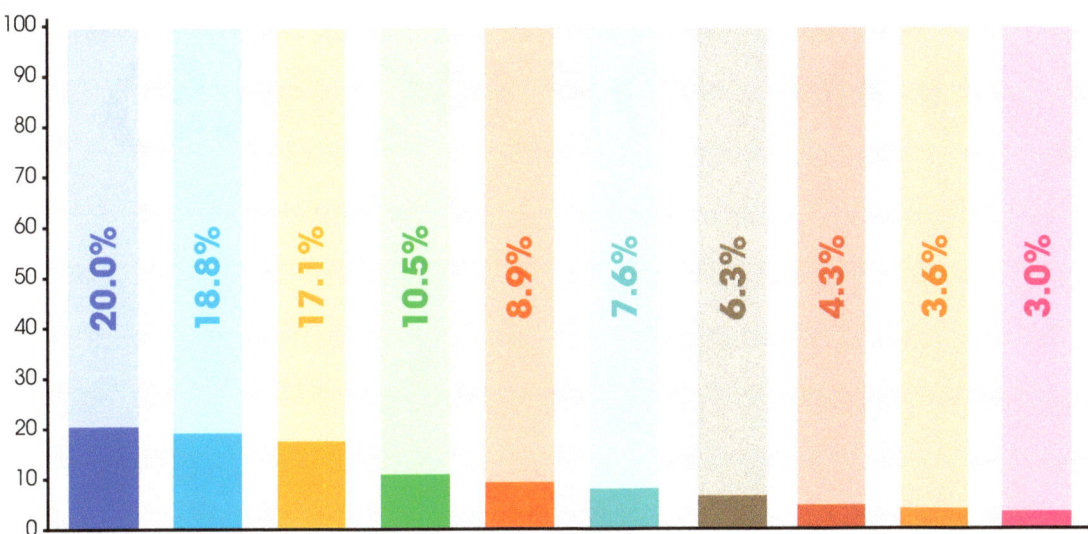

Cut Back	N/A	Through Pass	Simple Pass	Corner Kick
61 Goals	**57** Goals	**52** Goals	**32** Goals	**27** Goals

Deep Cross	Wide	Lay-off	By-line Cross	Long Pass
23 Goals	**19** Goals	**13** Goals	**11** Goals	**9** Goals

* N/A = Penalty/Free kick/Deflection/Rebound

TACTICAL EXAMPLES

2. CUT BACKS (20.0% OF GOALS)

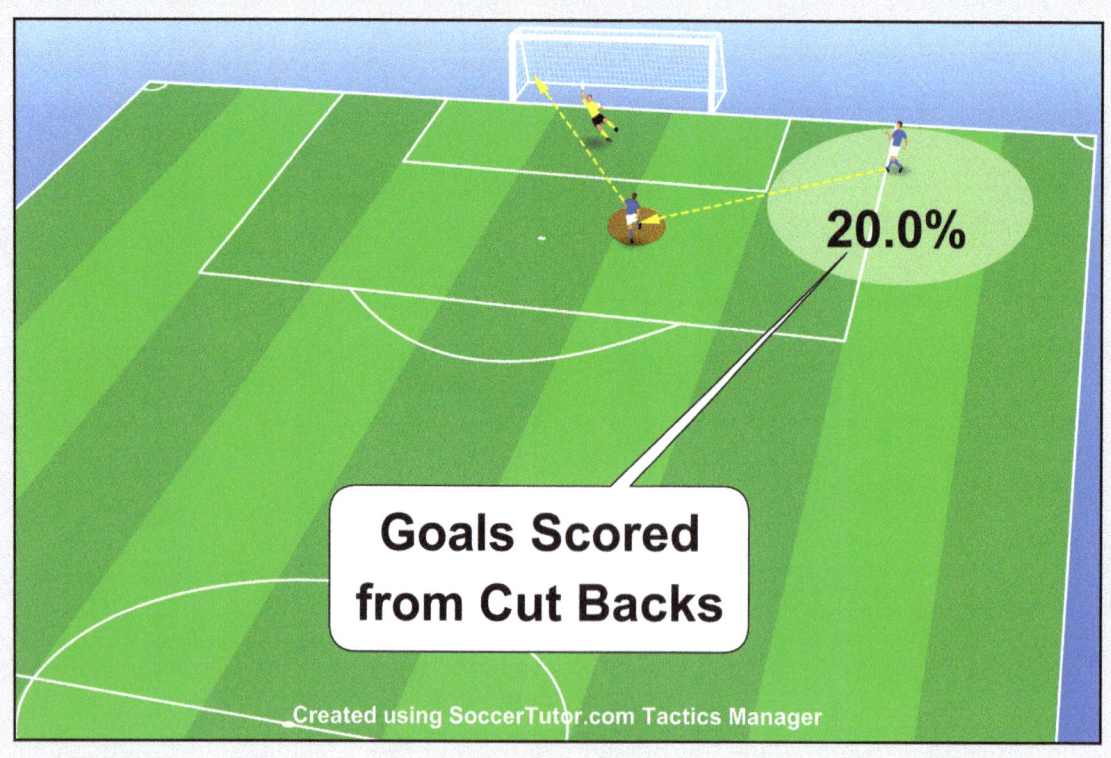

Goals Scored from Cut Backs

2. Cut Backs = 20.0% of All Goals Scored

RB Leipzig 3-2 Real Madrid (Vinicius Jr. 44') - 25/10/2022

Goal Example 1 (Real Madrid)
Cut Backs = 61 of 304 Goals Scored (20.0%)

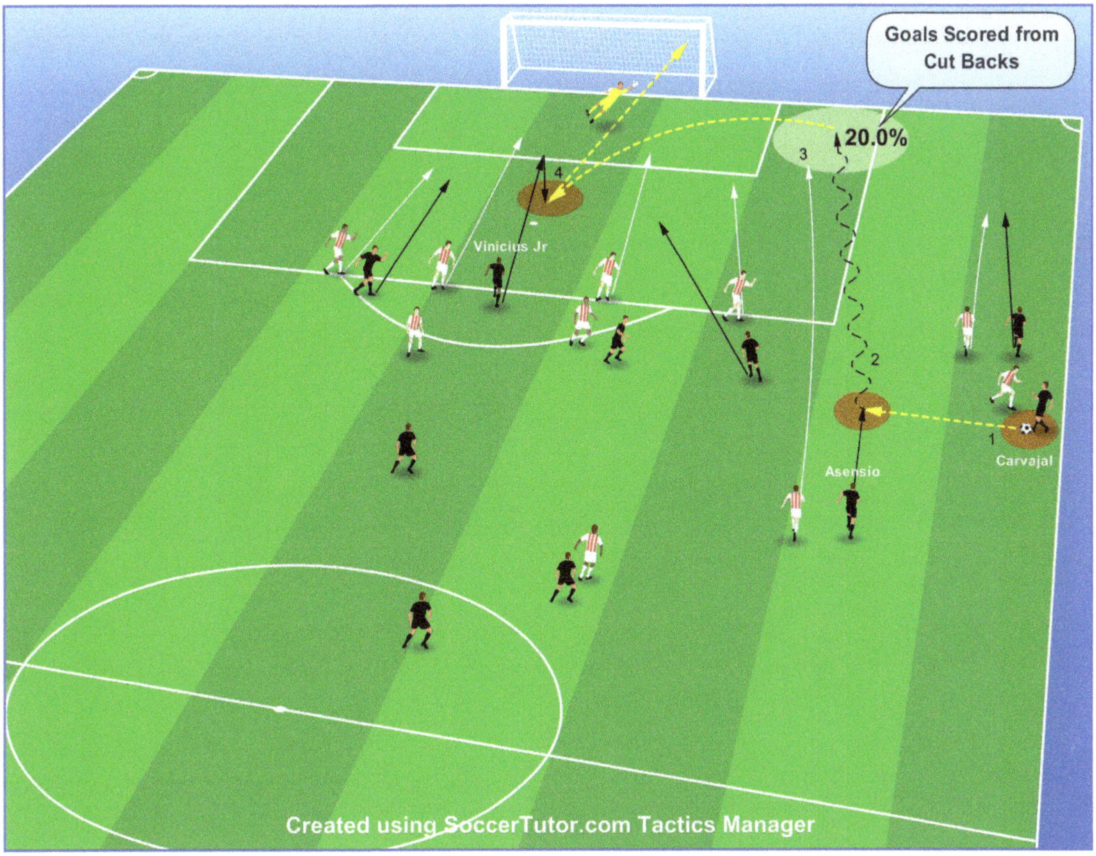

Description
The start of play is wide with the right back **Carvajal**. The attacking midfielder **Asensio** arrives from deep, receives the square pass, and dribbles the ball all the way to the by-line inside the box. From there, he plays an aerial cut back cross for the movement of left winger **Vinicius Jr**, who beats the defender to the ball to score with his head.

Key Aspects
1. **Carvajal's** wide position makes the RB Leipzig defence more open and Real Madrid have more space for their attack.

2. Another Real Madrid midfielder plays a key role by dragging a defender away from the play and towards the corner to create space for **Asensio** to exploit.

3. Attacking midfielder **Asensio** runs very quickly to take advantage of the created space and he is faster than the defender.

4. The winger **Vinicius Jr** anticipates the defenders' movement, arrives with perfect timing, and takes advantage of his speed in small spaces.

2. Cut Backs = 20.0% of All Goals Scored

Manchester City 5-0 Copenhagen (Álvarez 76') - 05/10/2022

Goal Example 2 (Manchester City)
Cut Backs = 61 of 304 Goals Scored (20.0%)

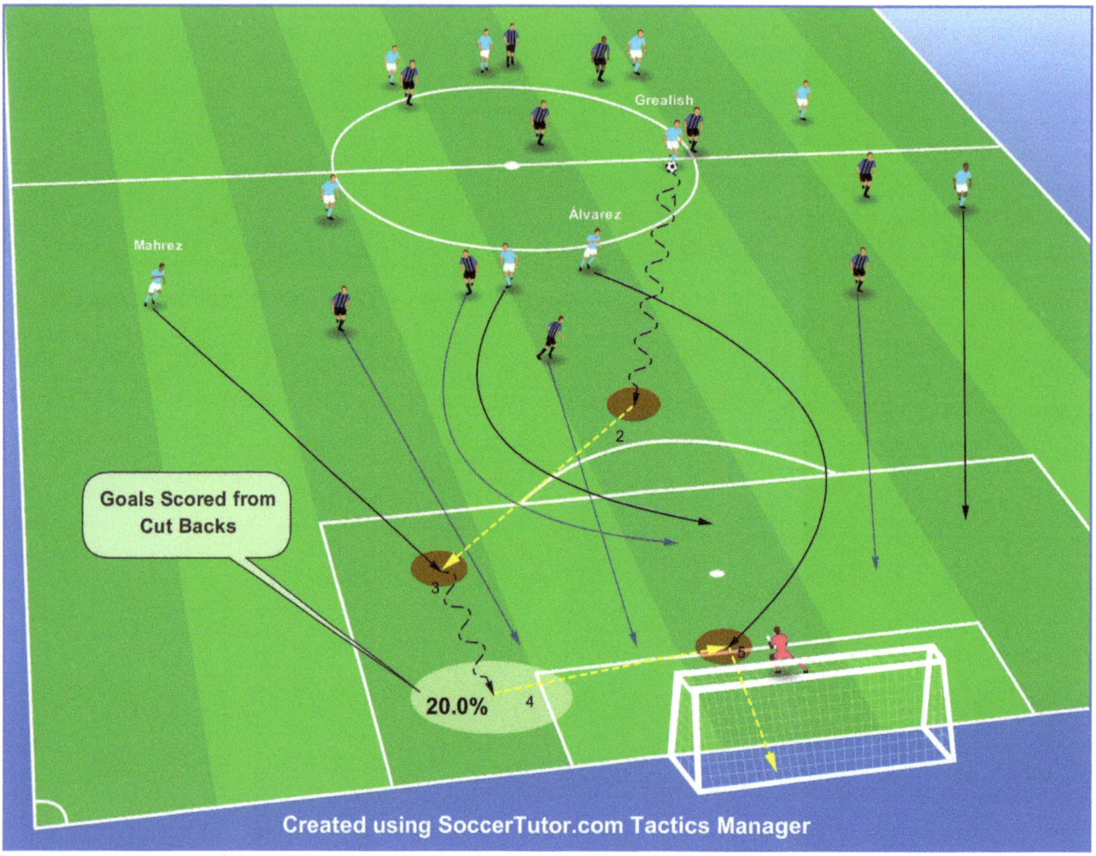

Description

Play begins with City's left winger **Grealish** dribbling past 2 defenders trying to win the ball from him. He advances forward with the ball and passes to the right for the well timed run of the right winger **Mahrez**, who then dribbles towards the by-line and plays a cut back pass between 2 defenders for the run of the forward **Álvarez** to score from close range.

Key Aspects

1. The attacking players ahead of **Grealish** do not stop and offer support, but instead all run forward and drag the opposing defenders away with them. This creates space for **Mahrez** to receive in the box on the right.

2. The forward **Álvarez** takes advantage of the defenders all running back towards their own goal to make his run into the centre of the box almost unnoticed.

3. Then **Grealish** looks and positions his body to the left to deceive the defenders before playing the pass to the right side.

TRAINING SESSION 2

Cut Backs: 61 Goals

FOR CUT BACKS (20.0% OF GOALS)

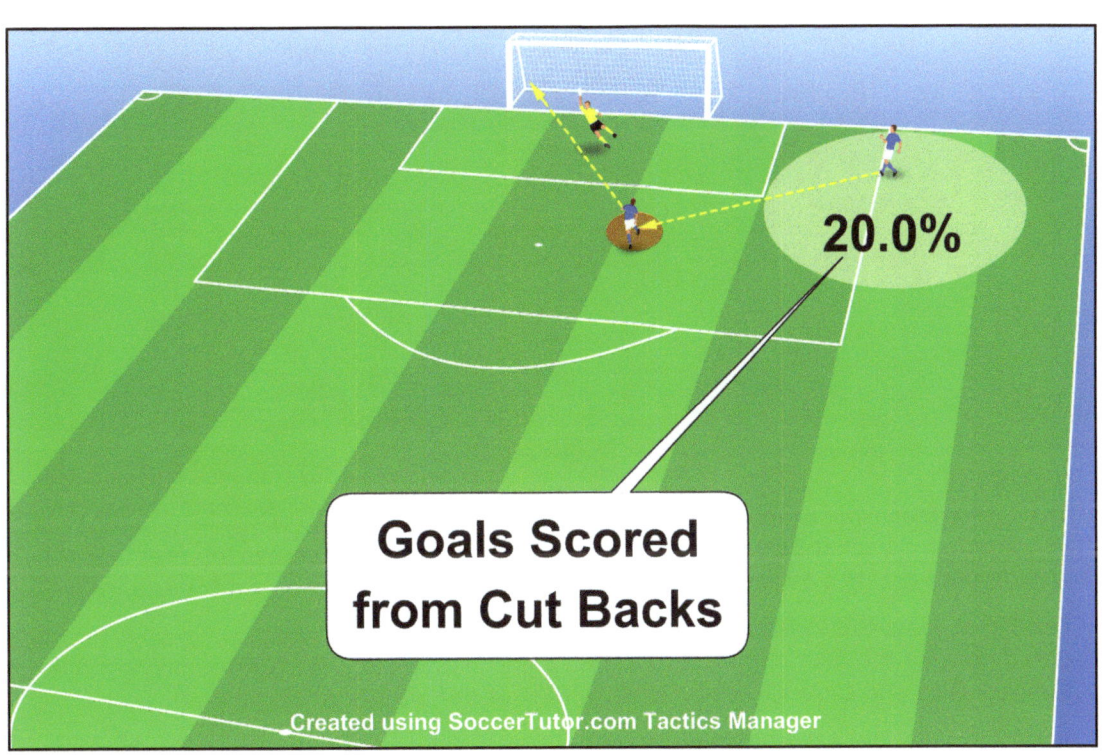

Goals Scored from Cut Backs

Training Session 2: **Cut Backs (20.0% of All Goals Scored)**

SESSION FOR THIS TACTICAL SITUATION (4 PRACTICES)
1. 3v1 in Wide Area, Overlapping Full Back Run and Cut Back for Oncoming Runners to Score

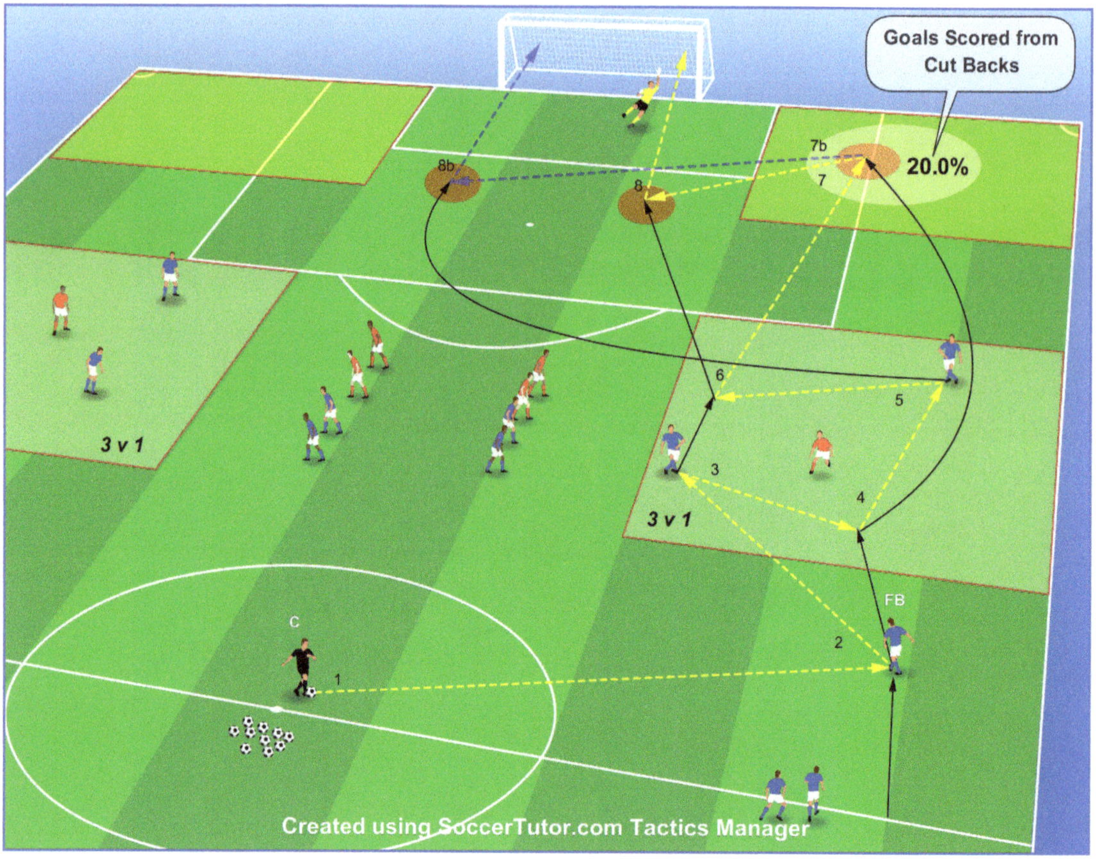

Description

- The Coach starts the practice with a pass to the blue full back **(FB)**, who enters the wide area to create a 3v1 situation.
- The 3 blue players combine and then play a pass for the overlapping run of the full back **(FB)** into the high corner area.
- After the pass, the 2 teammates run into box (one to the near post and the other to the far post).
- The full back **(FB)** receives and cuts the ball back for either teammate to score.
- When the phase ends, the practice continues with the next players waiting on the other side.
- The practice is performed on both sides of the pitch alternately.

Training Session 2: **Cut Backs (20.0% of All Goals Scored)**

2. Pass to Winger Out Wide for 1v1 and Cut Back for Oncoming Runners to Score

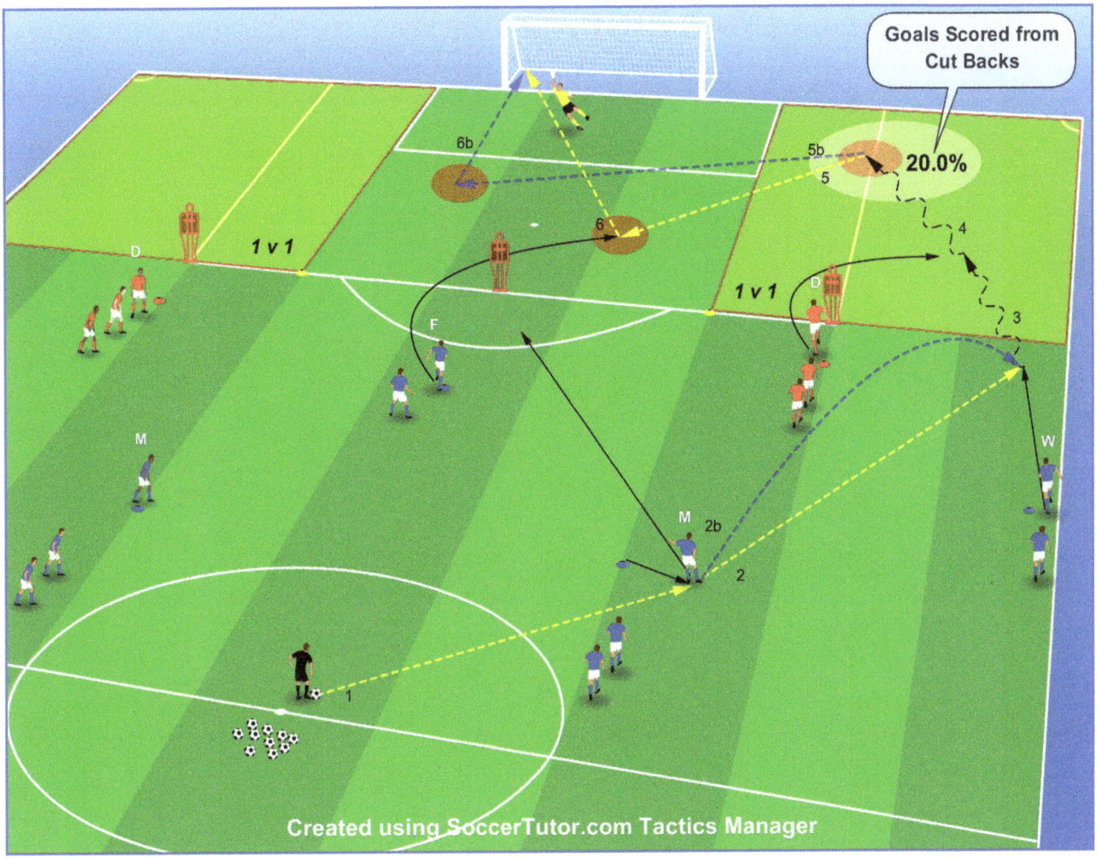

Description

- The Coach starts the practice with a pass to the blue midfielder **(M)**, who then passes out wide and in front of the winger **(W)** so they can run onto the ball.

- The red defender **(D)** runs around the mannequin and takes up a defensive position within the corner area.

- The winger **(W)** moves forward with the ball into the corner area and starts a 1v1 action.

- The winger's **(W)** aim is to beat the defender and then play a cut back pass for either the forward **(F)** or the midfielder **(M)**, who make runs to the near and far post areas respectively to score.

- After finishing the phase, the 3 participating players return to their starting positions. Alternatively, they can rotate positions.

- When the phase ends, the practice continues with the next players waiting on the other side.

- The practice is performed on both sides of the pitch alternately.

35

©SOCCERTUTOR.COM — COACH YOUR TEAM TO SCORE MORE GOALS

Training Session 2: Cut Backs (20.0% of All Goals Scored)

VARIATION

3. Pass to Winger for 1v1 High Up the Flank and Cut Back to Edge of the Box for Shot

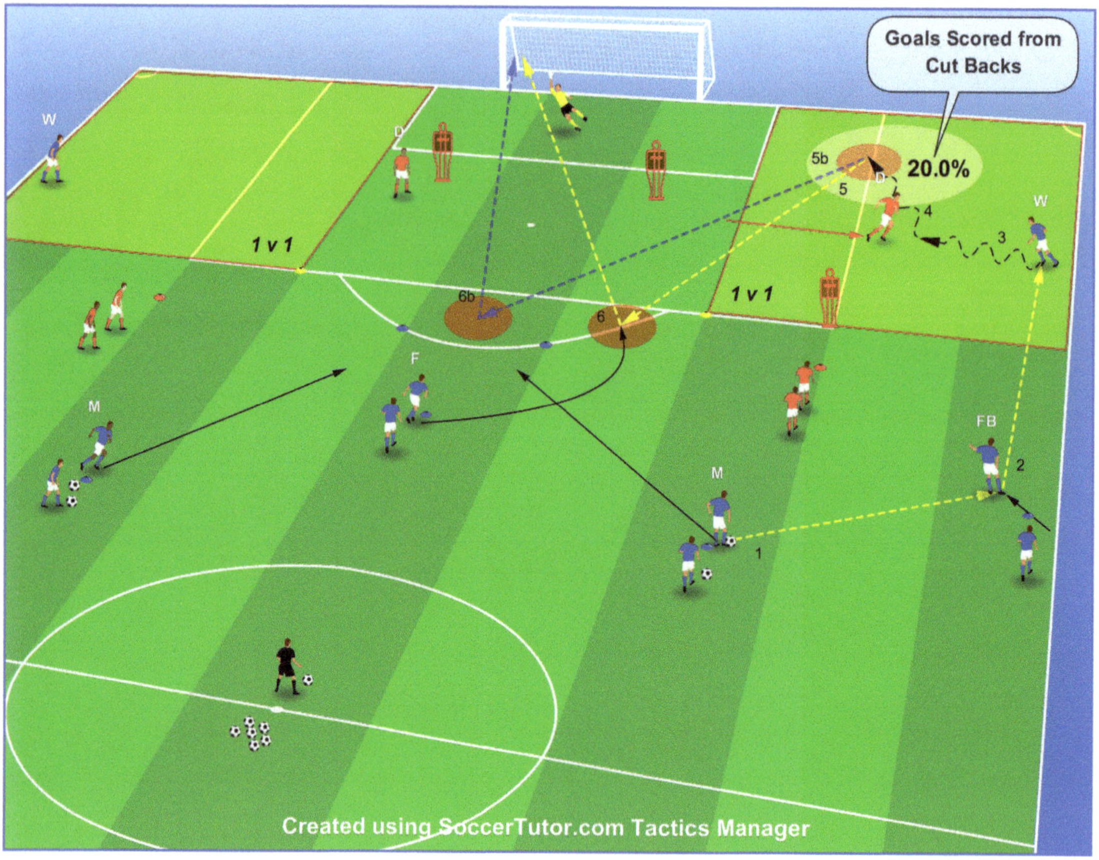

Description

- The practice starts with the midfielder's **(M)** pass to the full back **(FB)**.
- The full back **(FB)** passes to the winger **(W)** in the corner area.
- The red defender **(D)** on that side moves across into the corner area as soon as the winger **(W)** takes his first touch. We now have a 1v1 situation.
- The winger **(W)** aims to beat the defender and then cut the ball back to the edge of the box to a teammate.
- The forward **(F)** and the midfielder **(M)** both time their movements well to receive (one through middle of the 2 cones and one to the right side of them), so the full back **(FB)** has 2 good options.
- The player who performs the cut back has to raise his head and look where his teammates are located to play the ball into the correct position at the right speed.
- When the phase ends, the practice continues with the next players waiting on the other side.

Training Session 2: Cut Backs (20.0% of All Goals Scored)

PROGRESSION
4. Cut Backs and Finishing in a 6v6 (+2) Four Corner Area Game

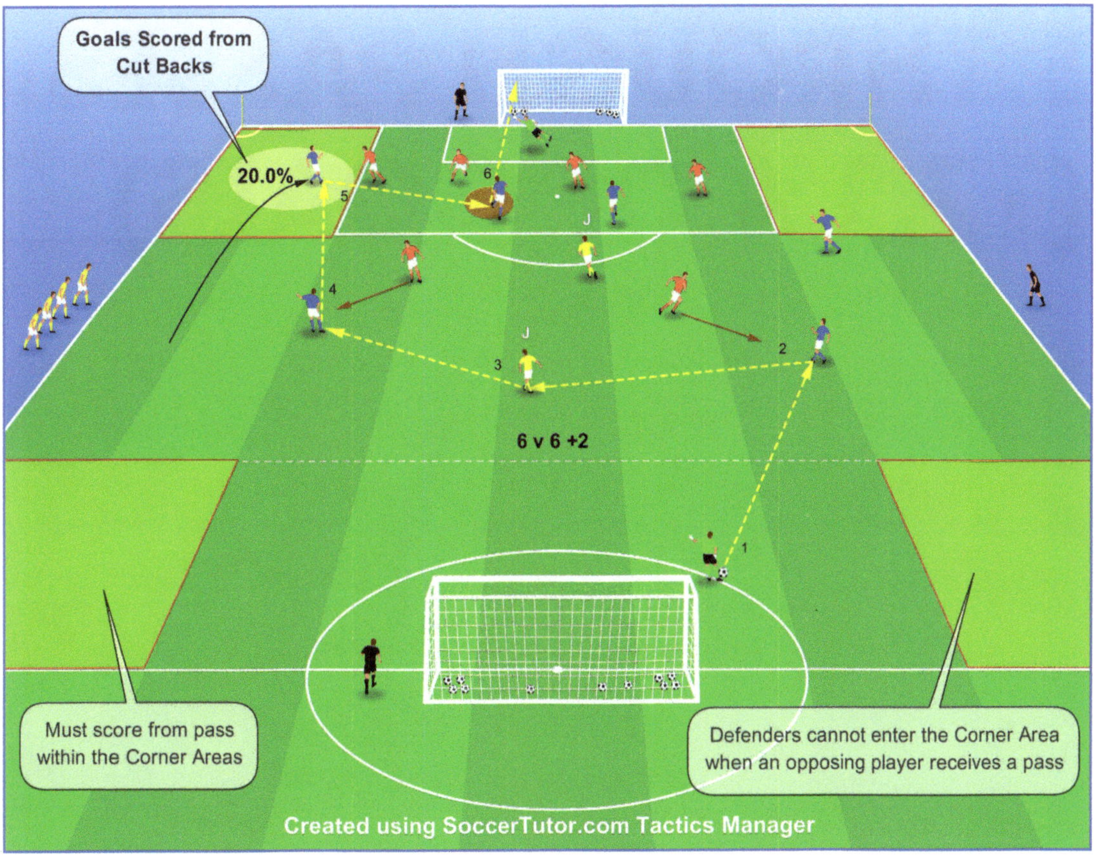

Diagram labels:
- Goals Scored from Cut Backs — 20.0%
- 6 v 6 +2
- Must score from pass within the Corner Areas
- Defenders cannot enter the Corner Area when an opposing player receives a pass
- Created using SoccerTutor.com Tactics Manager

Description

- Using half a full pitch, we mark out 4 corner areas as shown.
- We play a 6v6 (+2) game with one condition to score a goal: **The final pass has to come from a corner area**.
- The practice starts from either GK. The 2 yellow Jokers **(J)** always play with the team in possession.
- The defenders cannot enter the corner areas, they can only try to intercept passes played into them.
- When a goal is scored, restart from the GK of the team that just conceded.
- The teams play short 5-7 minute games. The outside resting team rotate in after each game, and the 2 Joker players must therefore switch roles too.
- The team that scores the most goals after a set number of games wins.

TACTICAL EXAMPLES

3. THROUGH PASSES (17.1% OF GOALS)

Goals Scored from Through Passes

3. Through Passes = 17.1% of All Goals Scored

FC Barcelona 0-3 Bayern Munich (Mané 10') - 26/10/2022

Goal Example 1 (Bayern Munich)
Through Passes = 52 of 304 Goals Scored (17.1%)

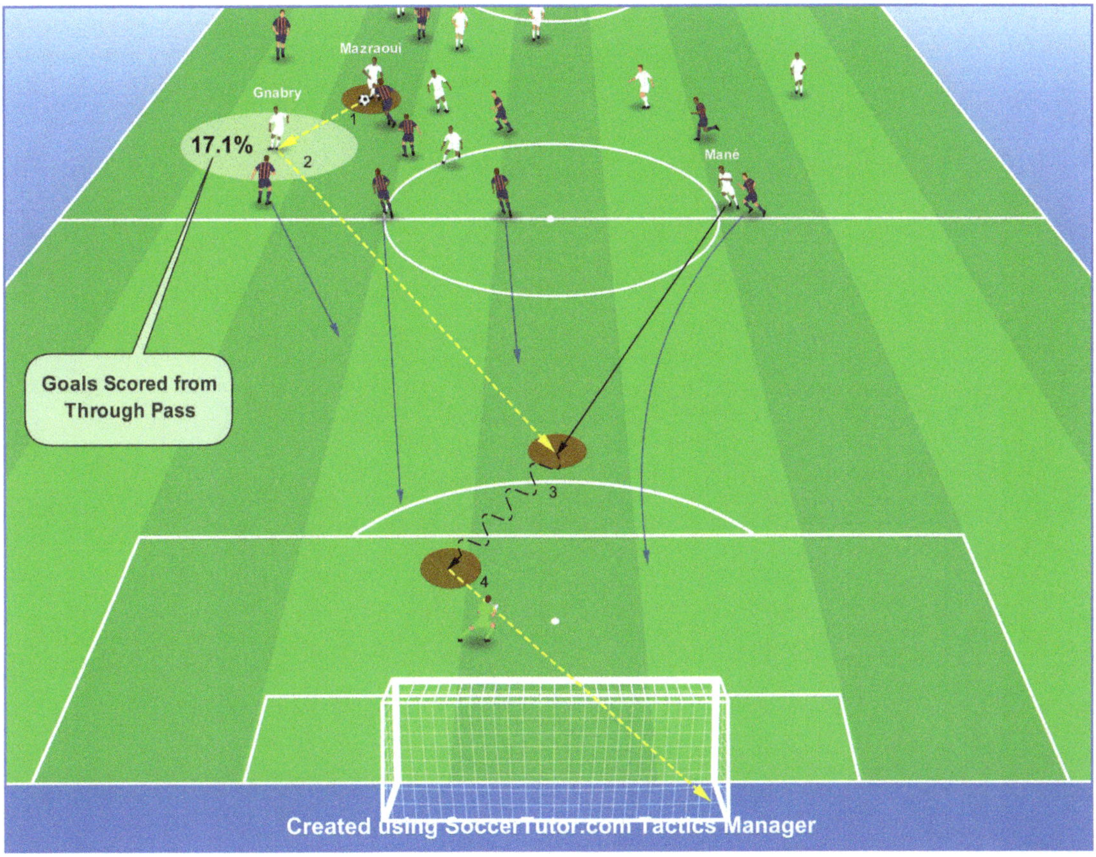

Description
The right back **Mazraoui** has won the ball and passes to the right winger **Gnabry** in space. Barcelona's defence is high up to the halfway line, so **Gnabry** plays a through pass in between the right back and centre back for the run of left winger **Mané**. He is able to receive, dribble into the box, and score past the goalkeeper.

Key Aspects
1. Bayern's aggressive defensive style enables them to win the ball initially.
2. When Barcelona lose the ball in the first phase of the game, it is a big problem because Bayern have very fast players. In this example, **only 2 passes (1 through pass) are needed** for them to enter Barcelona's box and score.
3. When the opposition play with a high line as Barcelona did here, the through pass is a very advantageous tactic because there is so much space to exploit in behind the defensive line, especially if you have fast attackers.

3. Through Passes = 17.1% of All Goals Scored

Napoli 4-1 Liverpool (Anguissa 31') - 07/09/2022

Goal Example 2 (Napoli)

Through Passes = 52 of 304 Goals Scored (17.1%)

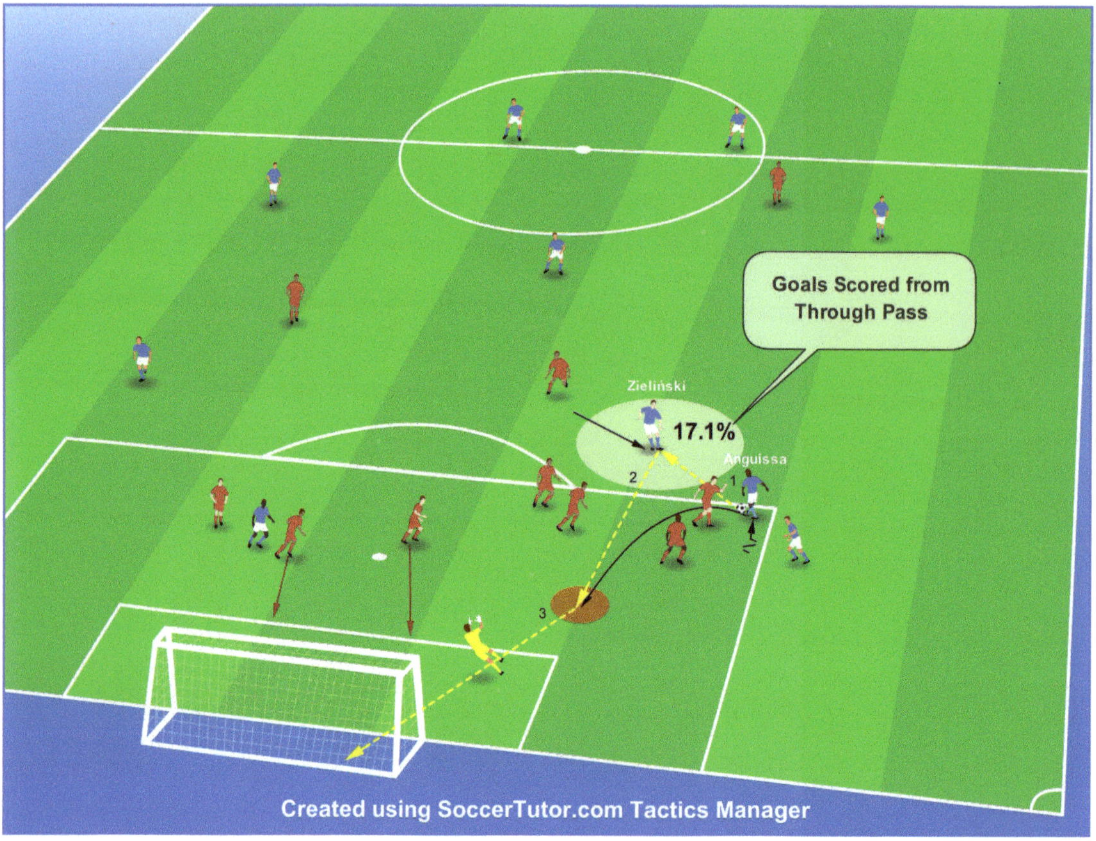

Description

Before this, Napoli's left winger **Kvaratskhelia** tried to beat the Liverpool centre back **J. Gomez** on the outside but had to turn back and pass to the central midfielder **Anguissa**.

Anguissa passes back outside the box to the attacking midfielder **Zieliński**, who then plays a through pass in between the Liverpool defenders for the run of **Anguissa** (one-two combination). From there, **Anguissa** is able to finish under the GK and score.

Key Aspects

1. The central midfielder **Anguissa** is put under pressure, so has no good individual route to goal. This is why he plays back to his teammate **Zieliński**.

2. It is then all about the through pass and the timing of the run. **Anguissa** appears to be surrounded by 4 Liverpool players, but **Zieliński's** precise pass is able to find the space in behind them. The perfect timing of **Anguissa's** run makes sure he stays onside and is able to get to the ball before the GK.

TRAINING SESSION 3

Through Passes

52 Goals

FOR THROUGH PASSES (17.1% OF GOALS)

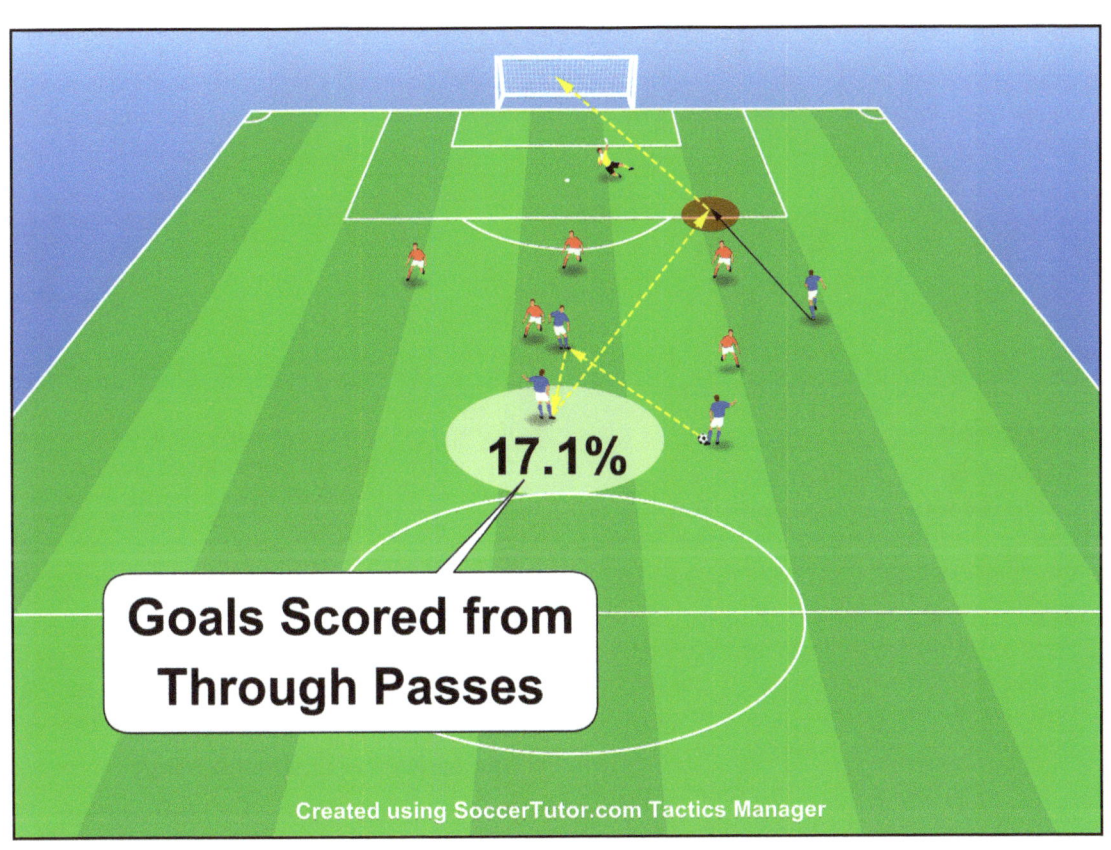

Goals Scored from Through Passes

Training Session 3: **Through Passes (17.1% of All Goals Scored)**

SESSION FOR THIS TACTICAL SITUATION (4 PRACTICES)

1. 4v4 Possession in Centre Circle + Through Pass to the Forward in a 1v1 (+GK) Situation

Description

- We start with 2 teams (blue vs reds). There is a 4v4 situation inside the centre circle + 1 additional outside player for each team on the halfway line, as shown.

- The Coach starts the practice with a pass to either team. That team (blues in diagram) aim to complete 3 passes before they are able to play a through pass for their outside player (forward).

- The blue forward sprints to receive the through pass and tries to score. The red outside player must run and try to defend the goal.

- If the reds win the ball inside the centre circle, they aim to complete 3 passes of their own, and then play a through pass for their forward.

- If the ball goes out of the centre circle, the Coach plays a new ball in for the other team.

- When the action ends, the other 2 teams (white and yellow) begin a new phase.

- The forwards constantly change.

- You can make it a 4 team competition and add up the goals scored by each team to determine the winners.

Training Session 3: **Through Passes (17.1% of All Goals Scored)**

PROGRESSION

2. 5 (+1) v 4 in Midfield Zone + Through Pass in Behind for Forward's 1 v 1 vs GK

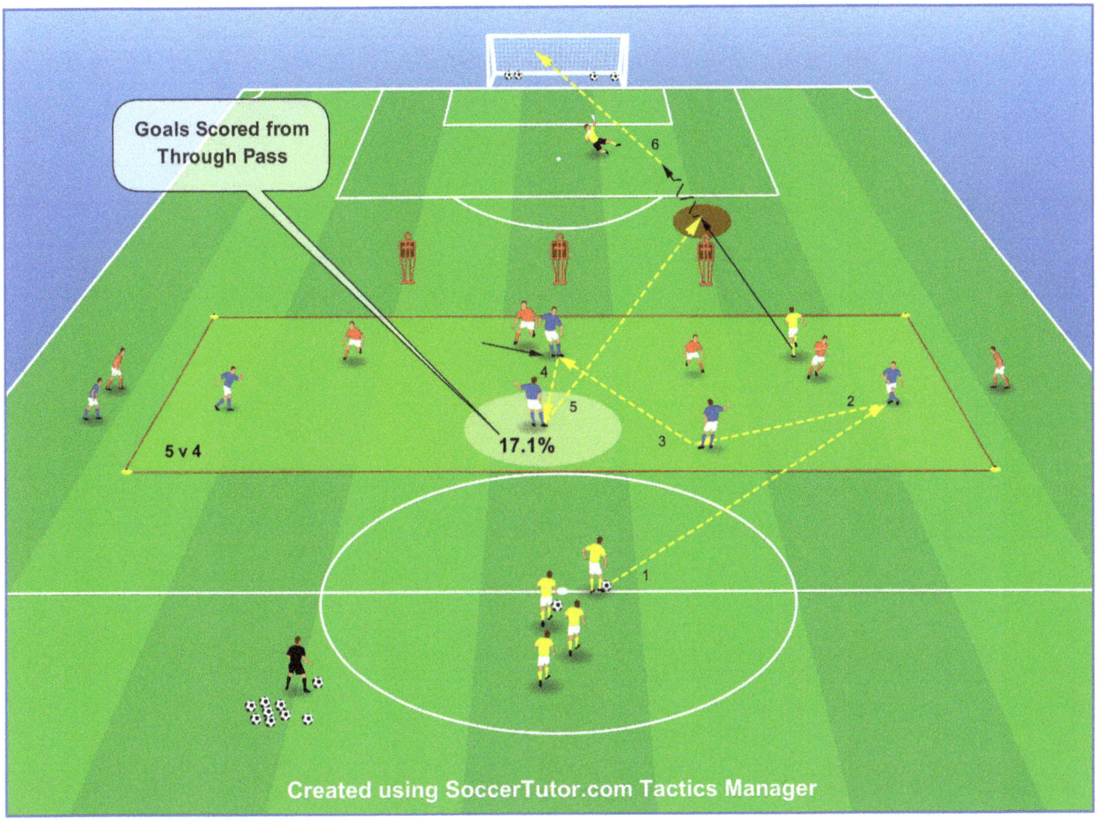

Description

- The yellow players are forwards, the blue players are the attacking team, and the reds are the defending team.

- The practice starts with an outside yellow player's pass into the marked out central zone. Inside the central zone, there are 5 blues + 1 yellow forward vs 4 red defenders.

- The blue players pass the ball within the central zone, trying to find a player with time and space on the ball, and a good passing lane to play a through pass.

- The red players work together to press and try to block any through passes.

- The 3 mannequins act as defenders so the pass has to be seen and accurately played. The yellow forward times his run well in behind, receives, and tries to score against the GK.

- After each action, 2 of the defenders rotate out so they can rest and recover well after their pressing and closing down. The yellow forward also changes and the practice continues with a new ball from the next outside yellow player.

Training Session 3: Through Passes (17.1% of All Goals Scored)

PROGRESSION
3. Build-up Play in Defensive Half + Through Pass into Attacking Half in a 4v4 (+2) +GKs Conditioned Game

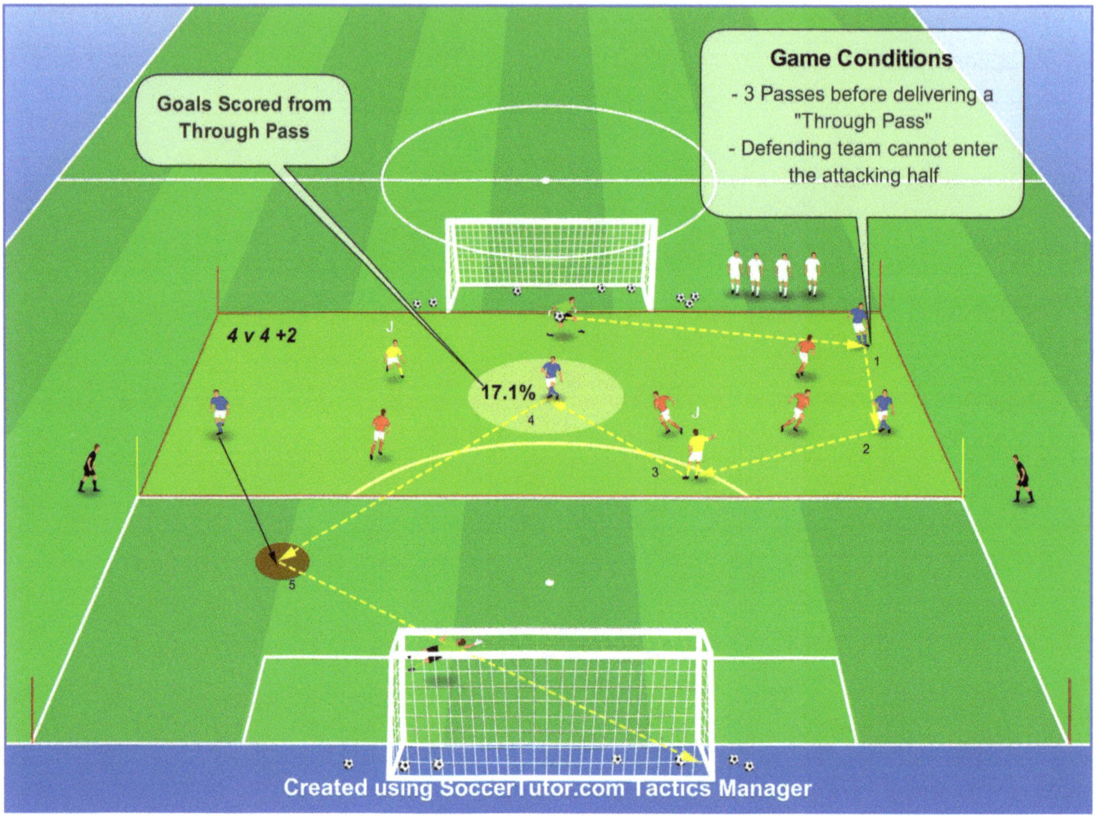

Game Conditions
- 3 Passes before delivering a "Through Pass"
- Defending team cannot enter the attacking half

Description

- The game starts from the blue team's GK and a 4v4 (+2) +GK situation in their own half.

- The aim is to complete at least 3 passes before playing a through pass into the attacking half for the run of one of their players. That player times his run into the attacking half to receive the pass and tries to score against the GK.

- The red defending team are not allowed to enter the attacking half even after the through pass, so it is just a 1v1 to finish.

- If the reds win the ball, they must complete 3 passes before attempting to score.

- When the action ends, the game restarts from the red team's GK and the red team are now the attacking team + 2 Jokers. The game works in the same way from the opposite end.

- The blues rotate out and the whites become the new defending team.

- You can make it a 3 team competition and add up the goals scored by each team to determine the winners.

44

COACH YOUR TEAM TO SCORE MORE GOALS

Training Session 3: Through Passes (17.1% of All Goals Scored)

PROGRESSION

4. Build-up Play in Defensive Half + Through Pass into Attacking Half in a 7v7 +GKs Conditioned Game

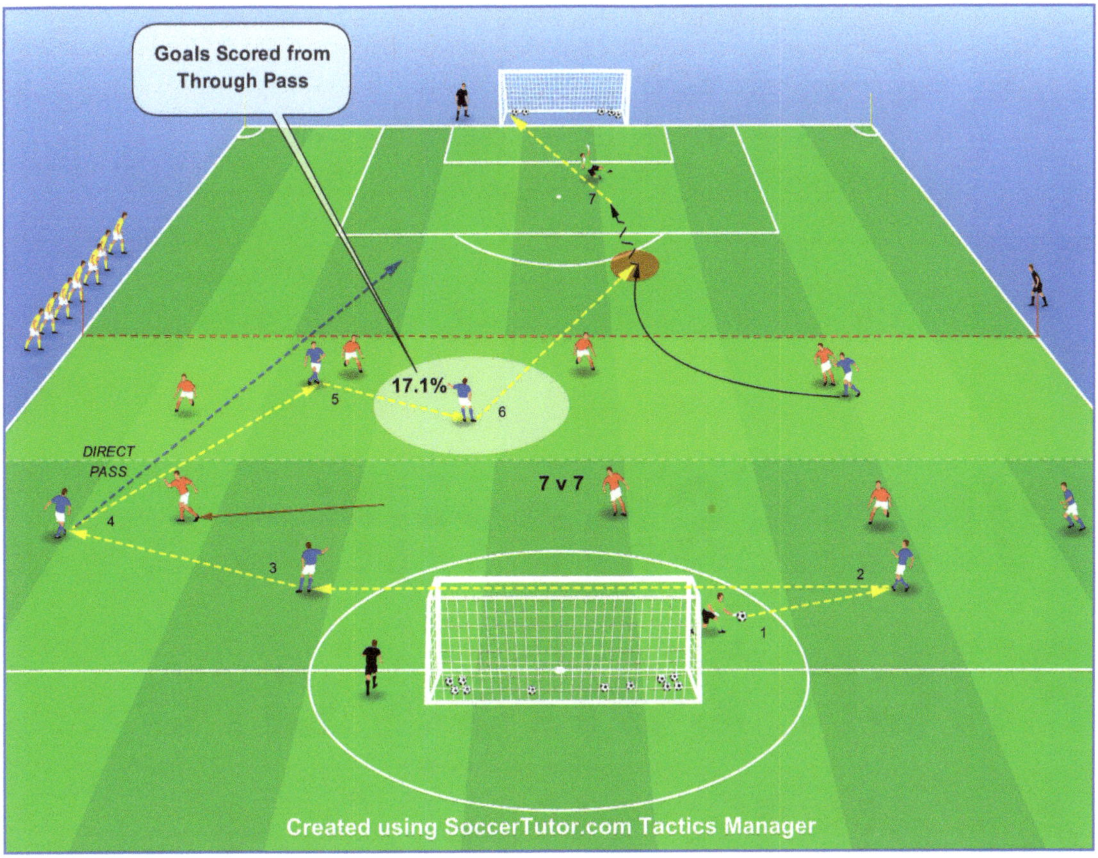

Description

- The game starts from the GK with all the players from both teams within the low area of the pitch in 4-3 formations.

- The attacking team (blues in diagram) build-up trying to play through the lines of their opponents. The red defending team press high to try and win the ball.

- The blue defenders either play into their 3 midfielders, who then play a through pass in behind, or they play a direct long through pass into the attacking half.

- The player that runs in behind moves to finish 1v1 against the GK unopposed.

- If the red defending team win the ball, they try to score a goal themselves.

- After a phase is complete, the teams switch ends, and the reds receive from the same GK (become attacking team).

- There is a third team (yellows) outside resting because the teams rotate after each 5-7 minute game. The team that scores the most goals after a set number of games wins.

ZONE OF ASSISTS

What Specific Pitch Zones are Assists Played from?

ZONE OF ASSISTS: WHAT SPECIFIC PITCH ZONE ARE ASSISTS PLAYED FROM?

The Pitch Zone Where Assists were Played from for All Goals During the Champions League Group Stages in the 2022-2023 Season (304 Total Goals)

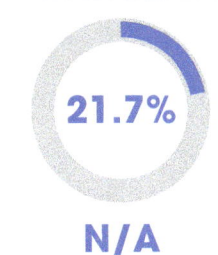

21.7%
N/A
66 GOALS

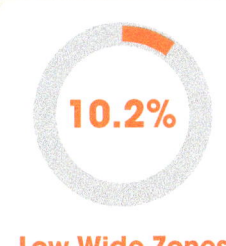

18.4%
Side of Box
56 GOALS

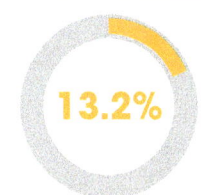

13.2%
Centre Space
40 GOALS

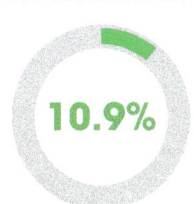

10.9%
Half Spaces
33 GOALS

10.2%
Low Wide Zones
31 GOALS

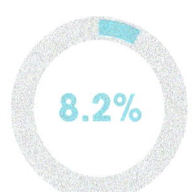

8.2%
High Wide Zones
25 GOALS

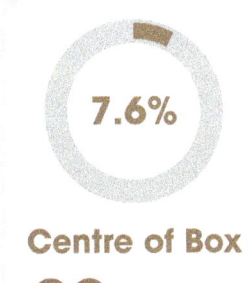

7.6%
Centre of Box
23 GOALS

6.6%
Corner Kick
20 GOALS

3.3%
Defensive Half
10 GOALS

* N/A = Penalty/Free kick/Deflection/Rebound

TACTICAL EXAMPLES

4. GOALS ASSISTED FROM SIDE OF BOX (18.4% OF GOALS)

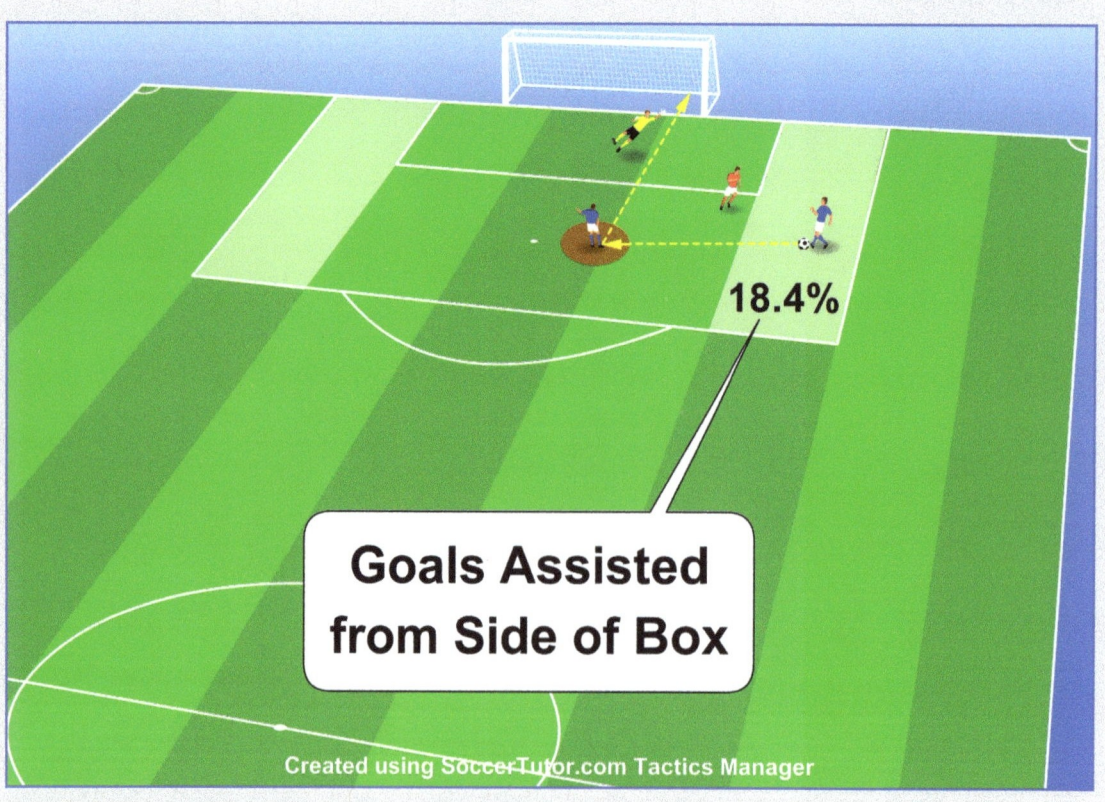

18.4%

Goals Assisted from Side of Box

4. Goals Assisted from Side of Box = 18.4% of All Goals Scored

Viktoria Plzen 2-4 FC Barcelona (Ferrán 54') - 01/11/2022

Goal Example 1 (FC Barcelona): Goals Assisted from Side of Box = 56 of 304 Goals Scored (18.4%)

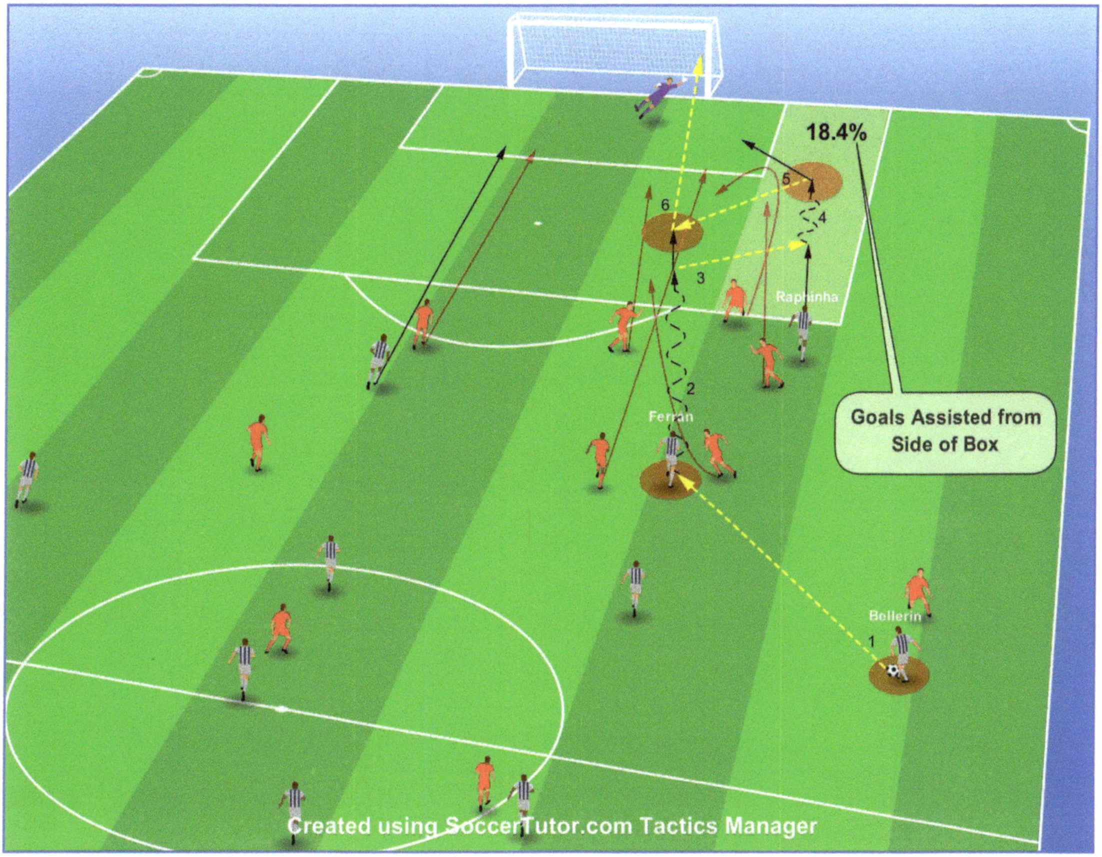

Description

The left winger **Ferrán Torres** receives in the centre from the right back **Bellerin**. He turns and dribbles forward between 3 opponents and is then able to pass to right winger **Raphinha** in the side of the box area (highlighted). **Raphinha** moves forward with the ball and then plays it back for **Ferrán** to score at the near post.

Key Aspects

1. The individual quality of **Ferrán** is key to dribbling the ball between 3 players. He protects the ball the whole time with his body, and with great technique, he makes sure that the ball is always under his control.

2. Right winger **Raphinha** understands the play very well to first create space and then waits for **Ferrán** to find the moment to give the correct pass. He quickly returns the ball to **Ferrán**, and the 2 players easily pass between the lines.

3. The forward **Fati** runs to the far post which creates more space in the centre.

4. Goals Assisted from Side of Box = 18.4% of All Goals Scored

Sevilla 0-4 Manchester City (Haaland 20') - 06/09/2022

Goal Example 2 (Manchester City): Goals Assisted from Side of Box = 56 of 304 Goals Scored (18.4%)

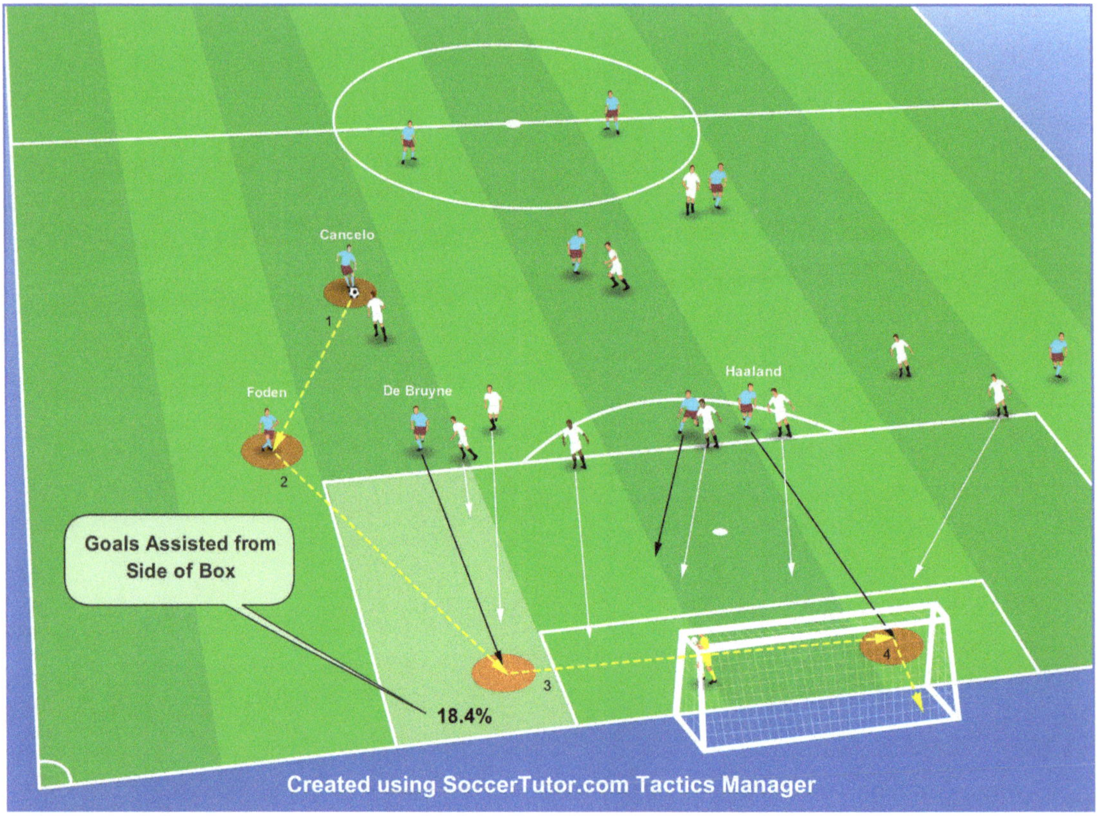

Description

The right back **Cancelo** passes to the right winger **Foden**, who looks up to see the key available space in the box. This space is used by attacking midfielder **De Bruyne**, who receives **Foden's** pass into the side of the box area. The centre forward **Haaland** anticipates well to score at the back post from **De Bruyne's** low cross across the box.

Key Aspects

1. **Foden's** vision is key as he quickly sees the empty space (side of the box). He then quickly sends a perfect pass for **De Bruyne** to take advantage of that space.

2. **De Bruyne** wastes no time and crosses very quickly. He crosses with speed to the far post, so that the ball can overcome the defenders and the GK.

3. **Haaland's** quickness to understand that the ball will go to the far post is key. Along with this mental speed, he also has fast physical reactions. With great speed, he manages to reach the correct position at the right moment to dive forward and finish on the volley with his left foot.

TRAINING SESSION 4

Side of Box — 56 Goals

FOR GOALS ASSISTED FROM SIDE OF BOX (18.4% OF GOALS)

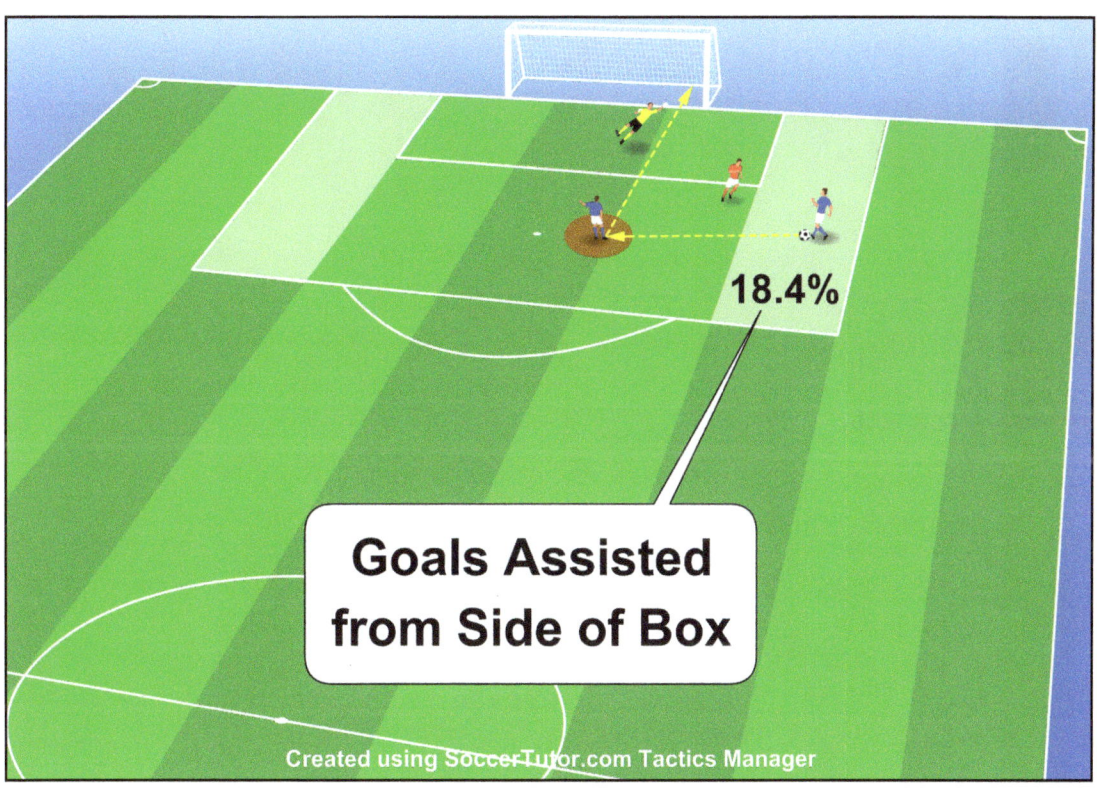

Goals Assisted from Side of Box

Training Session 4: Goals Assisted from Side of Box (18.4% of Goals Scored)

SESSION FOR THIS TACTICAL SITUATION (3 PRACTICES)
1. Double One-Two with Through Pass into Side of Box, Cut Back, and Finish in Pairs

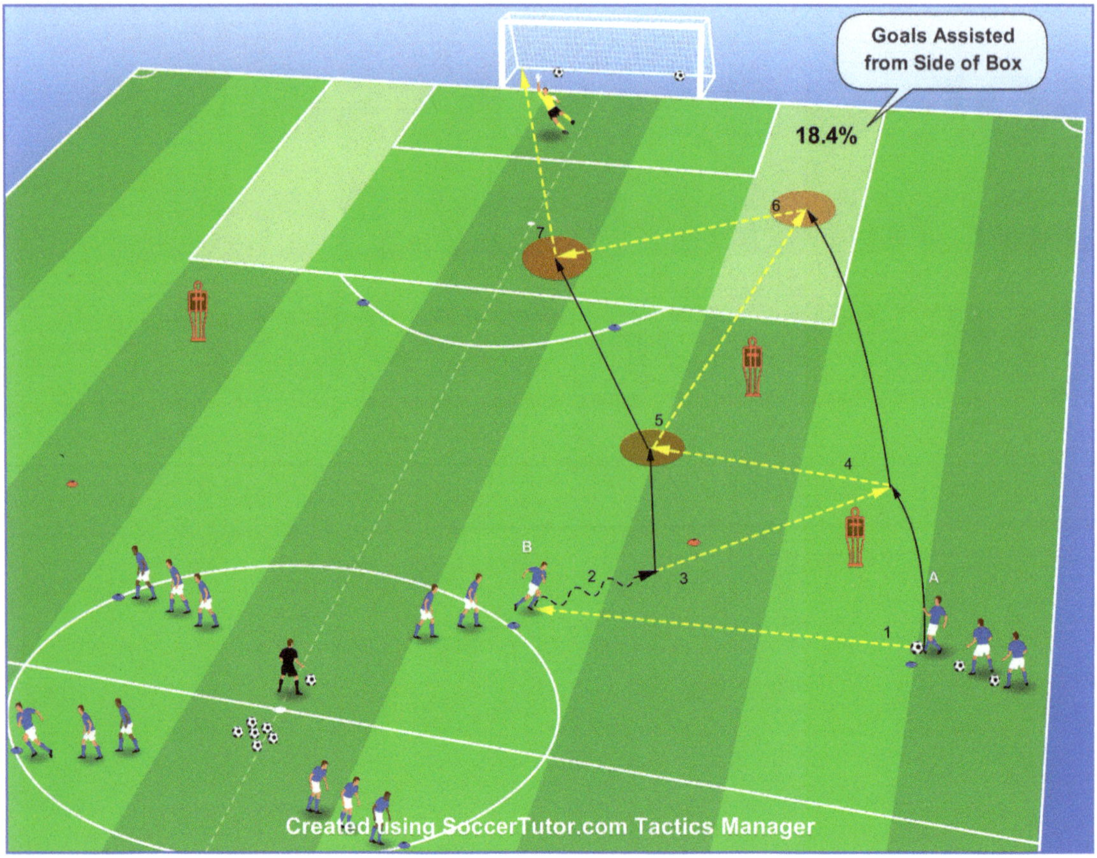

Description
- With a full pitch split into 4 sections, the players start in groups of 6.
- **A** passes to **B**, who carries the ball inside. **A** runs past the mannequin to receive **B's** return pass.
- **A** passes inside to **B** and then makes a fast advanced run to receive the return into the side of the box area (through pass to complete one-two).
- **B** runs through the 2 cones and into the box to finish from **A's** cut back.
- As soon as an action is finished, the next players waiting repeat the same sequence.
- All groups work at the same time.

Training Session 4: Goals Assisted from Side of Box (18.4% of Goals Scored)

PROGRESSION

2A. Wide Combination, Wing Play into Side of Box, and Cut Back for Finish in a 2v2 Situation

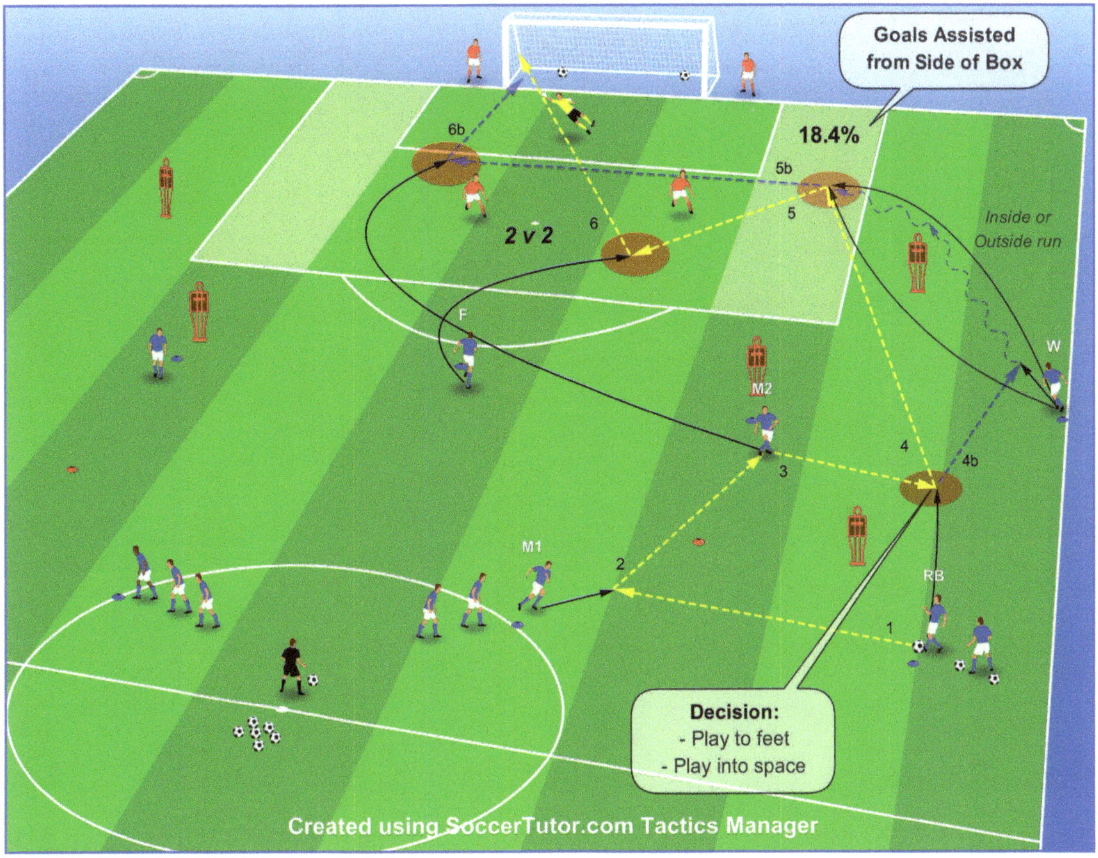

Description (2a)

- There are 5 blue players involved in the combination **(RB, M1, M2, W & F)** and 2 red defenders in the box, as shown.

- The right back **(RB)** passes inside to the first midfielder **(M1)**, who passes forward to the second midfielder **(M2)**. He passes wide for the forward run of the right back **(RB)** to receive.

- The right back either plays a through pass for the winger's **(W)** run in behind, or plays a short pass to the winger **(W)** who then dribbles past the mannequin and into the side of the box.

- When inside the side of the box area, the winger **(W)** looks up to find a teammate **(M2 or forward F)** with a cut back **(5)** or a low cross across the box **(5b)**. The 2 red defenders try to block or intercept.

- After the phase is finished, the same sequence is repeated from the left side and 2 new red defenders rotate in.

- The players all rotate positional roles throughout the practice.

Training Session 4: Goals Assisted from Side of Box (18.4% of Goals Scored)

2B. Wide Combination, Midfield Run into Side of Box, and Cut Back for Finish in a 2v2 Situation

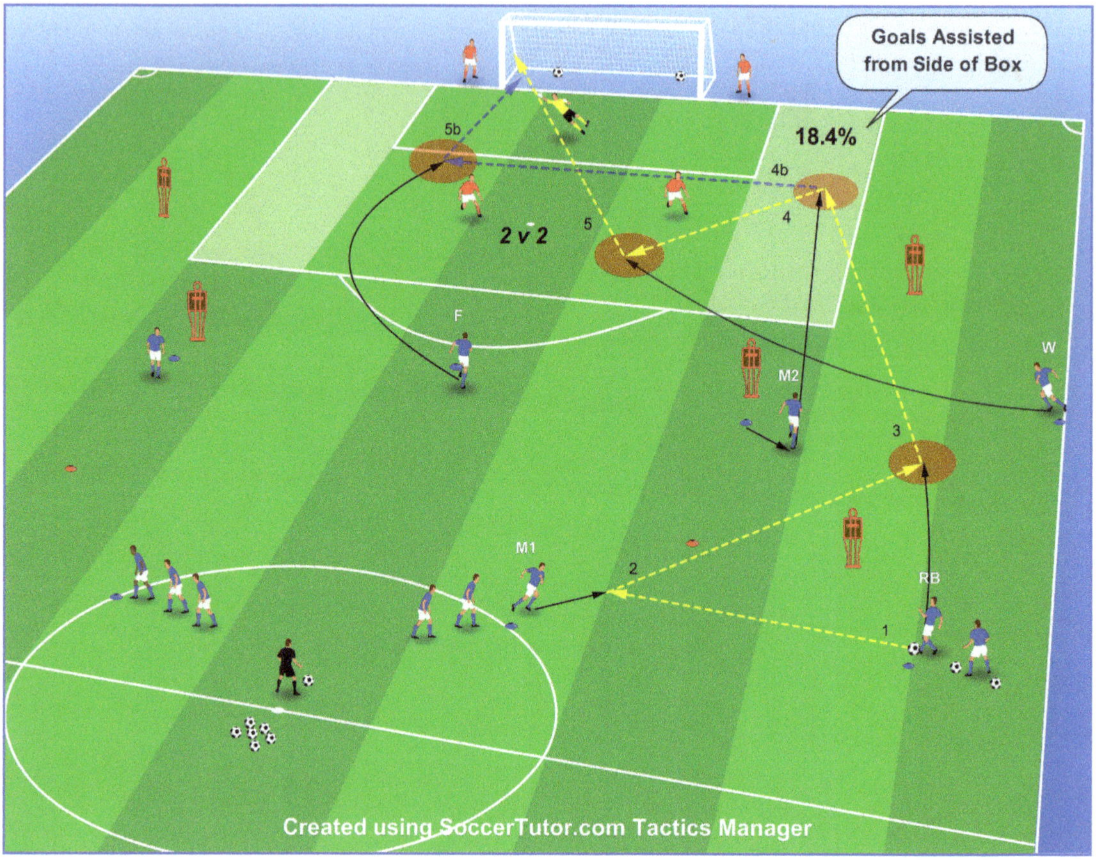

Description (2b)

- In this variation of the same practice, the right back **(RB)** starts by playing a one-two with the first midfielder **(M1)**, receiving beyond the mannequin.

- The second midfielder **(M2)** makes a forward run in behind towards the side of the box area. **RB** plays a through pass for **M2's** run, as shown.

- **M2** who receives in the side of the box area this time, the winger **(W)** makes a long run off the flank towards the box. Again, the forward **(F)** makes a run into the box too.

- When inside the side of the box area, **M2** looks up to find a teammate wither with a cut back (5) or a low cross across the box (5b).

- The 2 red defenders try to block or intercept the pass.

- After the phase is finished, the same sequence is repeated from the left side and 2 new red defenders rotate in.

- The players all rotate positional roles throughout the practice.

Training Session 4: Goals Assisted from Side of Box (18.4% of Goals Scored)

2C. Wide Combination, Third Man Run into Side of Box, and Cut Back for Finish in a 2v2 Situation

Description (2c)

- In this third variation, the right back **(RB)** starts by passing inside to the first midfielder **(M1)**, who passes forward to the second midfielder **(M2)**.

- **M2** passes inside to the forward **(F)**, who passes into the side of the box area for the run of the winger **(W)** off the flank.

- When inside the side of the box area, the **W** looks up to find a teammate **(M2 or forward F)** with a cut back (6) or a low cross across the box towards the front or near post.

- The 2 red defenders try to block or intercept.

- After the phase is finished, the same sequence is repeated from the left side and 2 new red defenders rotate in.

- The players all rotate positional roles throughout the practice.

Training Session 4: Goals Assisted from Side of Box (18.4% of Goals Scored)

PROGRESSION

3. Assists from the Side of Box Areas in a 6v6 (+2) + GKs Conditioned Small Sided Game

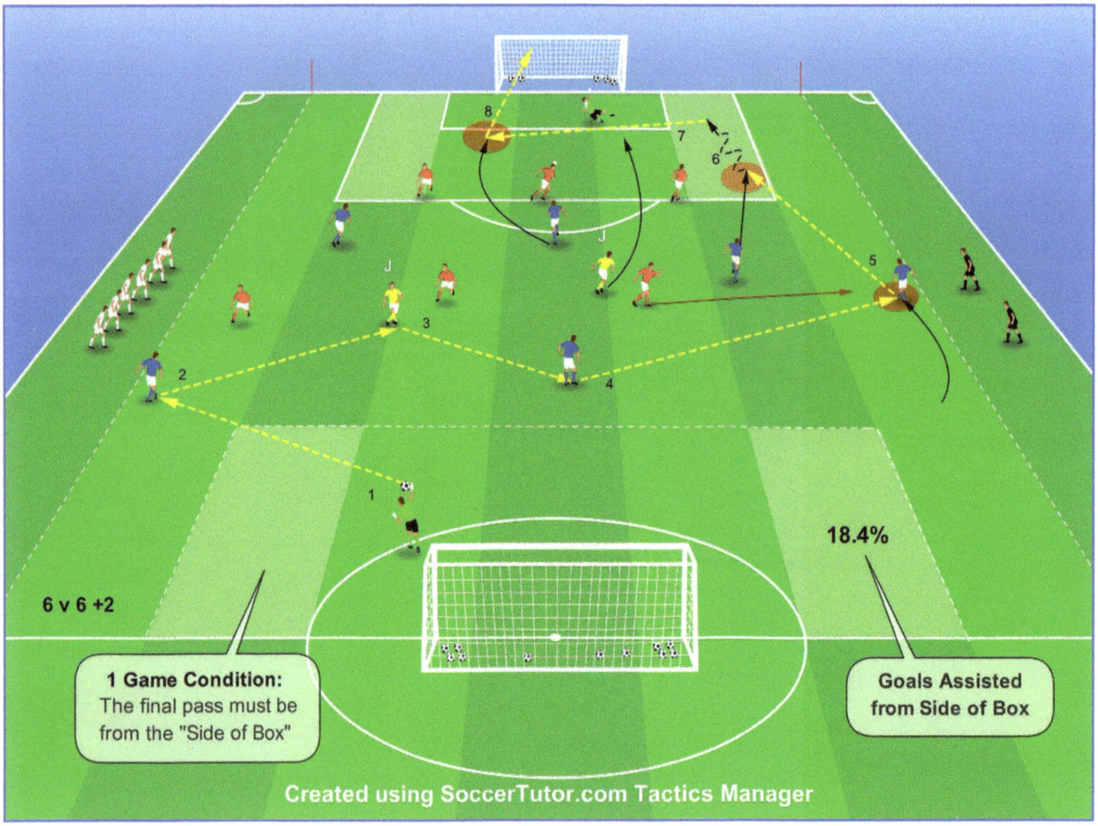

1 Game Condition: The final pass must be from the "Side of Box"

Goals Assisted from Side of Box

6 v 6 +2

18.4%

Description

- To finish the session, we play a 6v6 (+2) +GKs game using half a pitch with reduced width, as shown. The game starts from one of the GKs and that team (blues in diagram) build-up play with the help of the 2 Jokers and try to score.

- The only game condition is that teams can only score a goal if the assist is played from within the side of the box areas (highlighted).

- When a goal is scored, restart from the GK of the team that just conceded.

- Play short 5-8 minute games. There is a third team outside resting because the teams rotate after each game. The team that scores the most goals after a set number of games wins.

- If a set amount of time passes within a game without a goal being scored, the outside team enters and one of the other teams rotates out.

- When the outside resting team enters, (which would be the whites in the diagram), they become the attacking team with play starting from the GK.

TACTICAL EXAMPLES

5. GOALS ASSISTED FROM WIDE AREAS (18.4% OF GOALS)

Goals Assisted from Wide Areas

5. Goals Assisted from Wide Areas = 18.4% of All Goals Scored

Bayern Munich 5-0 Viktoria Plzen (Sané 50') - 04/10/2022

Goal Example 1A (Bayern Munich): Goals Assisted from Low Wide Zones = 31 of 304 Goals (10.2%)

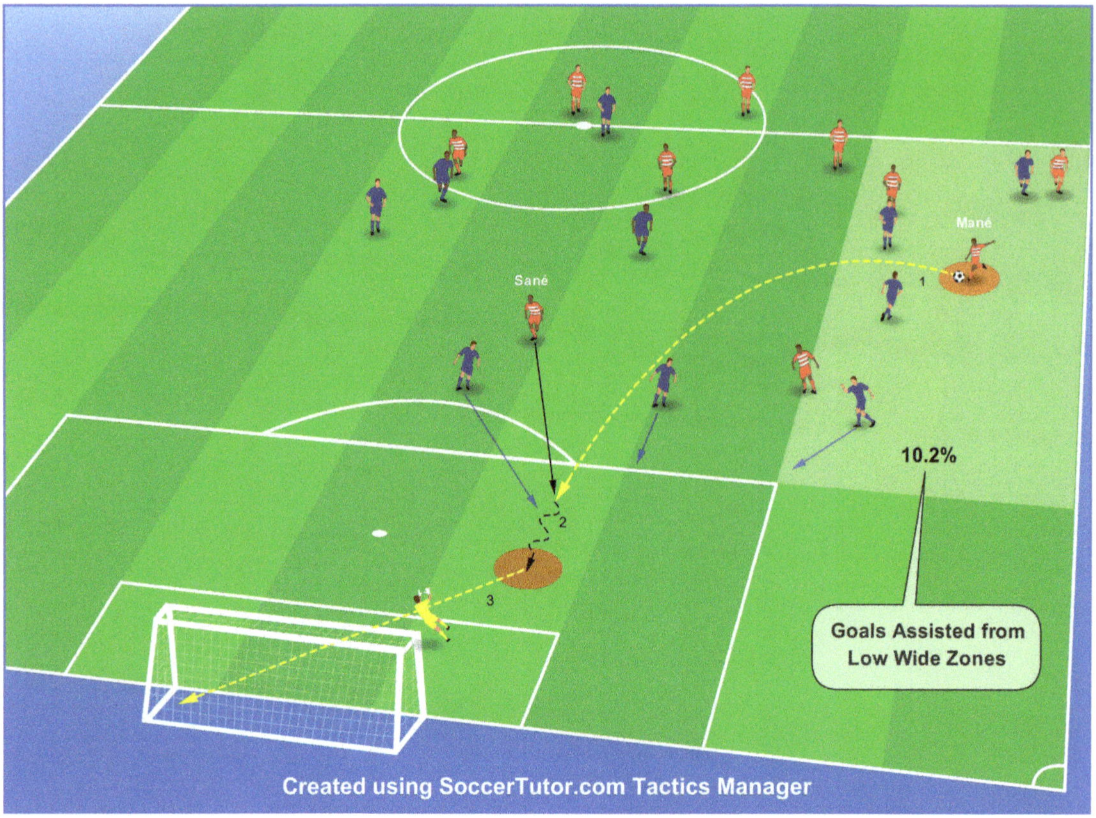

Description

Bayern's left winger **Mané** showed in many games that in addition to being a great finisher, he is also a very precise passer. In this example, he delivers a perfect high diagonal pass into the box from the low wide zone. The opposite winger **Sané** takes advantage of his great speed to get to the ball before the defender and strikes it into the far corner of the goal to score.

Key Aspects

1. The technique, the speed of decision, and the vision of **Mané** makes his long pass perfect for the ball to reach **Sané's** run at the exact right moment.

2. There is a connection and coordination between **Mané** and **Sané**. The great pass is matched by the timing of **Sané's** run.

3. The high quality of **Sané** is demonstrated to control the pass perfectly with his weaker right foot at speed, and then produce a firm and accurate shot across the GK into the far corner.

5. Goals Assisted from Wide Areas = 18.4% of All Goals Scored

PSG 7-2 Maccabi Haifa (Mbappe 64') - 25/10/2022

Goal Example 1B (PSG): Goals Assisted from Low Wide Zones = 31 of 304 Goals (10.2%)

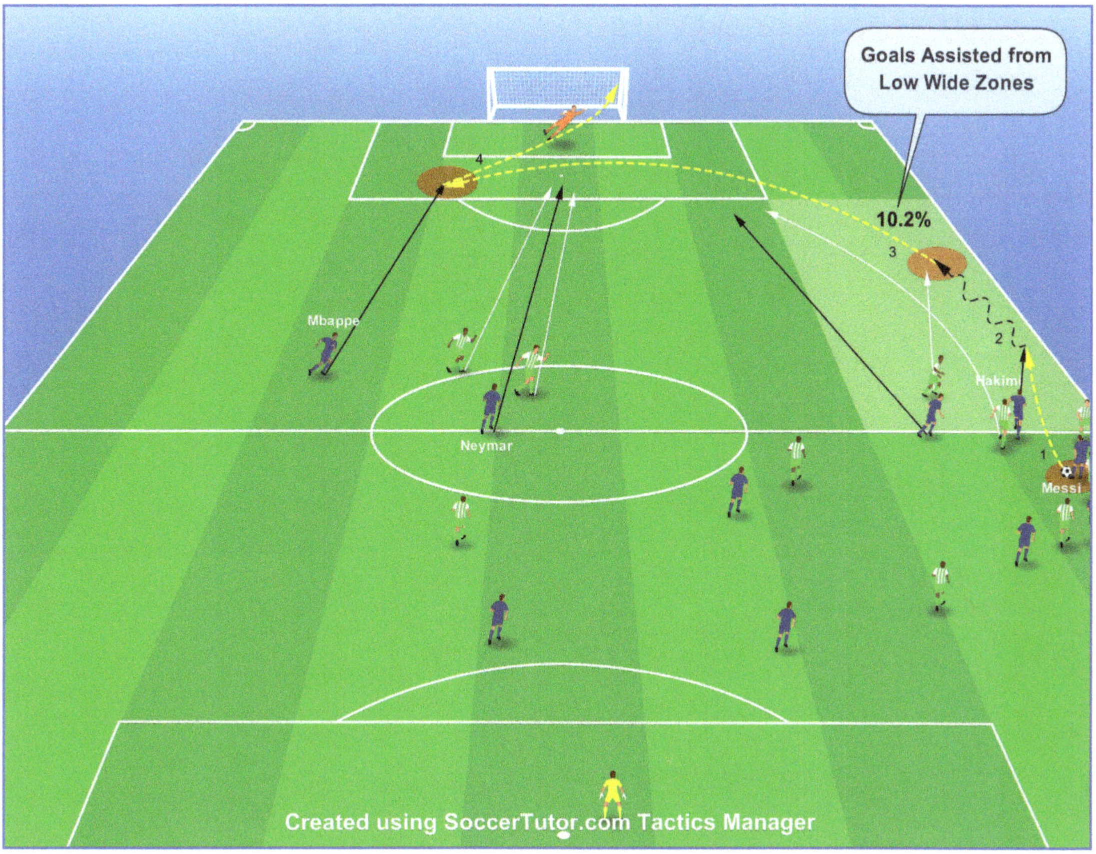

Description

We start with the forward **Messi** on the right very close to the sideline in his own half. He passes in between 2 opponents for the forward run of the right back **Hakimi**, who dribbles the ball forward higher up the flank. He looks up and sees the other forward **Mbappe** free in space.

Hakimi switches play to the left side of the pitch with a long pass for **Mbappe** inside the box. **Mbappe** controls the pass well and shoots into the far corner of the goal.

Key Aspects

1. **Messi's** first pass is very important as it breaks the defensive line of the opposition. **Hakimi** has time to carry the ball and look for available teammates.

2. **Hakimi** displays good vision and executes a perfect switch of play.

3. **Mbappe's** control is fantastic, but his curved finish into the far corner was even more impressive as it gave the GK no chance of producing a save.

5. Goals Assisted from Wide Areas = 18.4% of All Goals Scored

Manchester City 5-0 Copenhagen (Haaland 7') - 05/10/2022

Goal Example 2A (Manchester City): Goals Assisted from High Wide Zones = 25 of 304 Goals (8.2%)

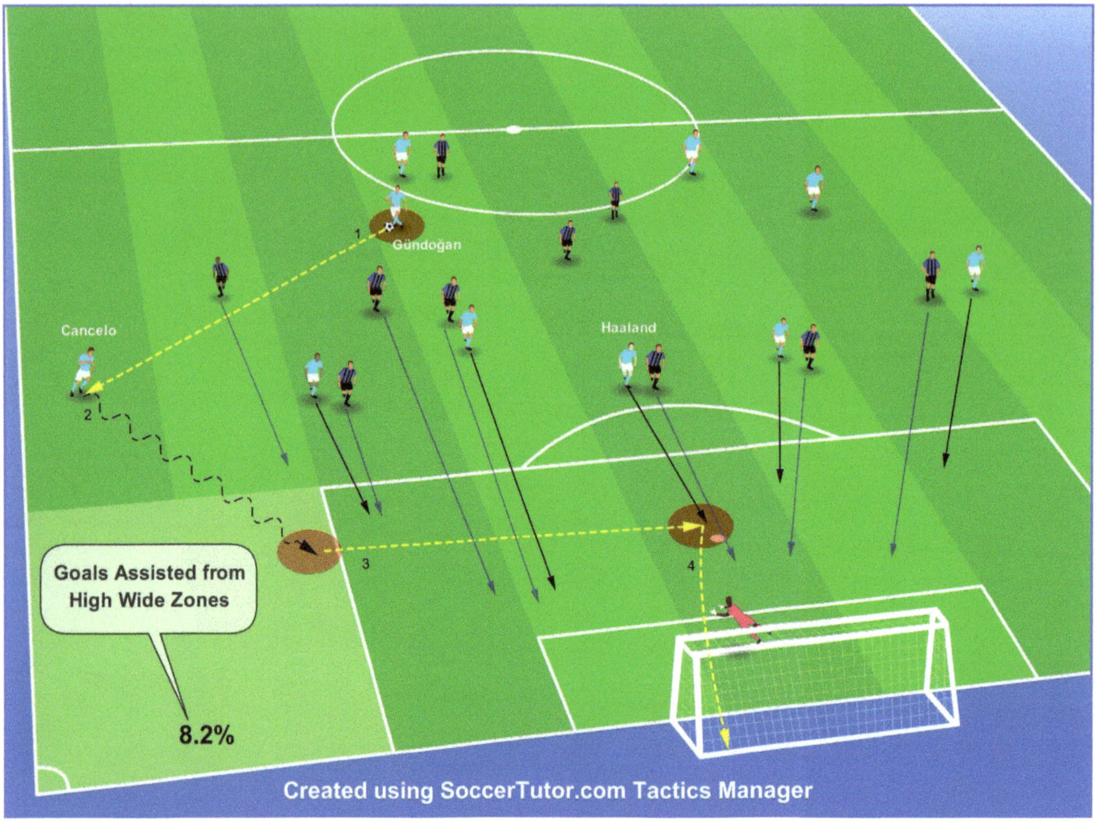

Description

The central midfielder **Gündoğan** passes from the centre to the right back **Cancelo**. He receives the ball and drives with it until he reaches the box. From there (high wide zone), he looks up and delivers a cross towards the penalty spot.

The forward **Haaland** first lets all the defenders run past him, stops at the right point (penalty spot), and then scores with a low shot into the corner from **Cancelo's** pass/cross.

Key Aspects

1. **Gündoğan's** vision discovers the space on the right side.

2. **Cancelo** takes advantage of the free corridor ahead of him, advances very quickly, stops, and looks for **Haaland**.

3. **Haaland** shows high intelligence to slow down his run and wait for 1 second on the penalty spot. This creates 2 metres of space for him. **Cancelo** picks him out and **Haaland** scores with great ease.

5. Goals Assisted from Wide Areas = 18.4% of All Goals Scored

Inter 4-0 Viktoria Plzen (Mkhitaryan 35') - 26/10/2022

Goal Example 2B (Inter): Goals Assisted from High Wide Zones = 25 of 304 Goals (8.2%)

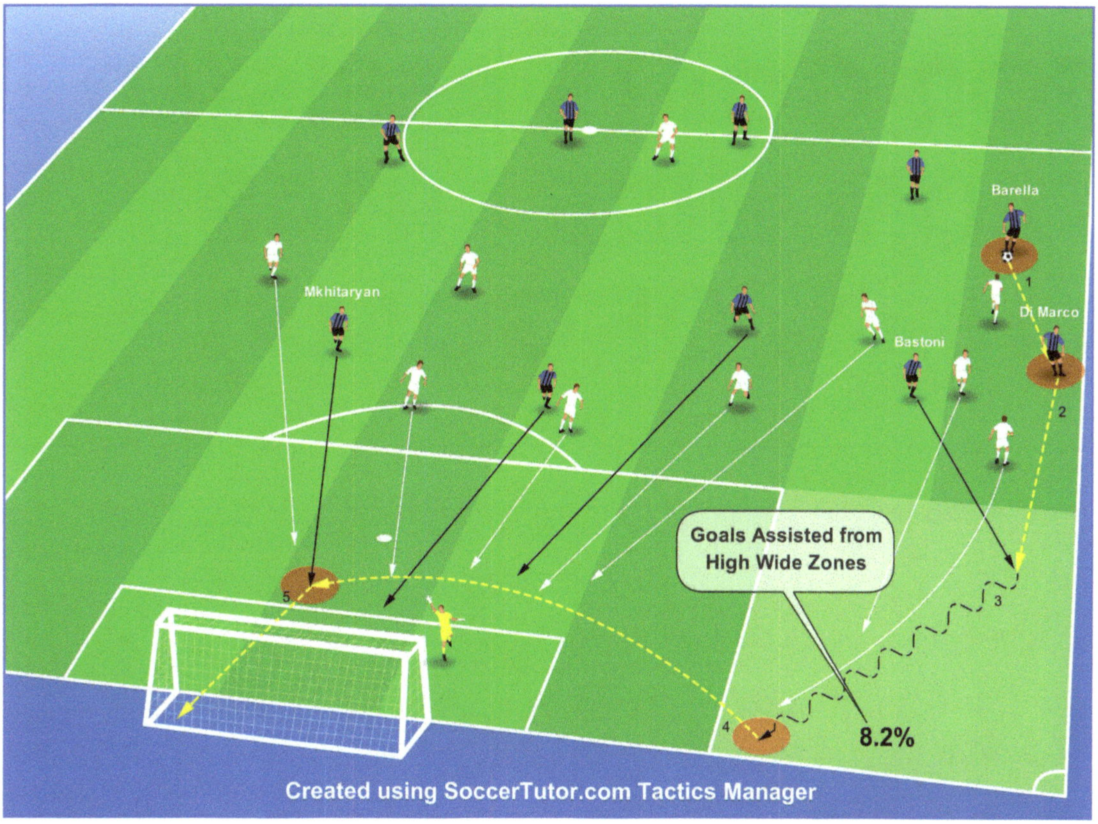

Description

The central midfielder **Barella** opens the game up and passes to the left wing back **Di Marco**. Without wasting any time, he passes in behind for the advanced run of left centre back **Bastoni**, who takes advantage of the space in the high wide zone, then dribbles to the by-line. **Bastoni** delivers a high cross over the GK for the central midfielder **Mkhitaryan** to score.

Key Aspects

1. **Barella** and **Di Marco** are quick to send the ball down the flank into the empty high wide zone, which is the perfect part of the pitch to gain an advantage over defenders.

2. **Bastoni** perfectly understands the play in good coordination with his teammates, picks up the ball and sends a great cross into the area. His great speed in executing the action is key to beating the opposition's defence.

3. **Dzeko** (the forward) makes a run to the near post and attracts defenders, which leaves **Mkhitaryan** free at the back post.

TRAINING SESSION 5

Wide Areas
56 Goals

FOR GOALS ASSISTED FROM WIDE AREAS (18.4% OF GOALS)

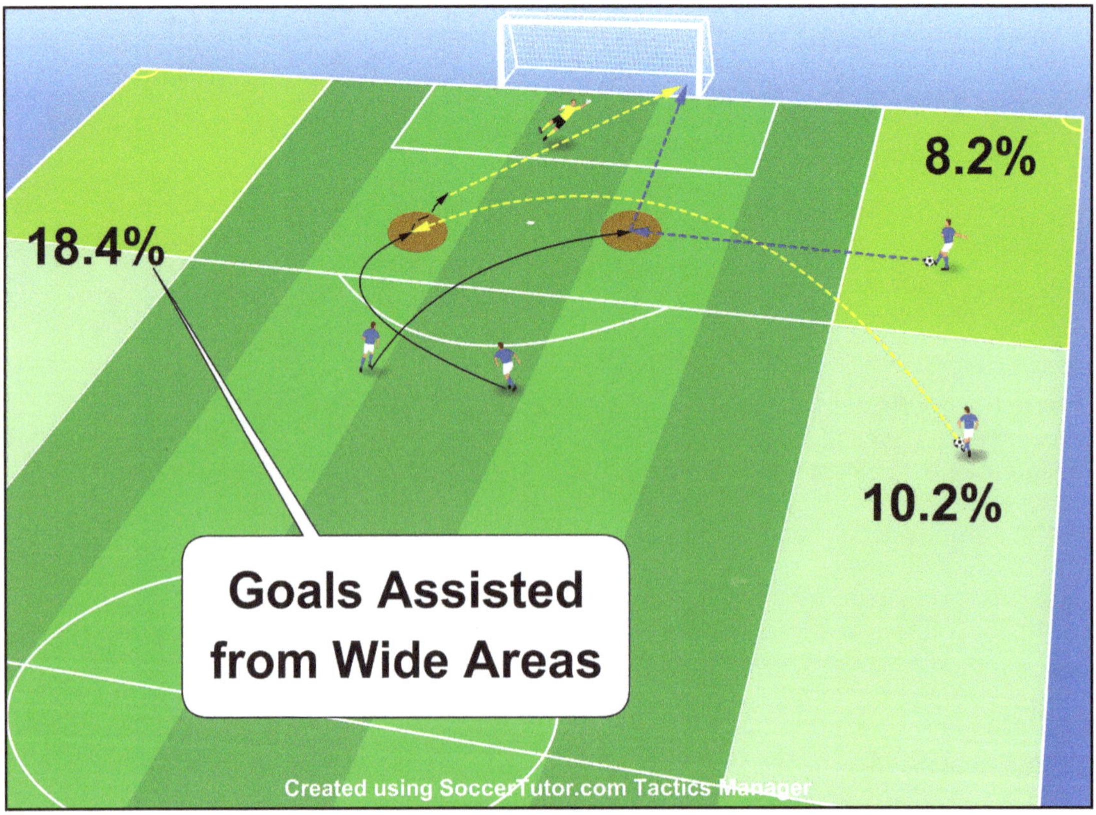

Goals Assisted from Wide Areas

18.4%

8.2%

10.2%

Training Session 5: **Goals Assisted from Wide Areas (18.4% of Goals Scored)**

SESSION FOR THIS TACTICAL SITUATION (4 PRACTICES)

1. One-Two to Receive Wide, Deep Cross into Box from Low Wide Zone, Control and Finish

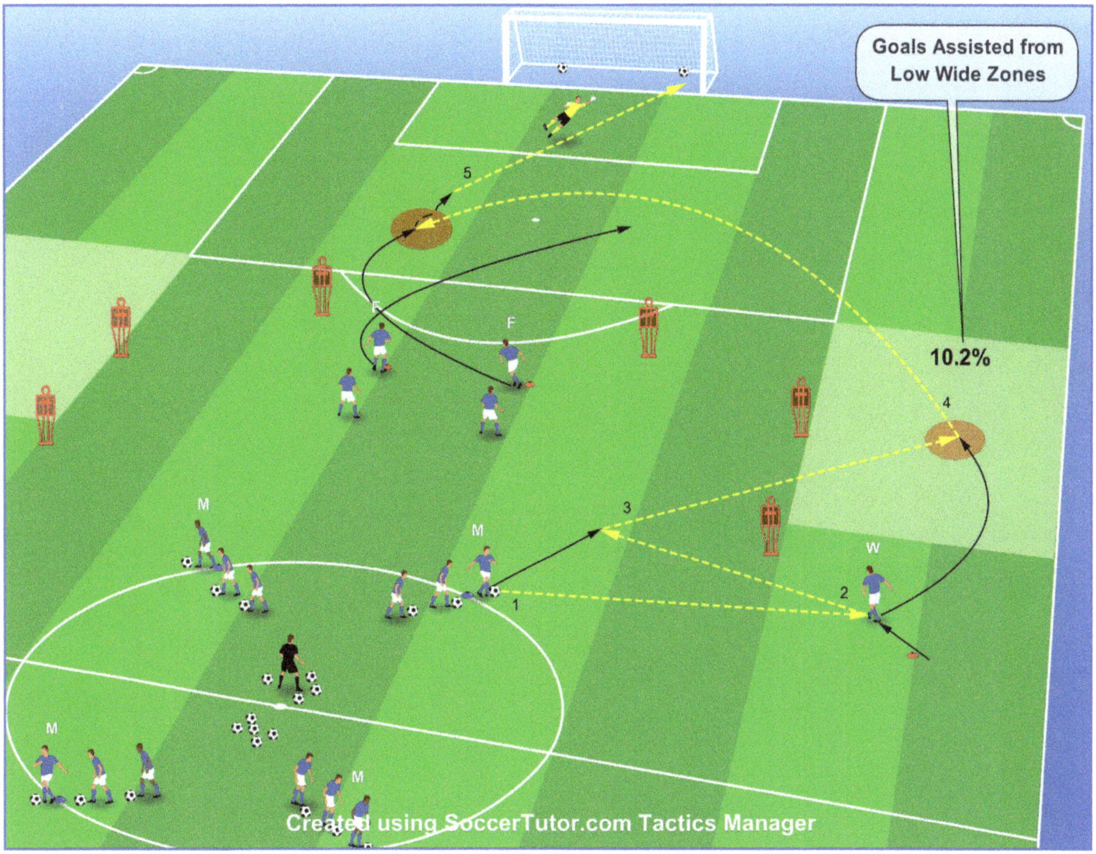

Description

- With a full pitch split into 4 sections, the players start in groups of 4. There are also 4 forwards at each end.
- The midfielder **(M)** passes to the winger **(W)**, who then plays a one-two with **M**, and receives within the low wide zone.
- From within the low wide zone, the winger **(W)** then delivers a cross into the box for the 2 forwards **(F)** who make opposite runs to the near/far post respectively.
- The forward **(F)** has to control the ball and then shoot at goal.
- When the phase is over, the winger **(W)** moves to the other side of the pitch to join the other group. This is to make sure the players practice deep crosses on both flanks.
- The midfielder **(M)** becomes the winger **(W)** and the sequence is repeated.

Training Session 5: **Goals Assisted from Wide Areas (18.4% of Goals Scored)**

VARIATION

2. One-Two, Pass Wide to Winger, Dribble into High Wide Zone, Cross and Finish

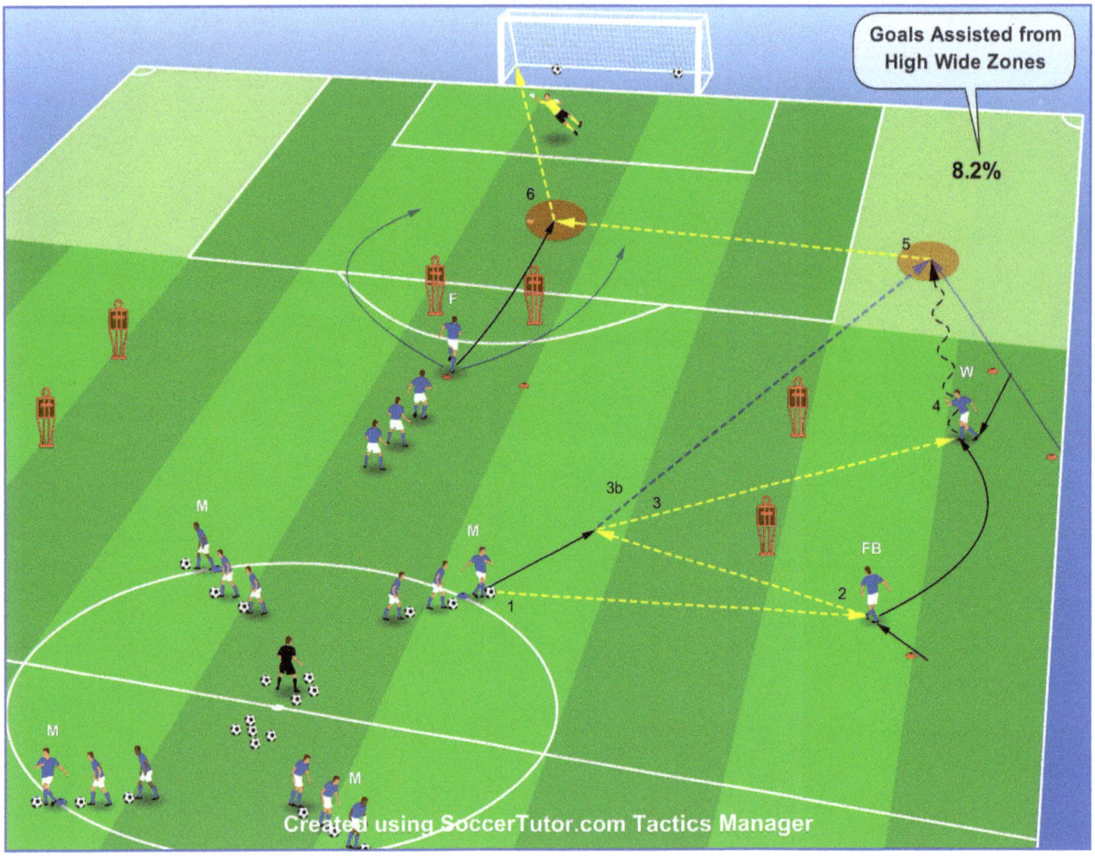

Description

- In this variation, we now work with 3 players in the wide area **(FB, M, & W)**.

- The midfielder **(M)** passes to the full back **(FB)**, who returns the ball back to **M** to complete the one-two.

- The midfielder **(M)** moves forward to receive and passes wide to the winger **(W)**, who drops back to receive. He dribbles the ball forward into the high wide zone. From there, he must locate the forward **(F)** and deliver a cross.

- The forward **(F)** has to decide between the 3 positions that he wants to try and meet the cross (left, right or centre).

- When the phase is over, the winger **(W)** moves to the other side of the pitch to join the other group. This is to make sure the players practice crosses on both flanks.

- The midfielder **(M)** becomes the full back **(FB)** and the full back becomes the winger **(W)**. The sequence is repeated.

Training Session 5: Goals Assisted from Wide Areas (18.4% of Goals Scored)

PROGRESSION

3. Conditioned 6v6 (+4) +GKs SSG with Diagonally Opposite Goals and Multiple Wide Zones for Assists

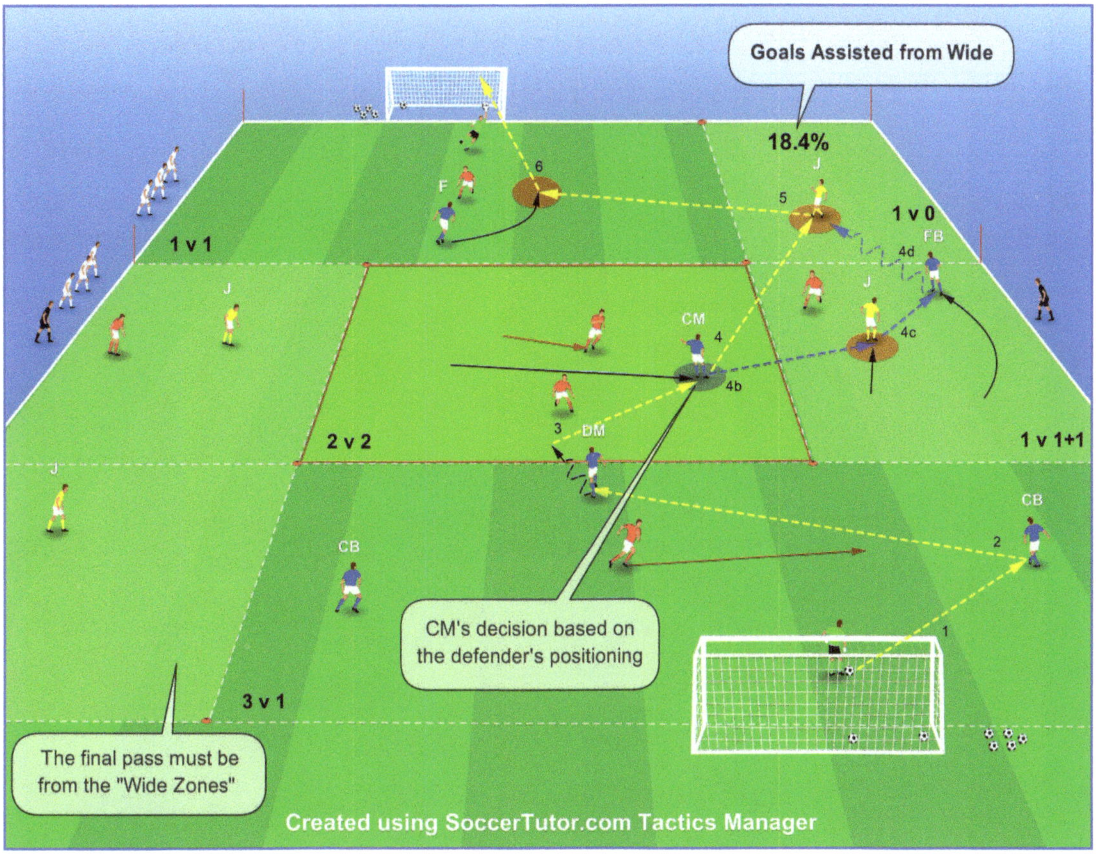

Description

- The size of the whole area used depends on the age/level of your players. There are 7 zones marked out in total, as shown in the diagram.

- Ideally, you want to use 2 mobile goals so they can be moved. In the first half of the game, the goals are positioned to the right and we practice assists with right backs. In the second half, they are moved to the left (still diagonally opposite each other) so we can practice assists with left backs.

- In each of the 4 wide zones, there is a yellow Joker, who always play with the team in possession.

- We play a 6v6 (+4) +GKs game starting from the GK. The blue attacking players can move across zones, but the red defenders cannot. To score a goal, the last pass (assist) must come from either the low or high wide zone. If the reds win the ball, they have the same aim.

- After each 5 minute game, rotate the team waiting (whites) in. Keep a total score to determine the winning team.

Training Session 5: Goals Assisted from Wide Areas (18.4% of Goals Scored)

PROGRESSION

4. Assists from Wide Areas in a Conditioned 7v7 +GKs SSG with Wide Zones

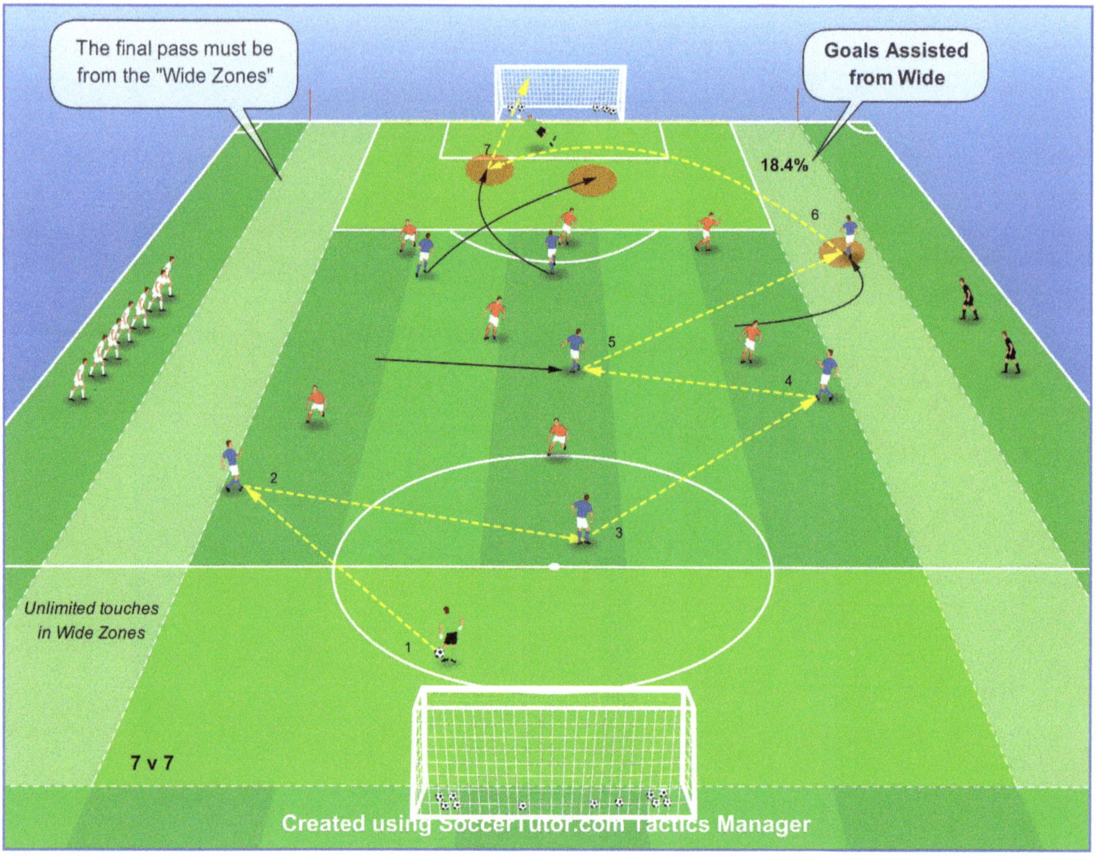

The final pass must be from the "Wide Zones"

Goals Assisted from Wide

18.4%

Unlimited touches in Wide Zones

7 v 7

Description

- In this final practice of the session, we play a 7v7 +GKs game starting from the GK.

- There are 2 wide zones marked out as shown. To score a goal, the last pass (assist) must come from a wide zone.

- Only 1 attacking player can enter a wide zone at a time, and no defending players can enter.

- If the red defending team win the ball, they have the same aim.

- When a goal is scored, the game restarts from the GK of the team that just conceded. This is important to speed up the game. The GK does not have to wait - he should play out very quickly.

- After each 5 minute game, rotate the team waiting (whites) in. Keep a total score to determine the winning team.

- When the new team enters to play, they start as the attacking team, receiving from their GK.

TACTICAL EXAMPLES

6. GOALS ASSISTED FROM CENTRE SPACE (13.2% OF GOALS)

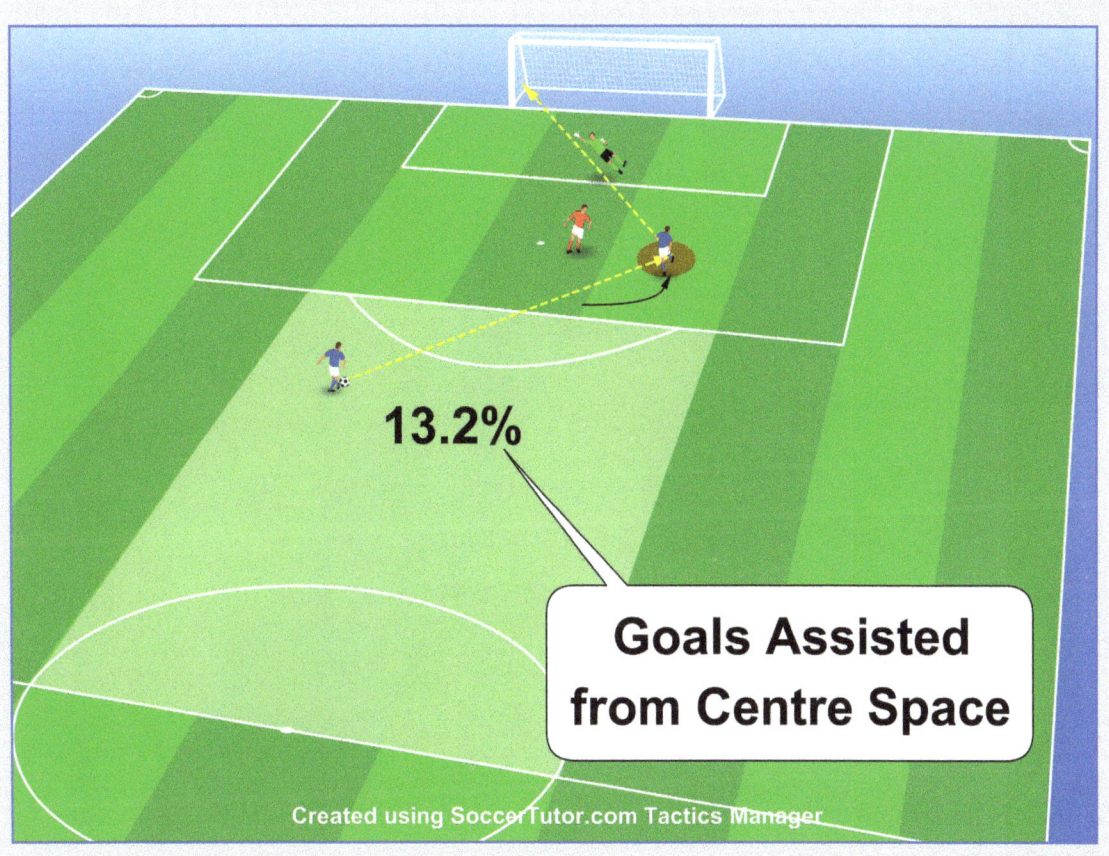

13.2%

Goals Assisted from Centre Space

6. Goals Assisted from Centre Space = 13.2% of All Goals Scored

Ajax 0-3 Liverpool (Elliott 51') - 26/10/2022

Goal Example 1 (Liverpool): Goals Assisted from Centre Space = 40 of 304 Goals (13.2%)

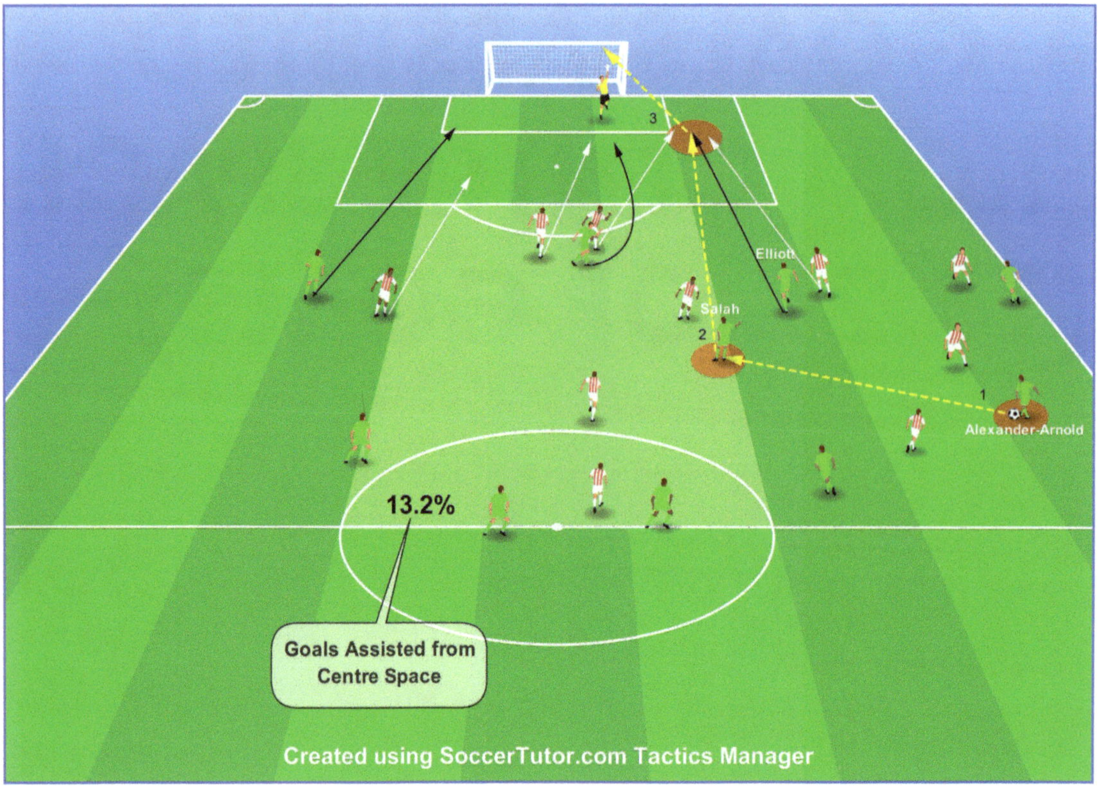

Description

This Liverpool goal is simple but has great technical execution. Only 2 two passes are needed to move the ball from out wide to the most dangerous area. The right back **Alexander-Arnold** passes to the right winger **Salah** inside the centre space, who receives and turns with 1 touch and then plays a though pass for the run of attacking midfielder **Elliott**. He finishes into the roof of the net with his first touch.

Key Aspects

1. **Alexander-Arnold** displays great vision to see **Salah** free in the key centre space.

2. **Salah's** technical quality means he can quickly turn and play a perfect through pass into the gap and empty space in the box. His awareness meant that he could see the space and movement of **Elliott** to create a fantastic opening.

3. **Elliott** exploits the poor positioning of the Ajax defenders who left a big gap in their defence. He is able to beat the first defender for speed and hold off the second defender who comes across to contest him. With a small angle available, his finish is quality into the high part of the goal which gives the GK no chance.

6. Goals Assisted from Centre Space = 13.2% of All Goals Scored

Benfica 1-1 PSG (Messi 22') - 05/10/2022

Goal Example 2 (PSG): Goals Assisted from Centre Space = 40 of 304 Goals (13.2%)

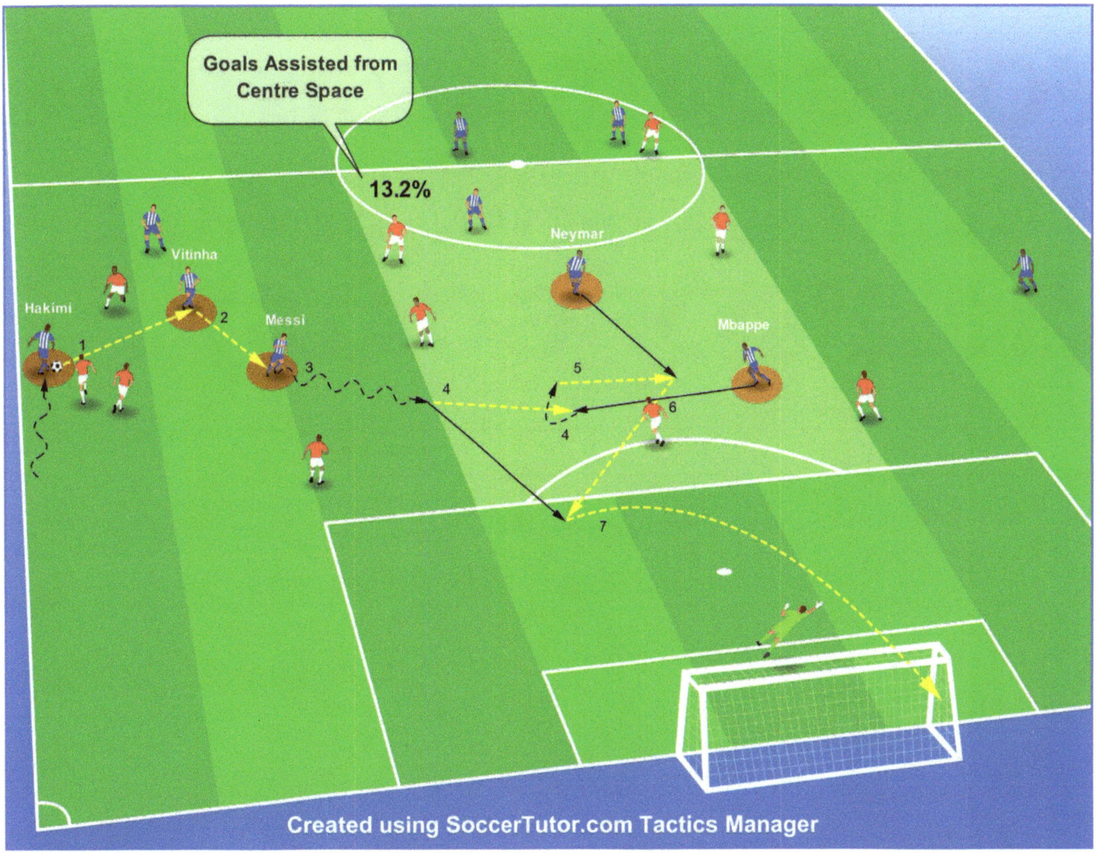

Description

The right back **Hakimi** passes to the central midfielder **Vitinha**, who plays a short pass to **Messi**. He dribbles inside and passes to the forward **Mbappe**, who has moved across to receive. **Mbappe** turns and passes to the oncoming **Neymar**, who plays a short diagonal pass for **Messi** to curl the ball into the far corner.

Key Aspects

1. The short and fast passes show the high technical quality of all the players.

2. There is very fast movement in attack with the players switching positions. **Messi** leaves the attack and comes into midfield to receive the ball. **Neymar** drops back close to the midfield line, and **Mbappe** moves to position himself in the centre. They all leave their zones at the same time, which throws off the defending team.

3. Finally, **Messi** displays great vision to see the GK's position and then send the ball over him. The whole play for the goal is exceptional.

TRAINING SESSION 6

Centre Space — 40 Goals

FOR GOALS ASSISTED FROM CENTRE SPACE (13.2% OF GOALS)

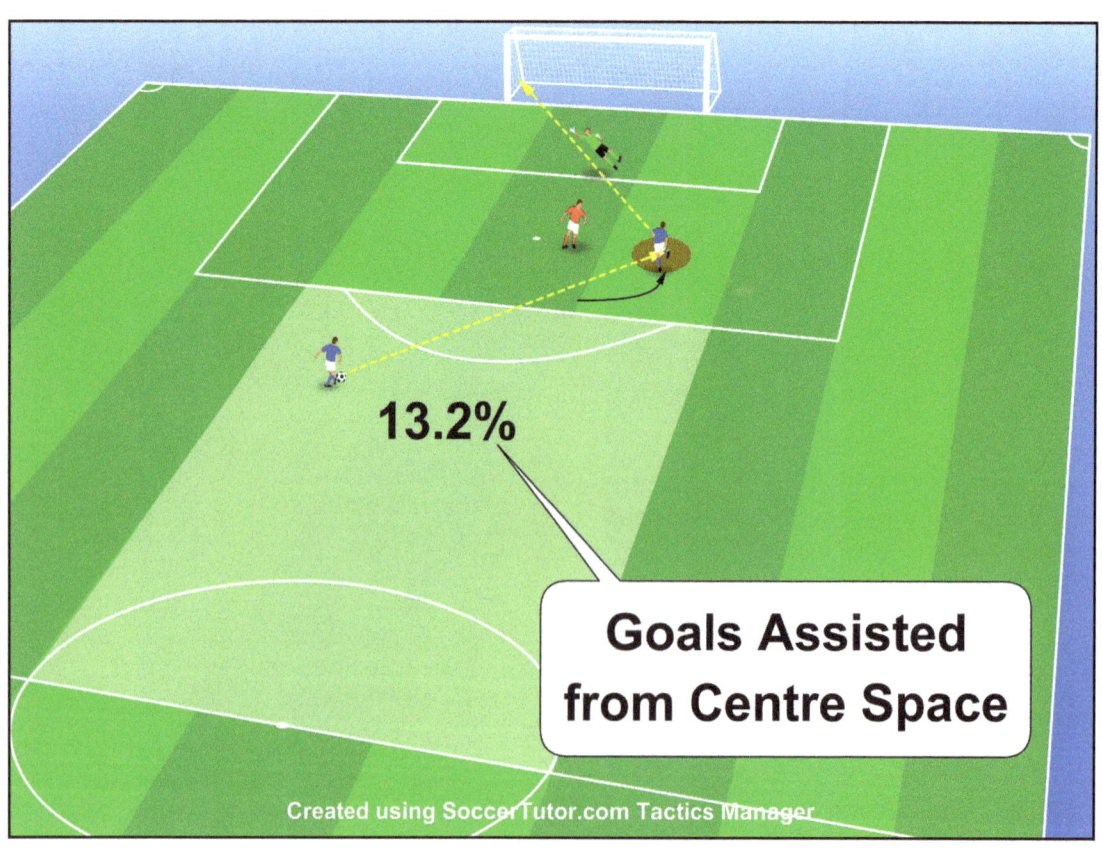

13.2%

Goals Assisted from Centre Space

Training Session 6: Goals Assisted from Centre Space (13.2% of Goals)

SESSION FOR THIS TACTICAL SITUATION (4 PRACTICES)

1. Pass, Turn in Centre Space, Through Pass for Run in Behind, and Finish

Description

- You can have 2 groups in either half of the pitch, as shown. **A** starts and can either pass to **B1** or **B2**.

- **B** must receive and decide if he wants to turn out to the left or right side of his cone.

- **B** then plays a through pass for the forward **C's** run in behind and into the box.

- The through pass can be either side of the 2 mannequins or in between them.

- **C** has to start from a central position between the 2 mannequins and makes a run at the correct time to indicate to **B** where he should play the through pass (make eye contact).

- **C** receives the pass inside the box and tries to score past the GK.

- The players rotate **A → B1 → B2 → C → A** and the same sequence is repeated with the next player waiting and a new ball.

Training Session 6: Goals Assisted from Centre Space (13.2% of Goals)

VARIATION

2. Different Passing Options in the Centre Space, Turn, Through Pass in Behind, and Finish

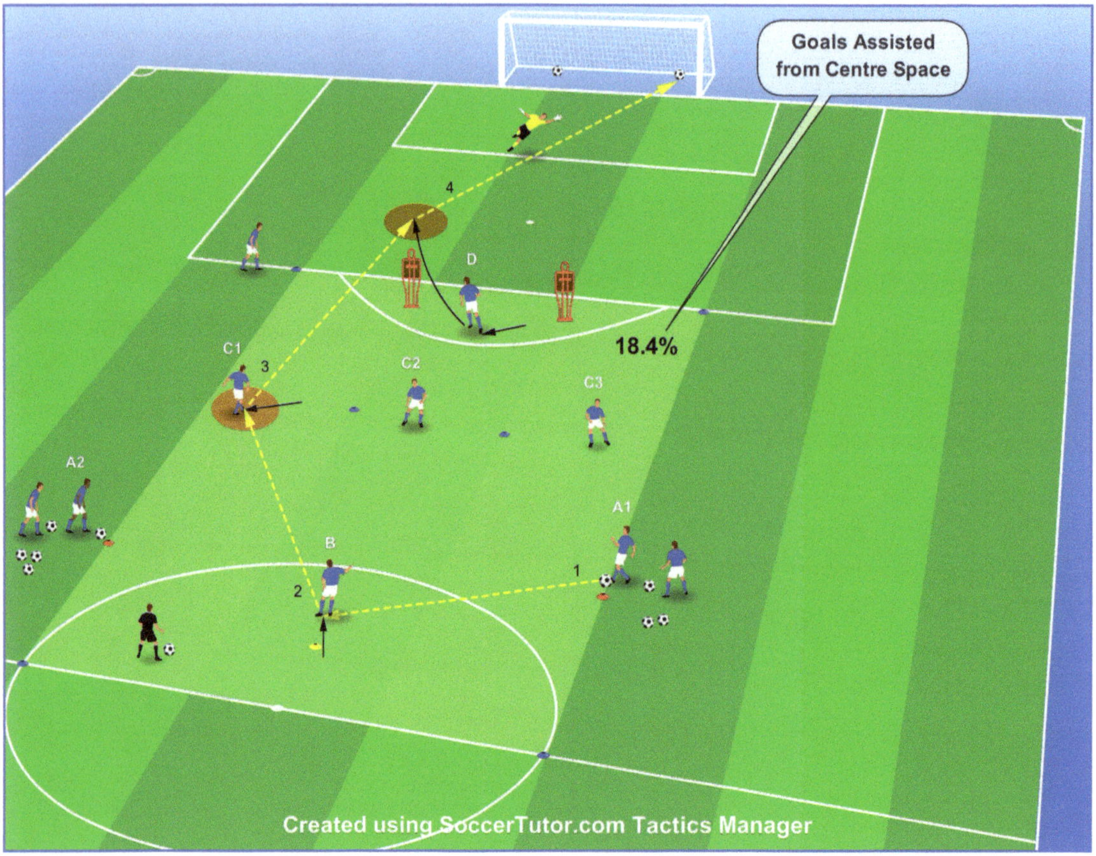

Description

- You can have 2 groups in either half of the pitch, as shown. **A1** or **A2** start and pass inside to **B**.
- **B** must receive and decide if he wants to pass to **C1**, **C2**, or **C3**. In the diagram example, **C1** receives and turns.
- **C** then plays a through pass for the forward **D's** run in behind and into the box.
- The through pass can be either side of the 2 mannequins or in between them.
- **D** has to start from a central position between the 2 mannequins and makes a run at the correct time to indicate to **C** where he should play the through pass (make eye contact).
- **D** receives the pass inside the box and tries to score past the GK.
- The players rotate **A1** → **A2** → **B** → **C1** → **C2** → **C3** → **D** → **A** and the same sequence is repeated with the next player waiting (**A2**) and a new ball.

Training Session 6: Goals Assisted from Centre Space (13.2% of Goals)

PROGRESSION
3. Play Through the Centre Space in a 4v2 Situation and Finish with 2v1 in the Box

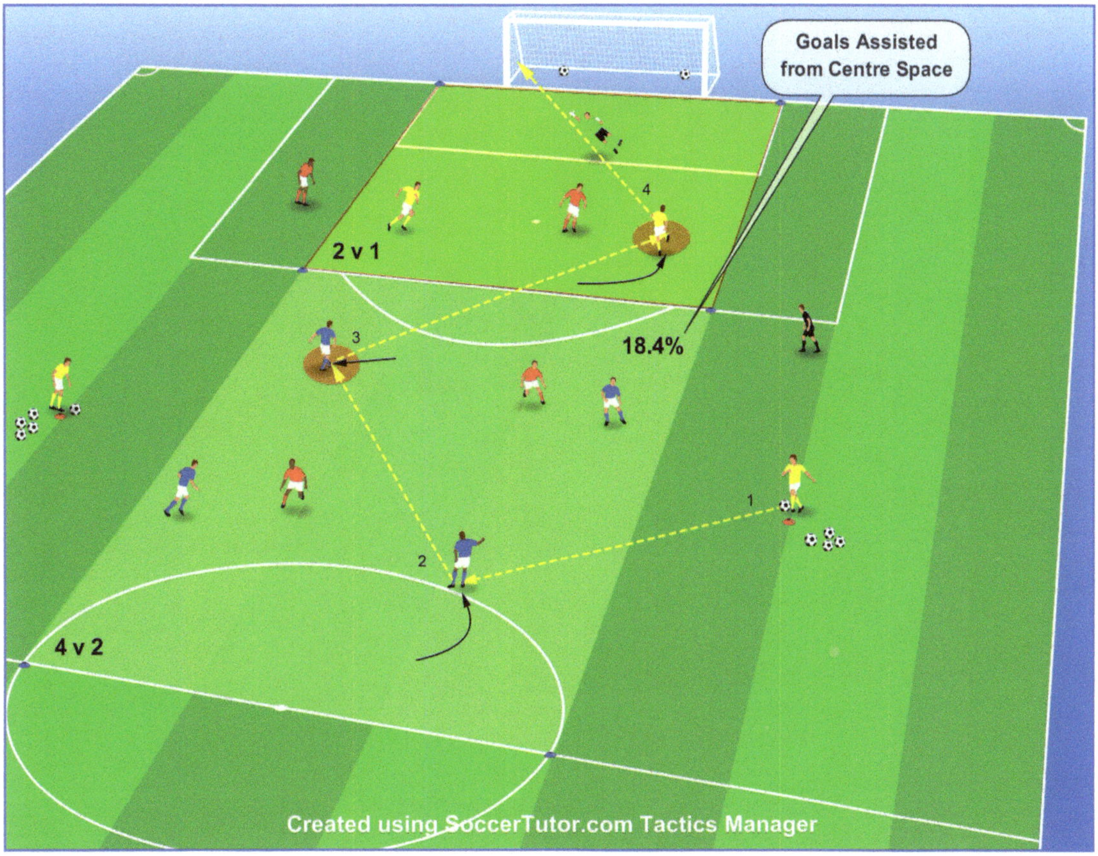

Description

- The practice starts with an outside yellow player passing to a blue player in the centre space (highlighted).
- In the centre space, there is a 4v2 situation. The aim is to pass to a free player who then passes forward to a yellow player in the box.
- In the box there are 2 yellow forwards vs 1 red defender (2v1 situation). They wait for the ball to reach them, receive, and then try to score a goal.
- The play restarts in the exact same way from the opposite outside yellow player.
- The red defender in the box rotates out and the resting player enters.
- After a set number of repetitions, rotate the team roles.

Training Session 6: **Goals Assisted from Centre Space (13.2% of Goals)**

PROGRESSION

4. Goals Assisted from the Centre Space in a 6v6 (+2) +GKs Narrow Conditioned Game

Description

- Using a full pitch but only the width of the box, we play a 6v6 (+2) +GKs game. The 2 yellow Jokers play with the team in possession. The 2 penalty boxes are used as end zones but there is no offside rule applied.

- The game starts with the GK's pass into the centre space. The attacking team aim to build-up play and move the ball into the end zone for their forward to score. The final pass must be played from within the centre space (condition).

- Only 1 blue player and 1 red player can enter the end zone once the pass has been struck.

- There is a third team outside resting because the teams rotate. The games are 3-5 minutes. The team that scores the most goals after a set number of games wins.

- Every time there is a goal, the GK starts the game with the team that conceded the last goal becoming the new attacking team.

COACH YOUR TEAM TO SCORE MORE GOALS

TACTICAL EXAMPLES

7. GOALS ASSISTED FROM HALF SPACES (10.9% OF GOALS)

10.9%

Goals Assisted from Half Spaces

Created using SoccerTutor.com Tactics Manager

7. Goals Assisted from Half Spaces = 10.9% of All Goals Scored

Manchester City 2-1 Borussia Dortmund (Haaland 84') - 14/09/2022

Goal Example 1 (Manchester City): Goals Assisted from Half Spaces = 33 of 304 Goals (10.9%)

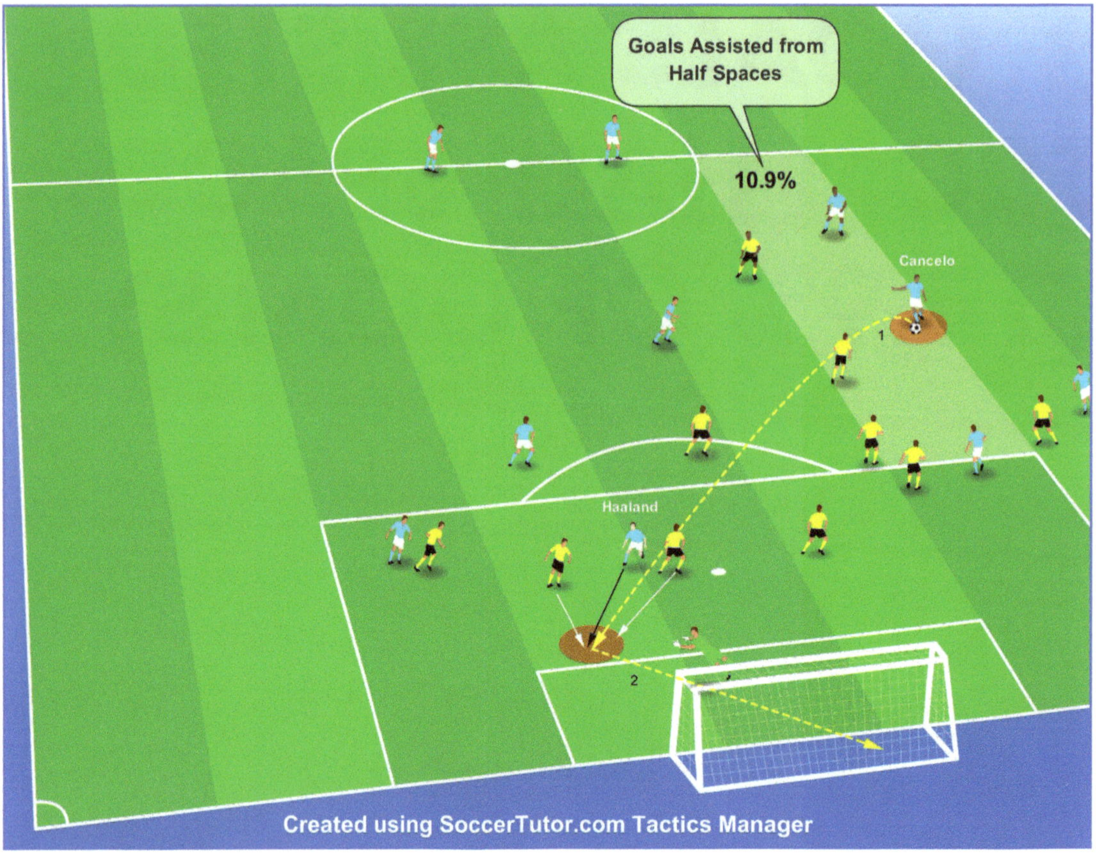

Description

This is an example of a simple goal executed brilliantly.

The left back **Cancelo** has the ball in the left half space. With the outside of his right foot, he delivers an incredible cross over the defenders to the far post.

The centre forward **Haaland** anticipates the cross perfectly and beats the Dortmund defender for speed to meet the ball with an "impossible" acrobatic outside of the left foot finish into the top of the goal.

Key Aspects

1. The left back **Cancelo** delivers the cross with minimum execution time. His vision is key, as he works out the best place to deliver the ball in less than a second.

2. When it comes to the finish, there are very few players in the world who can score a goal with these characteristics. **Haaland** shows incredible agility to meet the ball and perfect technique to make a true connection and score with the outside of his foot.

7. Goals Assisted from Half Spaces = 10.9% of All Goals Scored

Maccabi Haifa 1-3 PSG (Mbappe 69') - 14/09/2022

Goal Example 2 (PSG): Goals Assisted from Half Spaces = 33 of 304 Goals (10.9%)

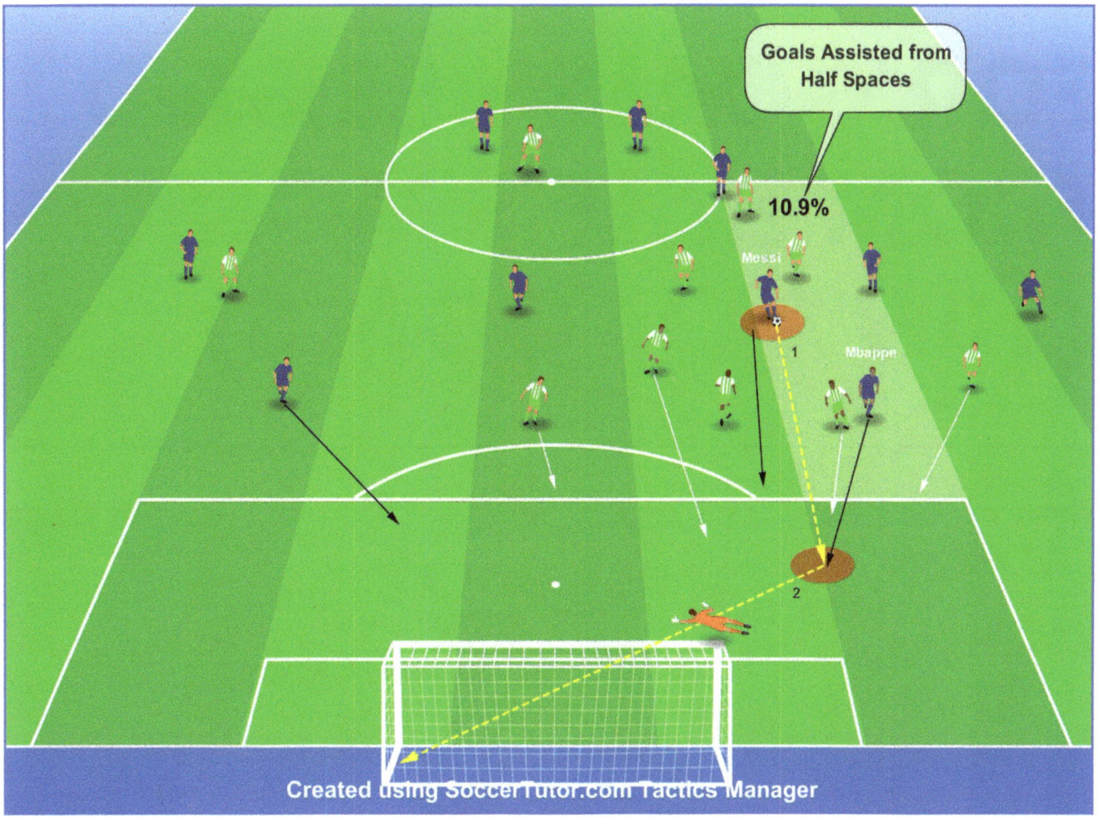

Description

The attacking midfielder **Messi** has the ball in the left half space. From there, he plays a very precise through pass in between the right back and centre back. The centre forward **Mbappe** receives the through pass inside the box and finishes with precision into the far corner of the goal.

Key Aspects

1. The excellent vision of **Messi** is the key for this goal. He has 2 easier options on either side, but instead chooses to thread a tight through pass to **Mbappe**.

2. A high passing skill is needed to play the ball through the small gap with the correct weight so **Mbappe** can get there before the GK and score.

3. The forward **Mbappe's** finishing is excellent. Even though it is initially a left foot finish, he turns his body and prepares his right leg with good agility to finish with his stronger foot. He places the ball in the exact spot he aims for into the far corner.

TRAINING SESSION 7

Half Spaces
33 Goals

FOR GOALS ASSISTED FROM HALF SPACES (10.9% OF GOALS)

10.9%

Goals Assisted from Half Spaces

Training Session 7: **Goals Assisted from Half Spaces (10.9% of Goals Scored)**

SESSION FOR THIS TACTICAL SITUATION (4 PRACTICES)

1. Receive in the Half Space and Deliver an Accurate Pass into the Box for a Finish

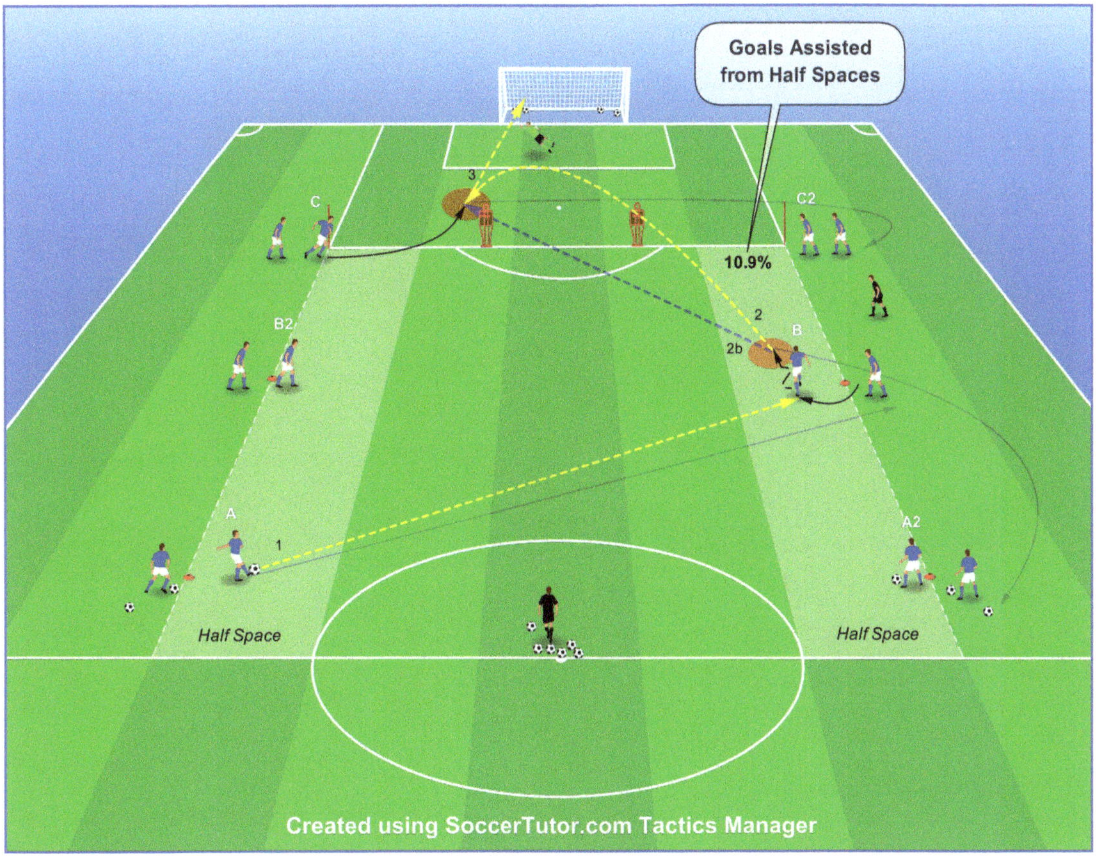

Description

- We start the session with a simple practice to start the progression of learning. However, precision is required in the passes as they are long passes, so that part is not simple.

- **A** starts by playing a long pass across to the opposite half space to **B**.

- When **B** receives the pass, he controls the ball and quickly sends an accurate final pass (assist) into the box.

- As you can see, this pass can be aerial **(2)** or along the ground **(2b)**.

- The forward **(C1)** controls the ball inside the box and tries to score.

- The players rotate **A → B → C → A** and the same sequence is repeated starting with **A2's** pass to **B2**.

- You can have 2 groups working in either half of the pitch.

Training Session 7: Goals Assisted from Half Spaces (10.9% of Goals Scored)

PROGRESSION
2. Pass Inside, then into the Half Space for a Through Pass into the Box for a Finish

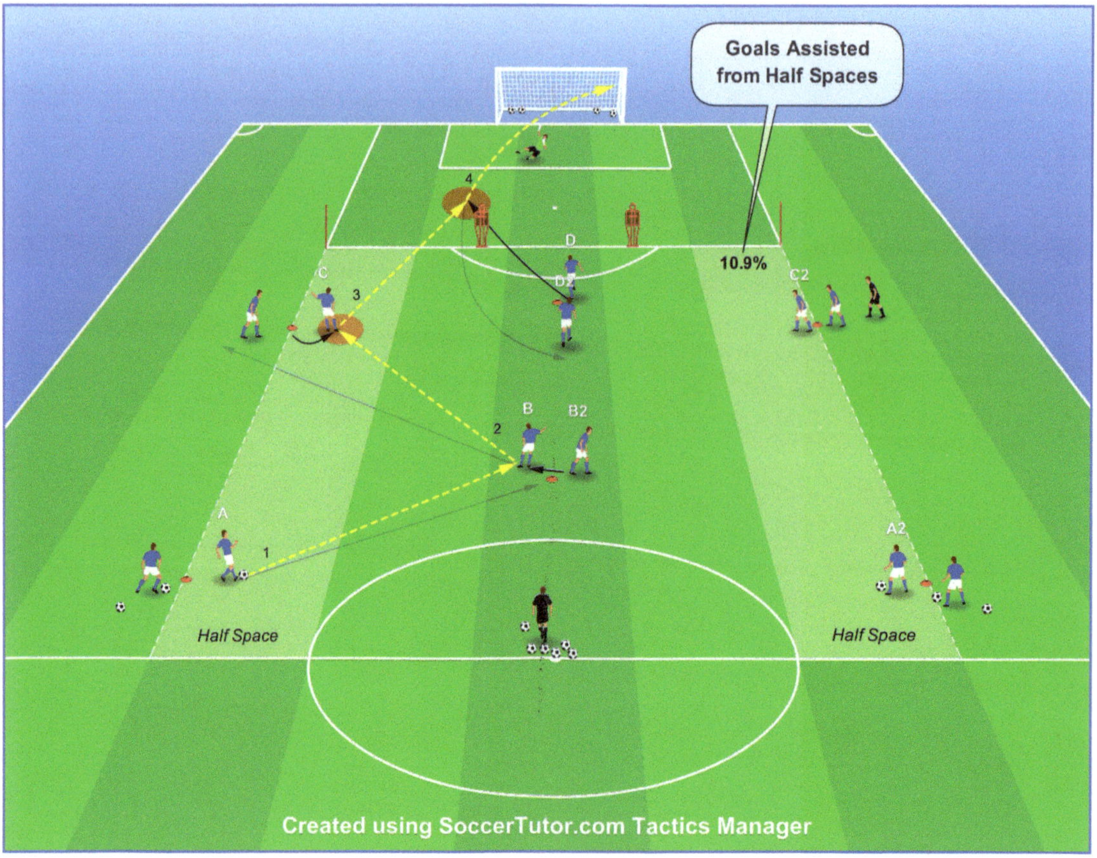

Description

- **A** starts by playing a diagonal pass to **B** in the centre.
- **B** passes to **C** in the half space.
- **C** plays a through pass to the left of the mannequin for the run of the **D** (forward) in between the 2 mannequins and into the box.
- **D** controls the ball inside the box and tries to score.
- The players rotate **A → B → C → D → A** and the same sequence is repeated starting with **A2's** pass to **B2**.
- You can have 2 groups working in either half of the pitch.

Training Session 7: Goals Assisted from Half Spaces (10.9% of Goals Scored)

PROGRESSION

3. Goals Assisted from the Half Space Zones in a 4v4 (+2) +GK Conditioned Small Sided Game

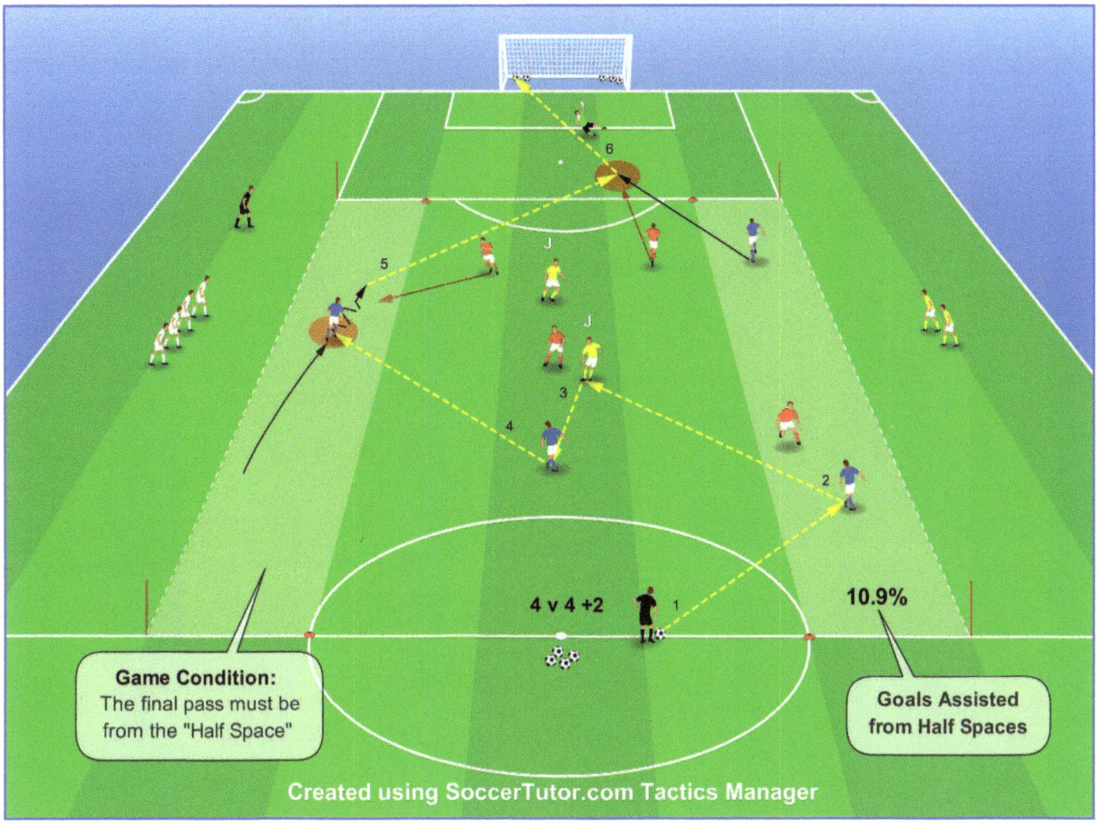

Game Condition: The final pass must be from the "Half Space"

Goals Assisted from Half Spaces — 10.9%

Description

- In half a pitch, we play only in the width of the box, and the box is used as an end zone. We also mark out the 2 half spaces.
- The Coach starts the game, and we play 4v4 (+2) +GK. The 2 yellow Jokers play with the team in possession.
- The aim is to score with an assist from within one of the half spaces.
- Only 1 blue player and 1 red player can enter the end zone (box) once the pass has been struck.
- After the phase is complete, the blues rotate out and are replaced by the white team. The 2 yellow Jokers rotate with the 2 resting outside.
- The Coach restarts with a pass to the reds who become the new attacking team, with the whites defending.
- All the goals are added up when the practice is finished. The team that scores the most total goals wins.
- The Jokers can also be a team, so all 4 teams rotate roles including becoming the Jokers.

Training Session 7: **Goals Assisted from Half Spaces (10.9% of Goals Scored)**

PROGRESSION

4. Goals Assisted from the Half Space Zones in an 8v8 +GKs Conditioned Game

Objective: Play the final pass from from the Half Spaces

Goals Assisted from Half Spaces

Description

- Using a full pitch but only the width of the box, we play an 8v8 +GKs game. The 2 penalty boxes are used as end zones but there is no offside rule applied. We also mark out the 2 half spaces.

- The game starts with the GK's pass and the attacking team (blues in diagram) aim to build-up play and move the ball into the end zone to score.

- The final pass (assist) must be played from within one of the half spaces.

- Players can enter the end zone once the pass directed in there has been struck.

- The reds aim to win the ball and then score themselves with an assist from a half space.

- There is a third team outside resting because the teams rotate. The games are 3-5 minutes. The team that scores the most goals after a set number of games wins.

ZONE OF GOALS

What Specific Pitch Zones are Goals Scored from?

ZONE OF GOALS: WHAT SPECIFIC PITCH ZONES ARE GOALS SCORED FROM?

Pitch Zone Where Goals were Scored from During the Champions League Group Stages in the 2022-2023 Season (304 Total Goals)

Front Centre of Box (FCB)
159 GOALS — 52.3%

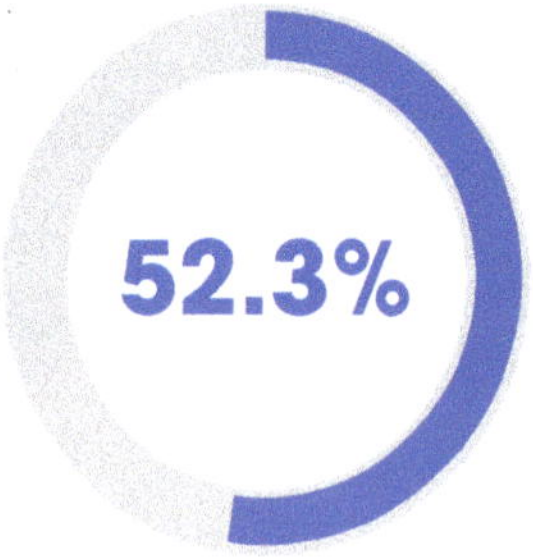

Back Centre of Box (BCB)
62 GOALS — 20.4%

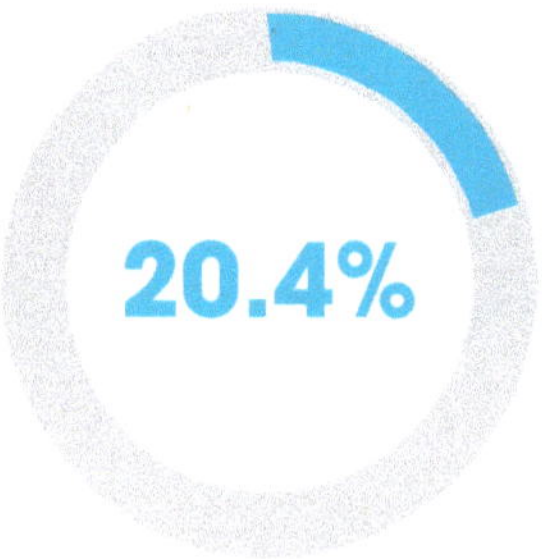

Outside Box
30 GOALS — 9.9%

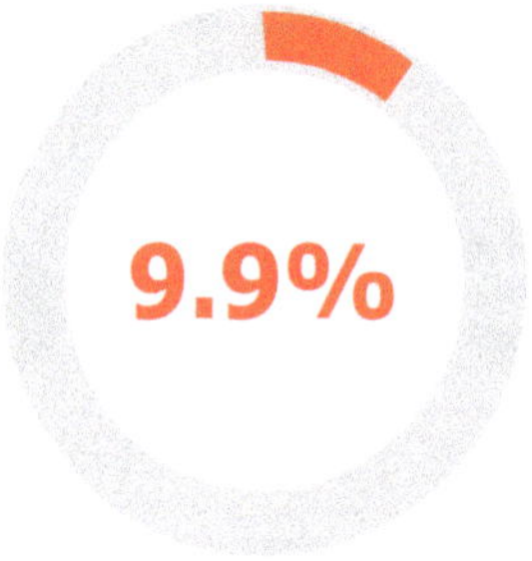

Penalty Spot
27 GOALS — 8.9%

Side of Box
26 GOALS — 8.6%

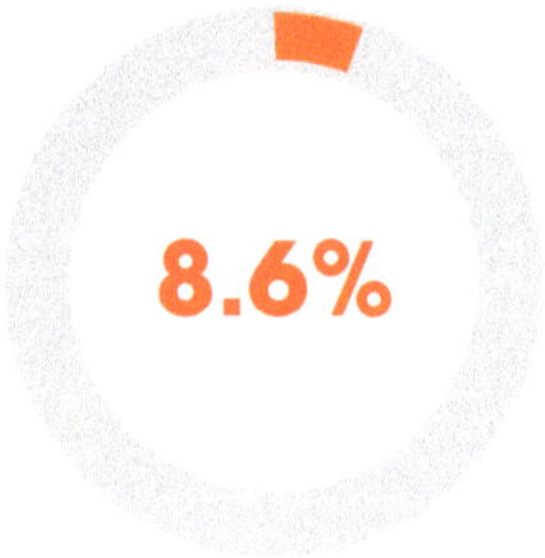

TACTICAL EXAMPLES

8. GOALS SCORED FROM CENTRE OF BOX (72.7% OF GOALS)

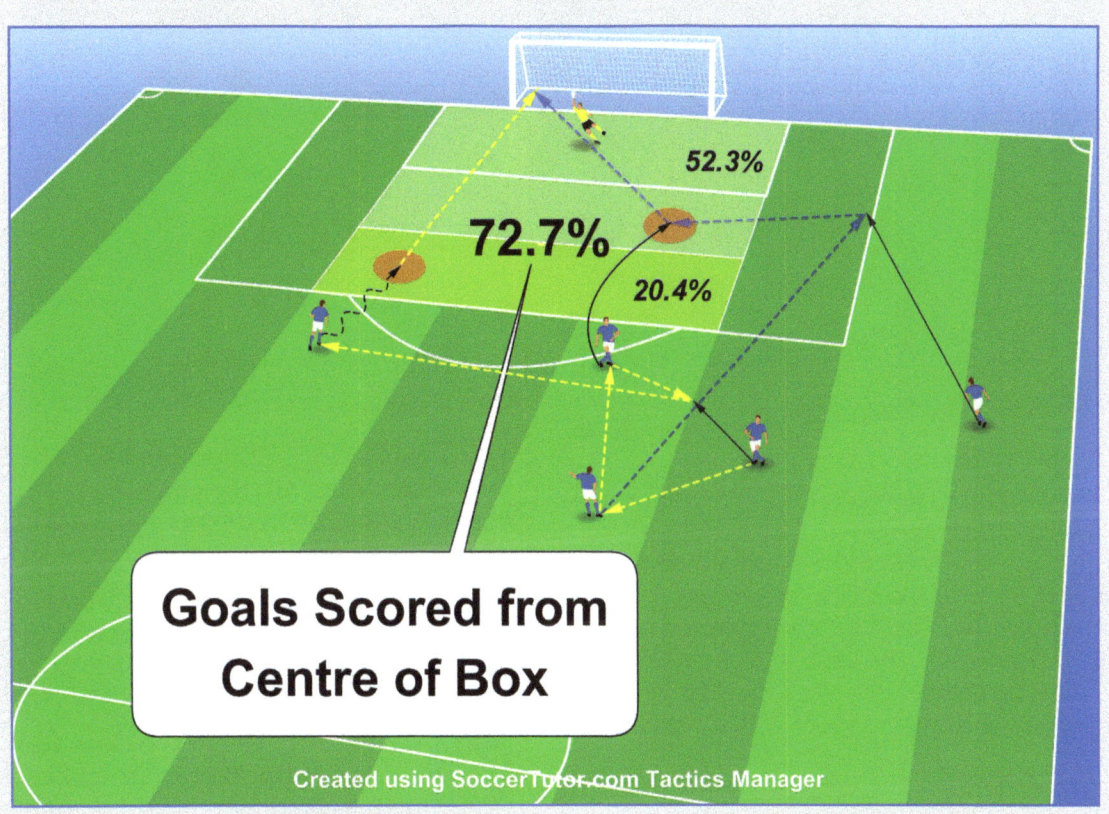

Goals Scored from Centre of Box

8. Goals Scored from Centre of Box = 72.7% of All Goals Scored

AC Milan 4-0 RB Salzburg (Krunic 46') - 02/11/2022

Goal Example 1A (AC Milan): Goals Scored from Front Centre of Box (FCB) = 159 of 304 Goals (52.3%)

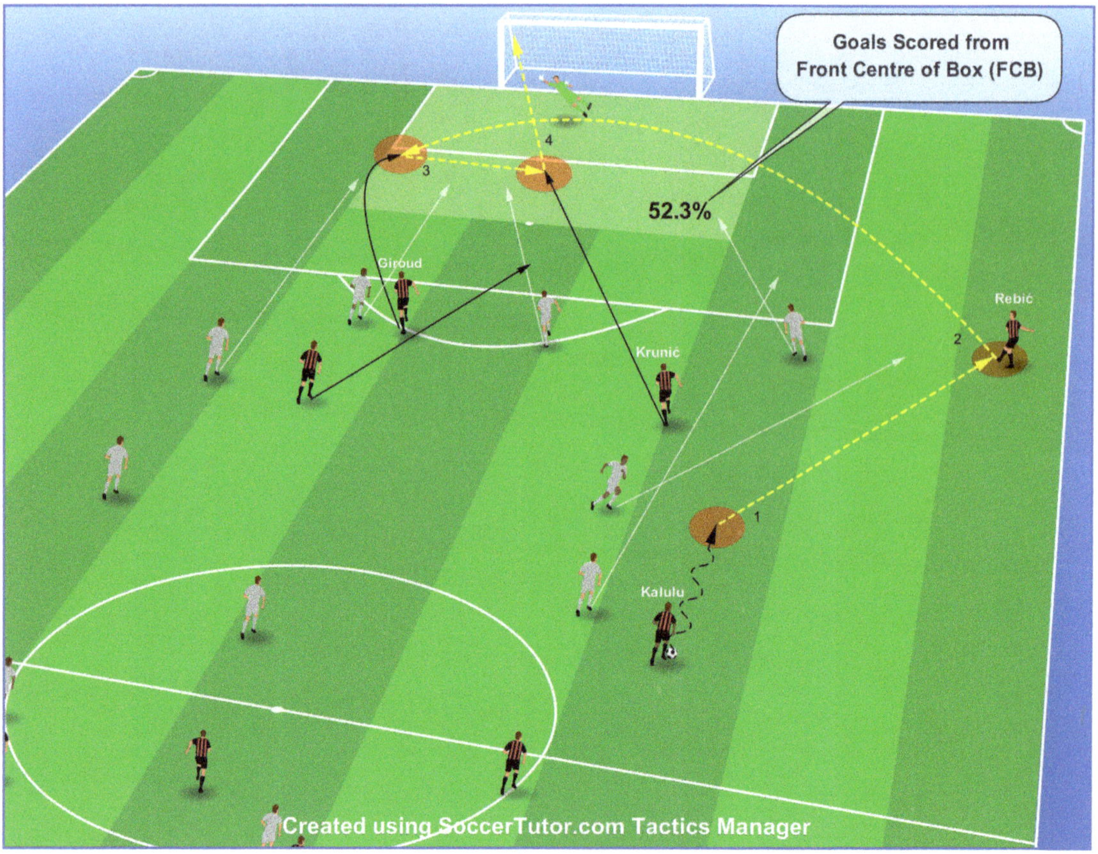

Description

The right back **Kalulu** dribbles forward into the centre and opens up play with a pass to the right winger **Rebić** high up on the flank. **Rebić** controls the ball, looks up towards the box and crosses into the front centre of the box area. The centre forward **Giroud** jumps up and heads across for attacking midfielder **Krunić** to score with a header.

Key Aspects

1. With only 2 passes, Milan move the ball from midfield to inside the box.

2. With **Rebić's** wide position and his teammates' runs into the box forcing the defenders to protect their goal, he has a lot of time and space to deliver his cross.

3. Inside the box, the height and attacking power of Milan in the air is evident. They take advantage of this and deliver high crosses into the box as often as they can.

4. The centre forward **Giroud** shows good awareness and composure to set up his teammate **Krunić** to score with a second header.

8. Goals Scored from Centre of Box = 72.7% of All Goals Scored

Viktoria Plzen 2-4 Bayern Munich (Goretzka 24') - 12/10/2022

Goal Example 1B (Bayern Munich): Goals Scored from Front Centre of Box (FCB) = 159 of 304 Goals (52.3%)

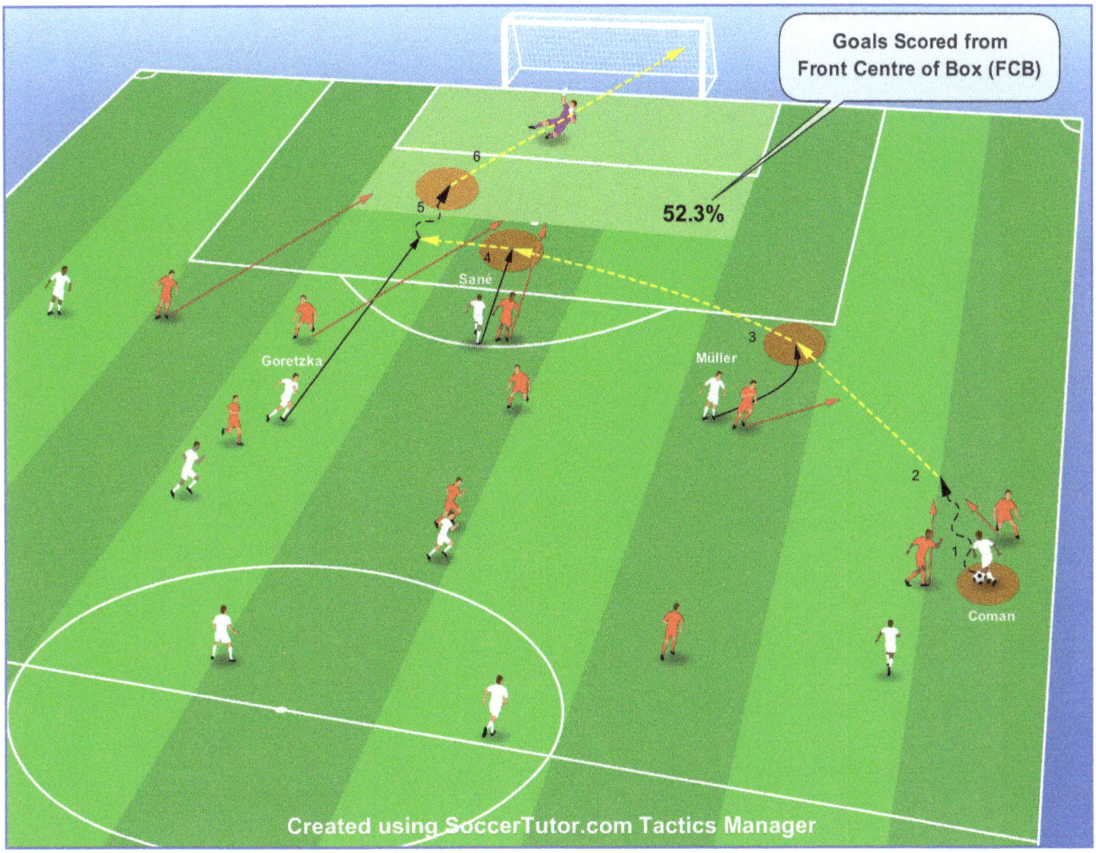

Description

The right winger **Coman** dribbles between 2 defenders on the wing and breaks through the opposition's midfield line easily. He then plays a through pass for the centre forward **Müller**, who runs behind his opponent to receive and crosses into the box. The N°10 **Sané** misses the ball, so the central midfielder **Goretzka** controls it and finishes into the far corner.

Key Aspects

1. The right winger **Coman's** dribbling skills take 2 defenders out of the game. A third defender who was marking **Müller** is now in a 2v1 situation which makes the pass to **Müller** easy.

2. The centre forward **Müller** takes advantage of the space he has to cross into the box.

3. After **Sané** misses the ball, **Goretzka** uses a single touch to control the ball and create space for himself in the centre of the box. From there, he is able to simply slot the ball home past the GK.

8. Goals Scored from Centre of Box = 72.7% of All Goals Scored

Viktoria Plzen 2-4 FC Barcelona (Pablo Torre 75') - 01/11/2022

Goal Example 2A (FC Barcelona): Goals Scored from Back Centre of Box (BCB) = 62 of 304 Goals (20.4%)

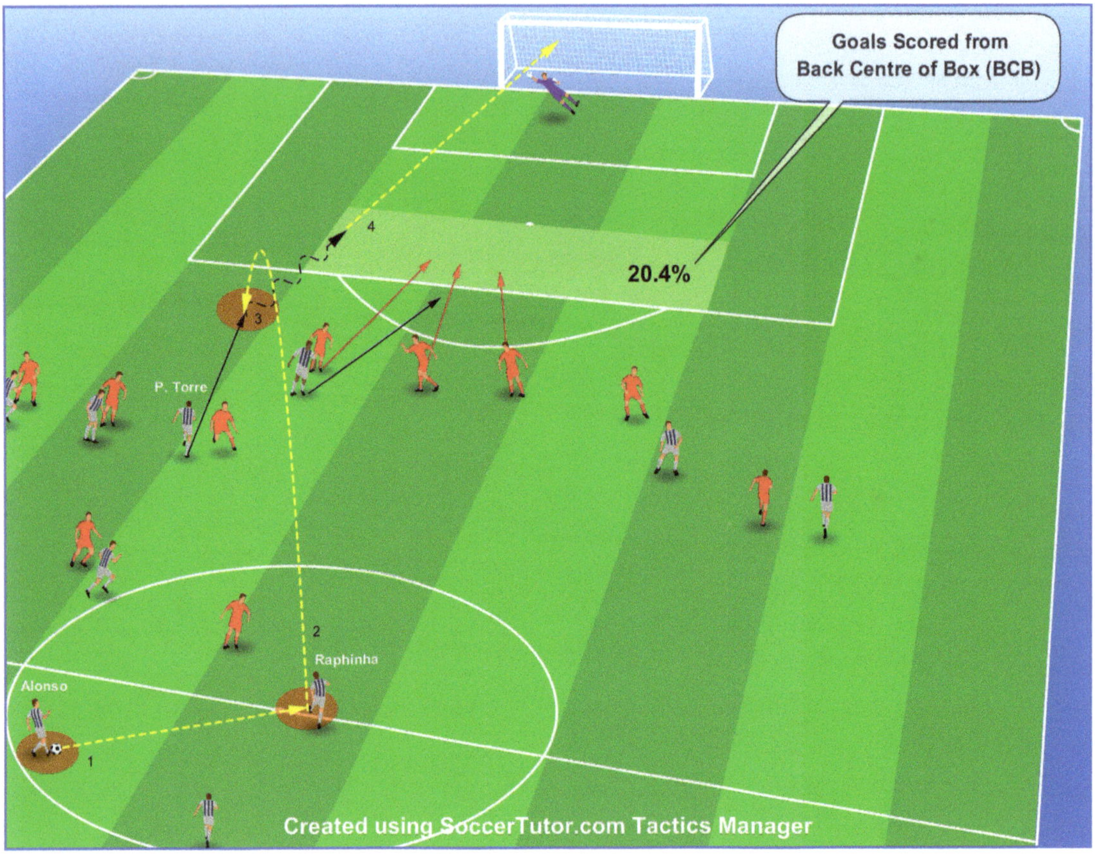

Description

The left back **Alonso** passes to right winger **Raphinha** in the central circle. He sends a long pass over the defensive line, so that central midfielder **Pablo Torre** can receive at speed with his third man run. He takes a very good first touch out in front with his right foot and smashes the ball into the top of the net with his left.

Key Aspects

1. Barcelona have many fast forwards and players with a lot of quality to send perfect passes in behind the defence.

2. The assist is played superbly by **Raphinha**, but the opposition allow him too much time and space to look up and pick the right pass for **Pablo Torre's** run.

3. Intelligence is displayed by **Pablo Torre** to attack the gap in the opposition's defence and make a run into the empty space behind the defensive line. He alerts **Raphinha** by pointing to where he wants the ball played, and then shows great speed to meet the pass.

8. Goals Scored from Centre of Box = 72.7% of All Goals Scored

RB Salzburg 1-1 AC Milan (Saelemaekers 40') - 06/09/2022

Goal Example 2B (AC Milan): Goals Scored from Back Centre of Box (BCB) = 62 of 304 Goals (20.4%)

Description

The central midfielder **Bennacer** drives with the ball into the attacking half of the pitch and passes wide to the left winger **Leão**. He drives the ball inside and into the box, slows down and passes across to the right winger **Saelemaekers**, who controls the ball and finishes at the near post.

Key Aspects

1. RB Salzburg had just lost the ball, so they did not have any defensive shape or organisation. They are unable to stop **Bennacer** as they are all running back towards their own goal. He plays the pass to **Leão** at the exact right time once he is free in space.

2. The final pass from **Leão** is played at the correct moment in front of the defenders who have all moved closer to the goal to defend it. This gives **Saelemaekers** time and space around the penalty spot, which he takes advantage of to score a goal.

TRAINING SESSION 8A

Front Centre of Box
159 Goals

FOR GOALS SCORED FROM FRONT CENTRE OF BOX (52.3% OF GOALS)

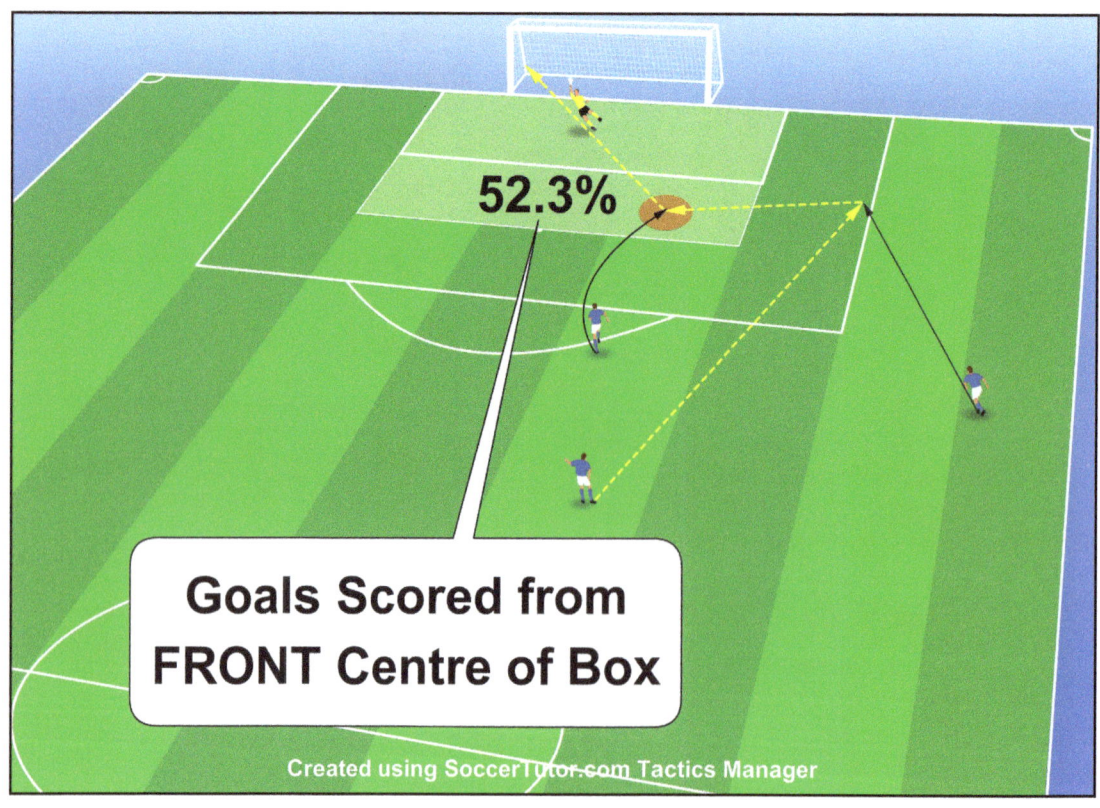

Goals Scored from FRONT Centre of Box

Training Session 8A: Goals Scored from **FRONT** Centre of Box (52.3% of Goals)

SESSION FOR THIS TACTICAL SITUATION (4 PRACTICES)
1. 3 (+1) v 1 Possession in the Centre + Play into the Front Centre of the Box for a 2v1 Finish

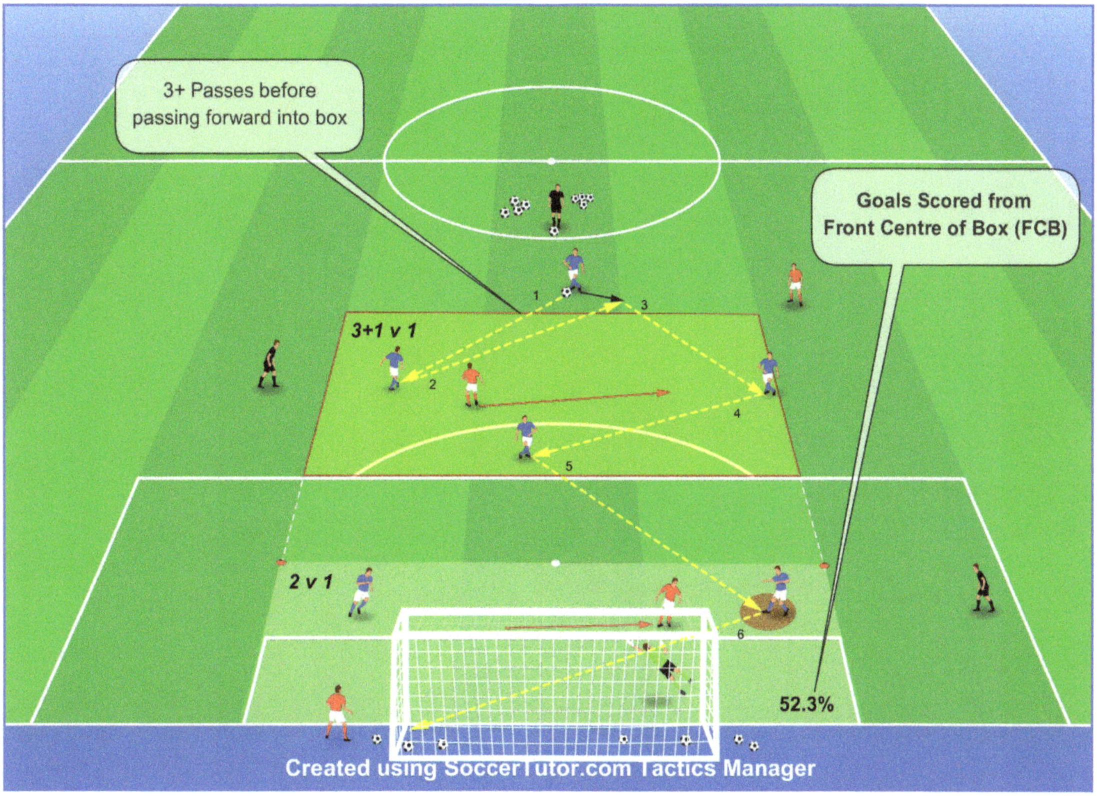

Description

- The practice starts with the outside blue player and a 3 (+1) v 1 situation in the first zone. The blues must complete 3 passes before passing forward to a teammate in the box.

- There is a 2v1 situation in the front of the box zone (highlighted).

- The 2 blue forwards try to find free space to receive the forward pass, control the ball, and score past the GK. If the defender closes them down, they have the option of passing to their teammate to score instead.

- The red defenders rotate with the players resting outside after each repetition.

- Change the defenders after a set amount of time.

Training Session 8A: Goals Scored from FRONT Centre of Box (52.3% of Goals)

PROGRESSION
2. 4v1 Possession in the Centre, Pass Wide, and Score in the Front Centre of the Box with a 1v1 Situation

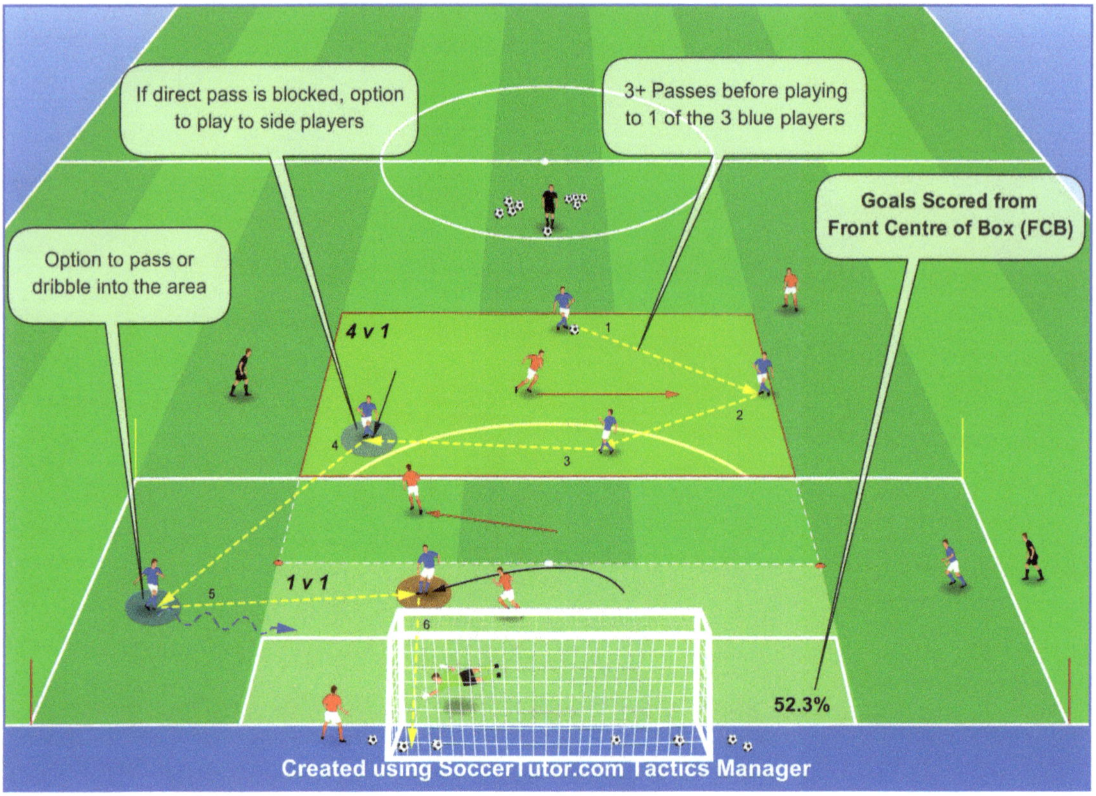

Description

- The practice starts with a 4v1 situation in the first zone. The blues must complete 3 passes before passing to the centre forward or wide to a teammate in the box.
- There is a red defender who tries to intercept the passes
- The wide blue players can either pass or dribble into the front centre of the box zone. The aim is to feed the blue forward who has a 1v1 situation against the red defender within the zone, trying to score a goal.
- When the forward receives from a wide player, he tries to score. However, if he is unable to find a good opportunity to shoot, he can pass back out to a wide player and the practice continues.
- The red defenders rotate with the players resting outside after each repetition. Change the defenders after a set amount of time.
- The blue players also rotate so they can practice the different roles.

Training Session 8A: Goals Scored from **FRONT** Centre of Box (52.3% of Goals)

PROGRESSION

3. Score in the Front Centre of the Box in a Multi-Zone 4v4 (+3) +GKs SSG with Wide Crossing Zones

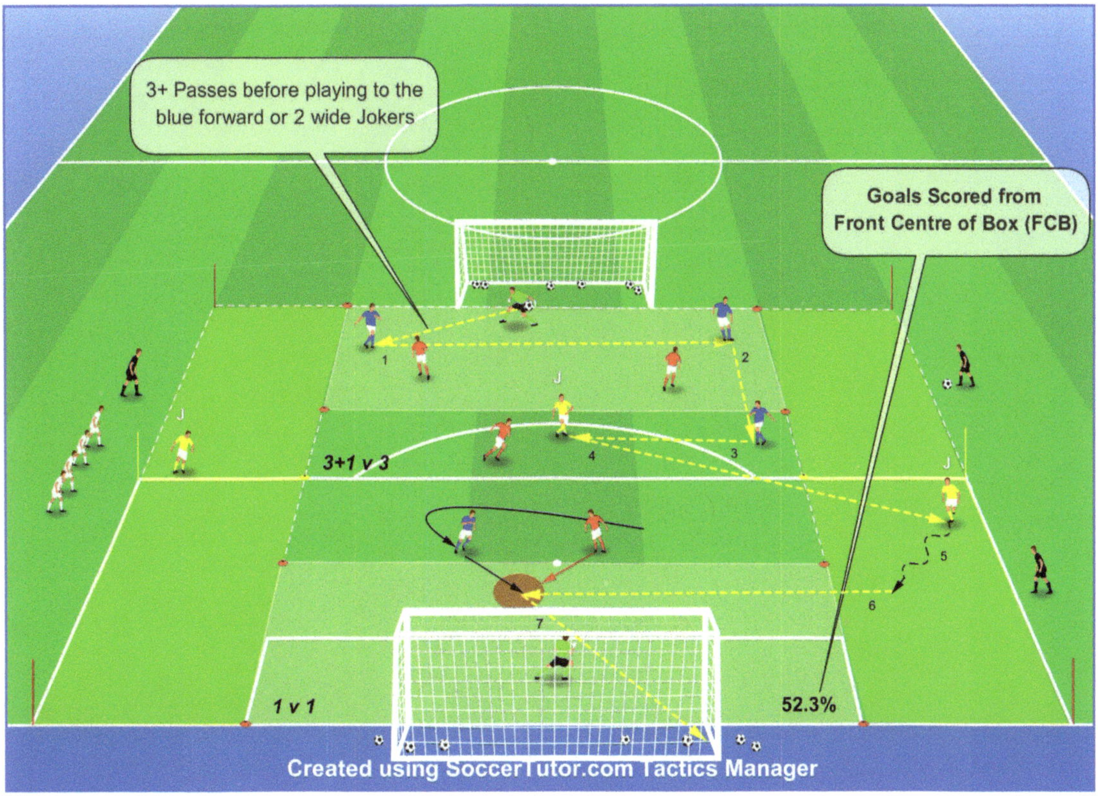

Description

- The GK starts the practice with a 3 (+1) v 3 situation played only within the central part of the defensive half. The blues must complete 3 passes before passing to the blue forward or a wide Joker.

- If the reds win the ball, they then have to complete 3 passes before passing forward and trying to score.

- The 2 wide Jokers play only within the wide crossing zones and no blue or red players are allowed to enter these zones.

- The aim is to feed the blue forward who has a 1v1 situation against the red defender within the front centre of the box, trying to score a goal. They start outside as shown and move into the front centre of the box to attack/defend the crosses.

- When the forward receives from a wide player, he tries to score. However, if he is unable to find a good opportunity to shoot, he can pass back out to a wide player and the practice continues.

- There is a third team outside (whites) resting because the teams rotate. Each game is 3-5 minutes. The team that scores the most goals after a set number of games wins.

Training Session 8A: Goals Scored from <u>FRONT</u> Centre of Box (52.3% of Goals)

PROGRESSION

4. Score in the Front Centre of the Box and Quick Changes of Direction in a 7v7 +GKs SSG

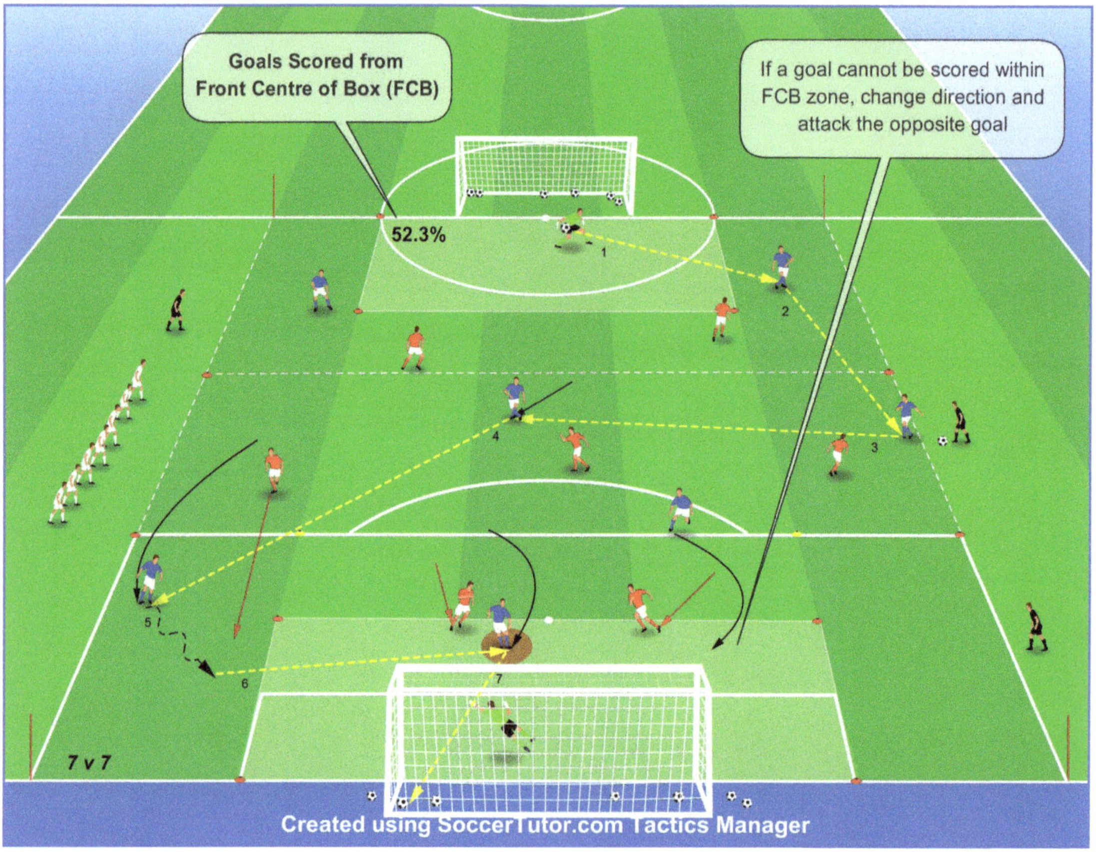

Description

- Within the area shown, there are 3 thirds marked out + 2 front centre of the box zones. We play a 7v7 +GKs game.

- The final pass (assist) must be played from outside the front centre of the box zone and the goals must be scored from within it (as shown in diagram example).

- If a goal cannot be scored after receiving a pass inside the front centre of the box zone, then the ball should be played back out to continue the game.

- When this happens, the team in possession completely change direction and attack the opposite goal. All of the players need to react quickly to the transition situation.

- Both teams can score in either goal but cannot have 2 consecutive attacks on the same goal.

- There is a third team outside (whites) resting because the teams rotate. Each game is 4-6 minutes. The team that scores the most goals after a set number of games wins.

TRAINING SESSION 8B

Back Centre of Box
62 Goals

FOR GOALS SCORED FROM BACK CENTRE OF BOX (20.4% OF GOALS)

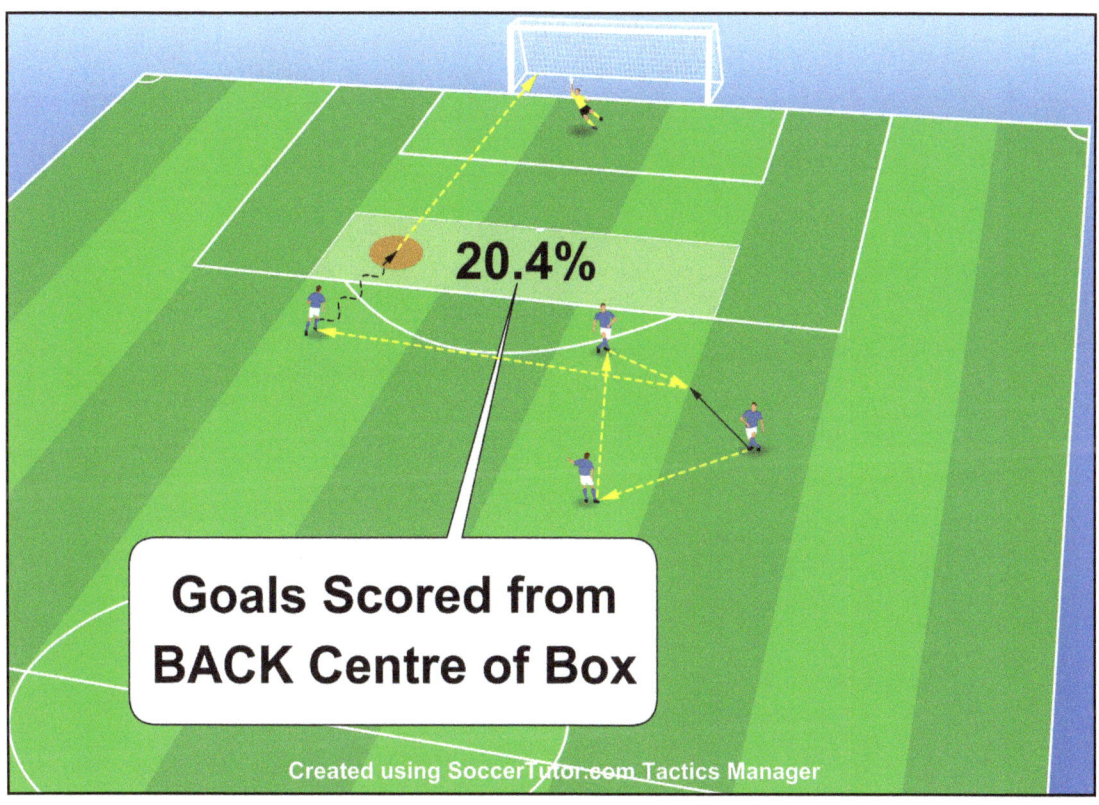

Goals Scored from BACK Centre of Box

Training Session 8B: Goals Scored from **BACK** Centre of Box (20.4% of Goals)

SESSION FOR THIS TACTICAL SITUATION (4 PRACTICES)

1. Attacking Pattern of Play with Finish in Back Centre of Box Zone with Assist or Individual Play

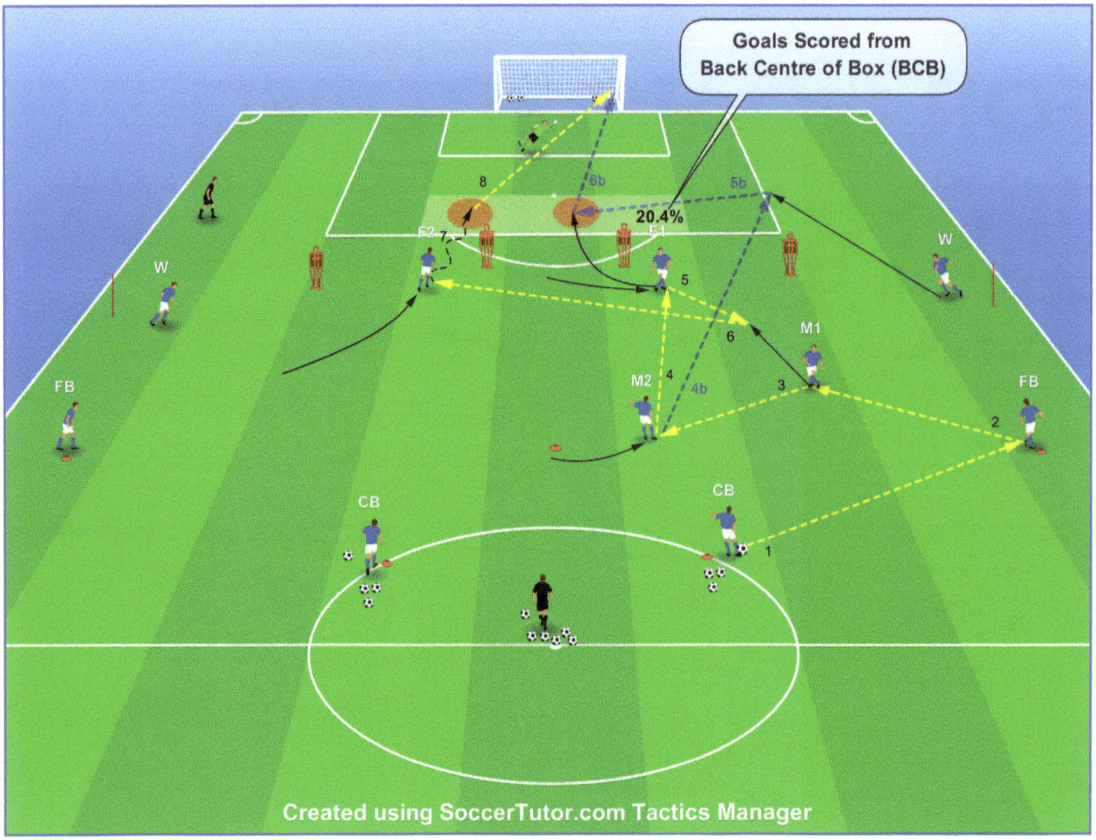

Description

- The players start in the positions shown, except for **M1** who floats. There are 4 mannequins to represent the opposition's defenders and the blues aim to score from within the highlighted back centre of box zone.

- The centre back **(CB)** passes wide to the full back **(FB)**, who passes inside to the midfielder **(M1)**. **M1** passes back to **M2**, who passes to the forward **(F1)**. **F1** lays the ball off for the forward movement of **M1**, who passes across to **F2**.

- From there, the second forward **(F2)** drives the ball into the back centre of the box zone and shoots.

- Alternatively, **M2** can pass to the winger **(W)**, who makes a run in behind and then passes across for the run of **F1** to score **(4b-6b blue arrows in diagram)**.

- The players can either rotate their positions or maintain them. After the pattern is complete, repeat on the other side (**M1** moves across).

- You can have 2 groups working in either half of the pitch.

Training Session 8B: Goals Scored from **BACK** Centre of Box (20.4% of Goals)

VARIATION

2. Attacking Pattern of Play with Finish in Back Centre of Box Zone with Assists from Wide Players

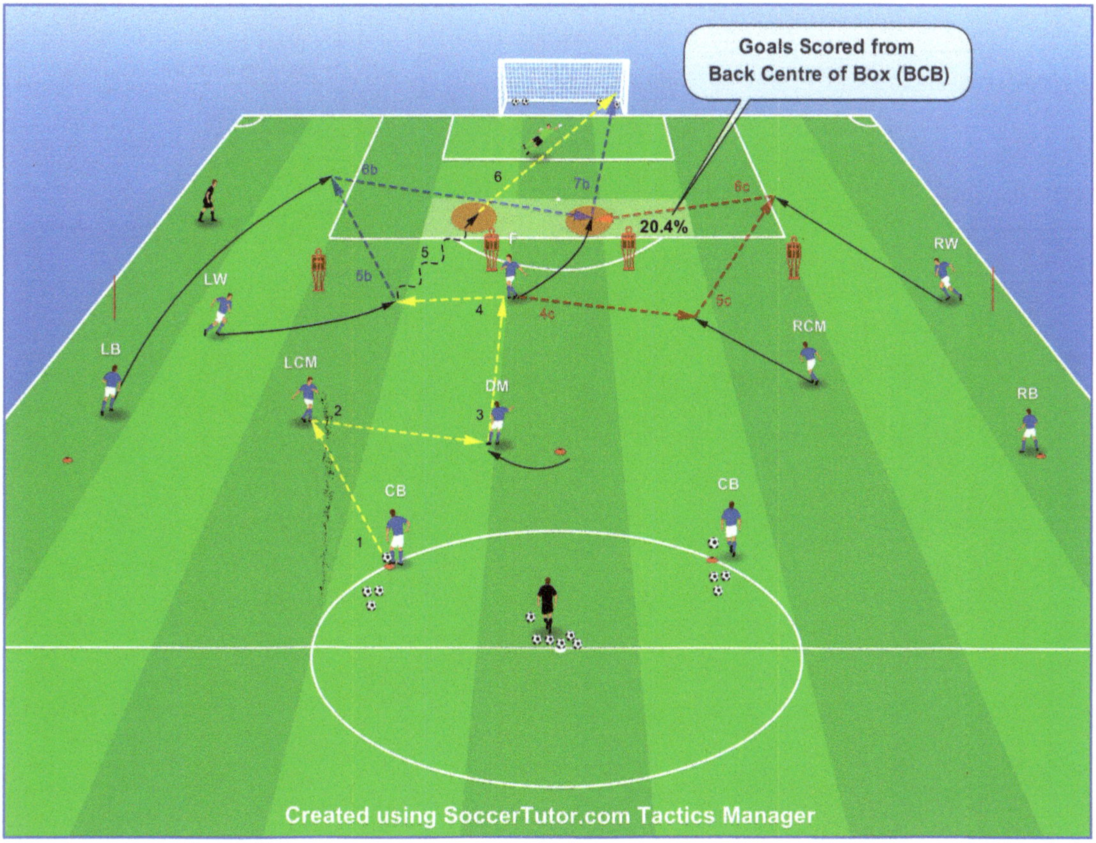

Description

- In this variation of the previous practice, we have the 10 blue players in a 4-3-3 formation for a combined pattern.

- The centre back **(CB)** passes wide to the left central midfielder **(LCM)**, who passes inside to the defensive midfielder **(DM)**. The **DM** passes to the forward **(F)**.

- There are 3 options to finish the attack. **Option 1 (4-6)** is **F's** lay-off for the inside run of the left winger **(LW)**, who drives into the back centre of the box zone and shoots at goal.

- For **Option 2 (5b-7b)**, **LW** plays a through pass for the overlapping run of the left back **(LB)**, who delivers a low cut back cross for the forward **(F)** to score within the back centre of box zone.

- For **Option 3 (4c-6c)**, **F** passes back to the right central midfielder **(RCM)**, who plays a through pass for the right winger **(RW)** to provide the assist.

- Players can either rotate their positions or maintain them. After the pattern is complete, repeat starting from the opposite side.

Training Session 8B: Goals Scored from **BACK** Centre of Box (20.4% of Goals)

PROGRESSION

3. Score Goals from Back Centre of Box Zone in an 8v8 (+1) +GKs Game with Corner Crossing Zones

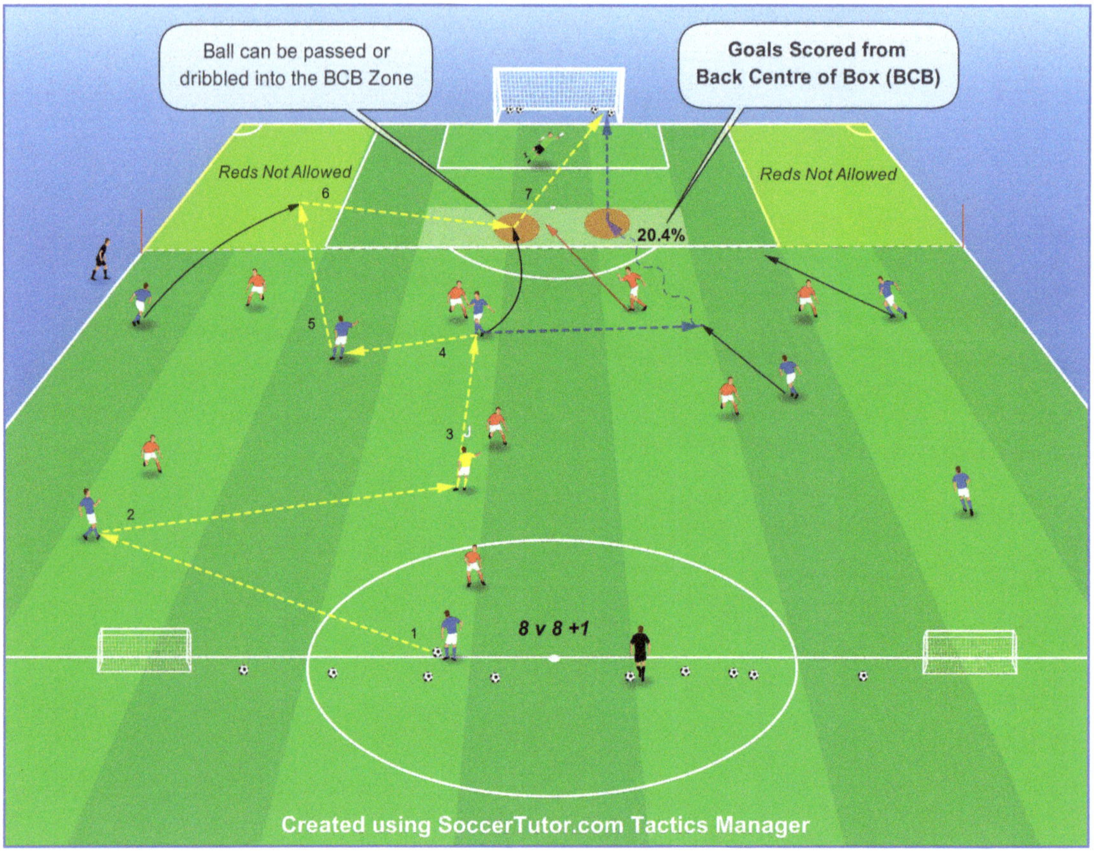

Description

- Using half a pitch, we mark out 2 corner zones where the red players are not allowed to enter at any time. There are 2 small goals positioned on the halfway line, as shown.

- The game starts with the deepest player on the halfway line and the blue team build-up play and try to score in an 8v8 (+1 Joker) situation.

- All goals must be scored from within the back centre of box zone (BCB).

- If the assist is played from within a corner zone (as in diagram example), then the goal counts double.

- Only 1 red defender can move into the box and only after the ball has been played in there.

- If the reds win the ball, they try to score in the 2 small goals.

- If the GK saves a shot or the ball goes out of play, restart the game from the deepest blue player on the halfway line.

Training Session 8B: Goals Scored from BACK Centre of Box (20.4% of Goals)

PROGRESSION

4. Score Goals from Back Centre of Box Zone in a Conditioned Tactical Game with Corner Zones

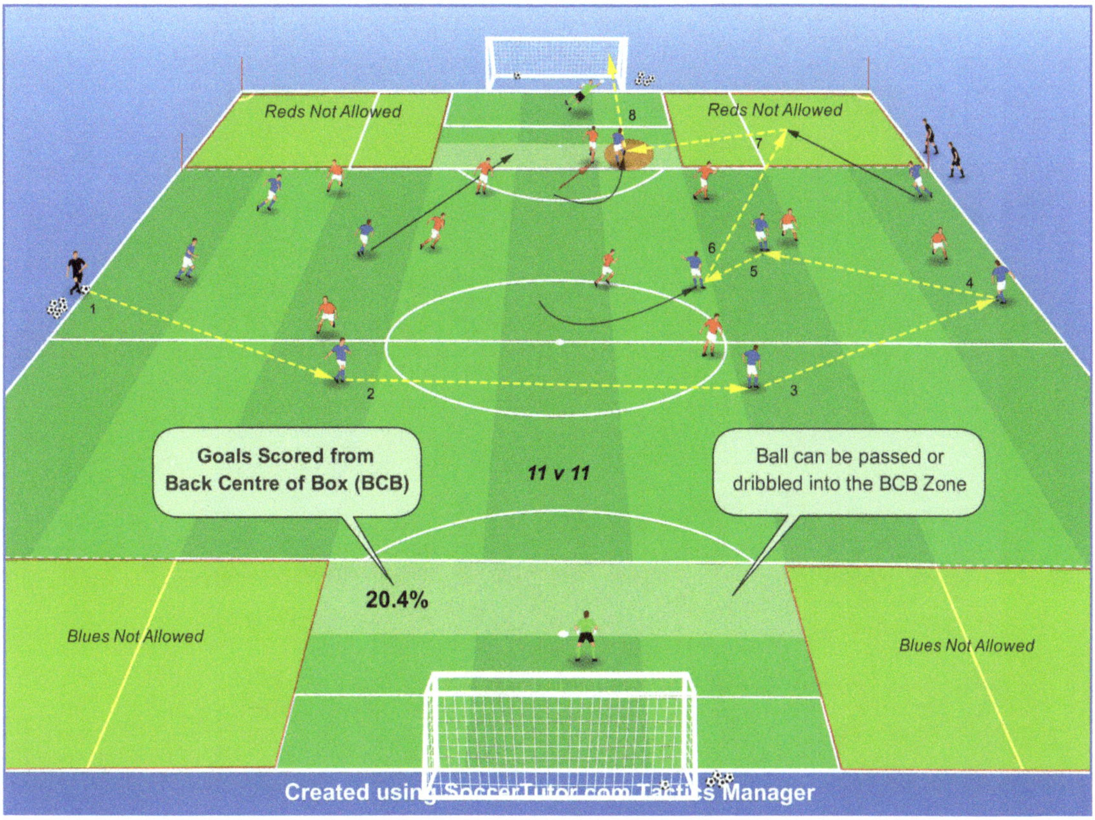

Description

- To complete the session, we play an 11v11 game on a full pitch.
- We mark out 4 corner zones where the defending players are not allowed to enter at any time. The offside rule is not applied.
- The game starts with the Coach's pass and the attacking team (blues) try to score.
- All goals must be scored from within the back centre of box zone (BCB).
- If the assist is played from within a corner zone (as in diagram example), then the goal counts double.
- If the GK saves a shot or the ball goes out of play, restart the game from the red team's GK. The red team continue the game with the exact same aims attacking in the opposite direction.

TACTICAL ASPECT

What Tactics are Used to Score the Most Goals?

Tactical Aspect: What Tactics are Used to Score the Most Goals?

TACTICAL ASPECT: WHAT TACTICS ARE USED TO SCORE THE MOST GOALS?

Tactical Aspect for Goals Scored During the Champions League Group Stages in the 2022-2023 Season (304 Total Goals)

Tactic	Percentage	Goals
Attacking Combination Play (Centre)	14.1%	43 Goals
Play Through Lines	8.2%	25 Goals
Switch of Play	6.9%	21 Goals
Attacking Out Wide / Crossing	6.9%	21 Goals
Attacking Combination Play (Wide)	4.9%	15 Goals
Attack Through Centre	4.9%	15 Goals
Long Pass	4.6%	14 Goals
Corner Kick	10.9%	33 Goals
Penalty	8.9%	27 Goals
Indirect Free Kick	2.3%	7 Goals
Direct Free Kick	1.0%	3 Goals
Counter (Middle Zone)	11.2%	34 Goals
High Press + Counter	4.9%	15 Goals
Counter (Low Zone)	4.6%	14 Goals
N/A	5.6%	17 Goals

* **Attacking Combination Play** = In the Final Third of the Pitch (at least 3 passes)
* **Play Through Lines** = Break 2 Opposition Lines of Defence

Tactical Aspect: What Tactics are Used to Score the Most Goals?

Categorisation of Tactics Used to Score Goals During the Champions League Group Stages in the 2022-2023 Season (304 Total Goals)

Build-up Play / Attacks
96 GOALS — 31.6%

Set Plays & Penalties
70 GOALS — 23.0%

Counter Attacks
63 GOALS — 20.7%

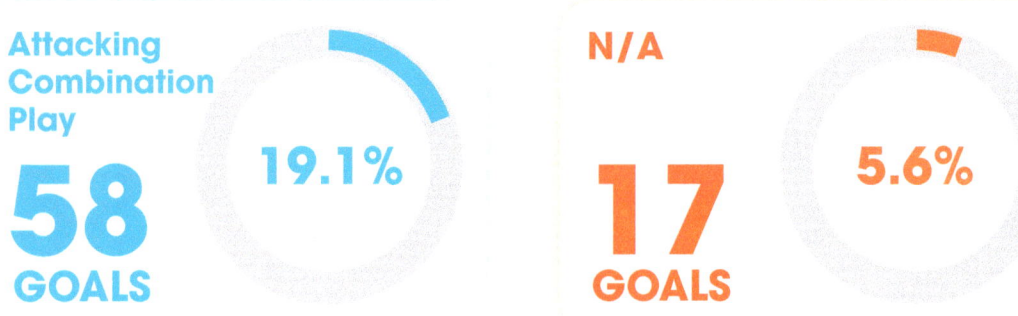

Attacking Combination Play
58 GOALS — 19.1%

N/A
17 GOALS — 5.6%

* **Attacking Combination Play** = In the Final Third of the Pitch (at least 3 passes)

TACTICAL EXAMPLES

9. BUILD-UP PLAY / ATTACKS (31.6% OF GOALS)

Play Through Lines
= 25 of 304 Goals Scored (8.2%)

Switch of Play
= 21 of 304 Goals Scored (6.9%)

Attack Wide / Crossing
= 21 of 304 Goals Scored (6.9%)

Attack Through Centre
= 15 of 304 Goals Scored (4.9%)

Long Pass
= 14 of 304 Goals Scored (4.6%)

9. Build-up Play / Attacks = 31.6% of All Goals Scored

Real Madrid 2-1 Shakhtar Donetsk (Vinicius Jr. 28') - 05/10/2022

Goal Example 1/5 (Real Madrid)
Play Through Lines = 25 of 304 Goals Scored (8.2%)

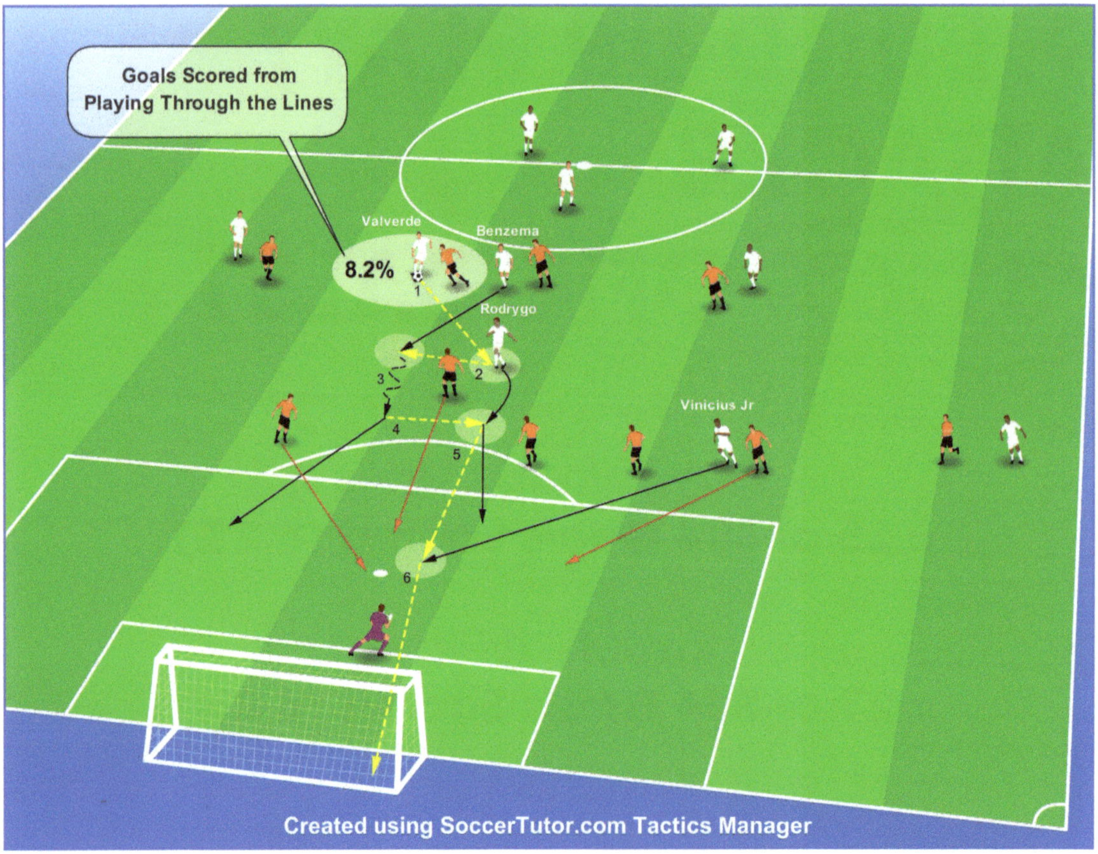

Description

The attacking midfielder **Valverde** passes forward to the centrally positioned right winger **Rodrygo**. He sets the ball for the oncoming centre forward **Benzema** to receive, drive forward, and then play a through pass in behind and into the centre of the box for the diagonal run of **Vinicius Jr**, who scores with a near post finish.

Key Aspects

1. The centre forward **Benzema** is a complete player and helps progress play in midfield. He influences his teammates with a game of short passes. This leads to the opposition's defence being disorganised with a gap in the centre.

2. Real Madrid's short passing game is very fast, so they are able to overcome the 2 lines (defence and midfield) to play through.

3. The left winger **Vinicius Jr** takes advantage of his speed. Starting from far behind, he still knows he will beat the defenders to the ball.

9. Build-up Play / Attacks = 31.6% of All Goals Scored

Celtic 0-3 Real Madrid (Hazard 77') - 06/09/2022

Goal Example 2/5 (Real Madrid)
Switch of Play = 21 of 304 Goals Scored (6.9%)

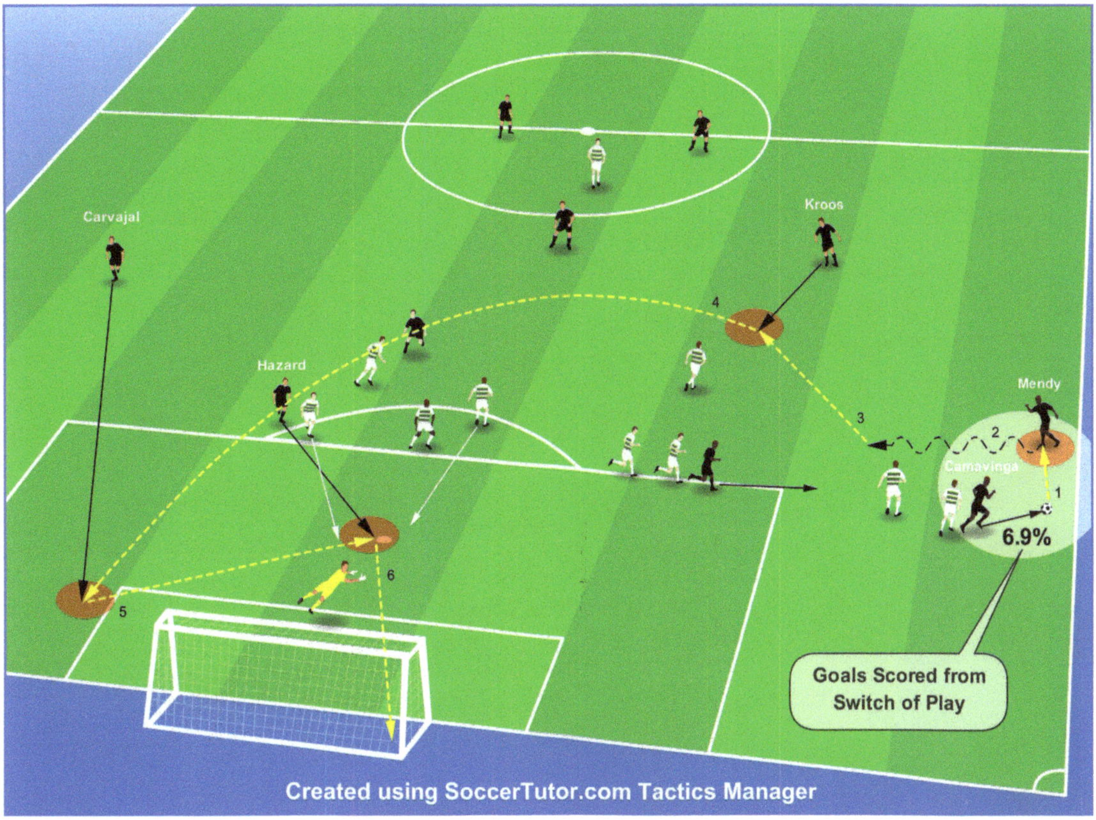

Description
The left back **Mendy** receives from the central midfielder **Camavinga**, dribbles inside and passes to defensive midfielder **Kroos**, who plays a high pass to the back post for the advanced run of the right back **Carvajal**. From there, **Carvajal** cuts the ball back to the penalty spot for the centre forward **Hazard** to finish.

Key Aspects
1. The key to the play is the accumulation of 4 Real Madrid players on one side of the pitch. This leads the opponents towards that side, leaving a large free space on the other side of the pitch.

2. This free space on the right side of the pitch is exploited by the right back **Carvajal**, as he makes a run towards the byline.

3. The expert vision of **Kroos**, together with a great technique, sends a long pass from one side of the pitch to the other where there is a lot of space.

4. The centre forward **Hazard** anticipates the cut back quicker than the defenders to get to the ball first and score.

9. Build-up Play / Attacks = 31.6% of All Goals Scored

Real Madrid 5-1 Celtic (Vinicius Jr. 61') - 02/11/2022

Goal Example 3/5 (Real Madrid)
Attack Wide / Crossing = 21 of 304 Goals Scored (6.9%)

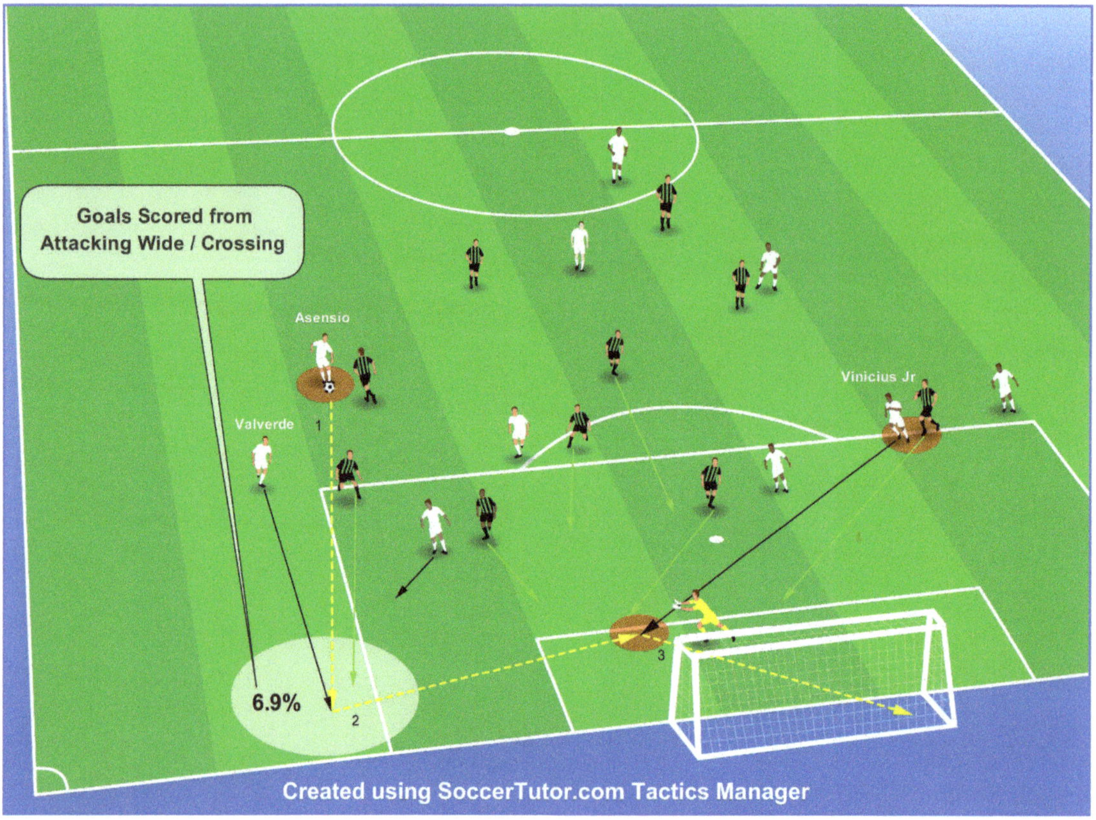

Description

The right winger **Asensio** has the ball and plays a pass for attacking midfielder **Valverde** to run onto on the outside. He shows great speed to get to the ball before the defender and delivers a low cross to the near post. The left winger **Vinicius Jr** is very quick to anticipate the cross ahead of the defenders and finishes first time at the near post.

Key Aspects

1. The pass of **Asensio** into the free space near the byline gives **Valverde** space to run into. **Asensio** knows that **Valverde** is quick over distance, so decides to send a deep pass for him to chase.

2. The attacking midfielder **Valverde** wastes no time and delivers the cross with his first touch, which prevents the defenders having time to get into positions to defend the box properly.

3. The left winger **Vinicius Jr** is intelligent and anticipates the area the ball will be played into. He reaches the near post with an advantage and finishes with one touch, so the GK has no time to react.

9. Build-up Play / Attacks = 31.6% of All Goals Scored

Inter 4-0 Viktoria Plzen (Lukaku 87') - 26/10/2022

Goal Example 4/5 (Inter)

Attack Through Centre = 15 of 304 Goals Scored (4.9%)

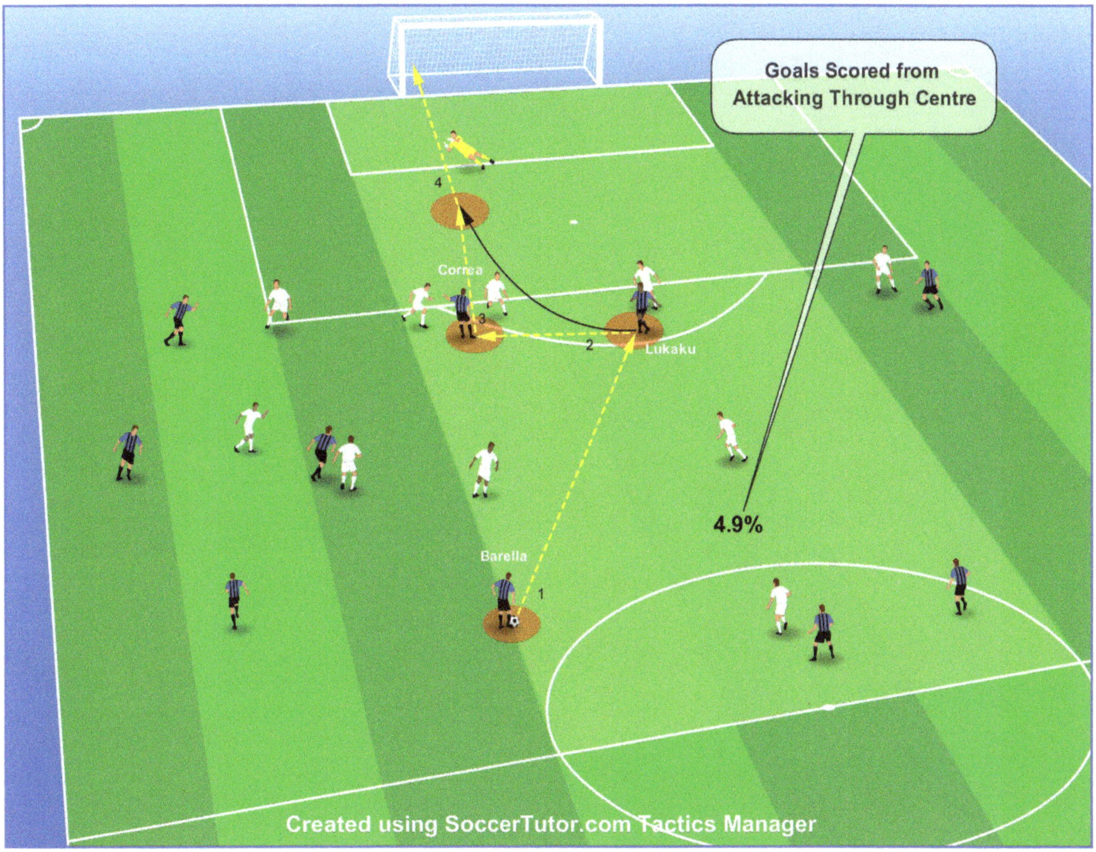

Description

The play begins with central midfielder **Barella** playing a long through pass to bypass the opposition's midfield line and play into the centre forward **Lukaku's** feet near the edge of the box.

Lukaku receives with his back to goal and turns. He plays a short pass to the other forward **Correa**, who plays quickly between 2 defenders into the box to complete the one-two with **Lukaku**, who has run in behind to score with a low finish.

Key Aspects

1. The central midfielder **Barella** shows good vision and accuracy to find **Lukaku** in a very dangerous position.

2. With **Lukaku's** big body, he does not let the defender see the ball at any time. He can therefore turn with no chance of the ball being stolen.

3. The other forward **Correa** uses only one touch to play through for **Lukaku** to receive alone inside the box. It is a simple touch but one of great quality.

9. Build-up Play / Attacks = 31.6% of All Goals Scored

Liverpool 2-1 Ajax (Salah 17') - 13/09/2022

Goal Example 5/5 (Liverpool)
Long Pass = 14 of 304 Goals Scored (4.6%)

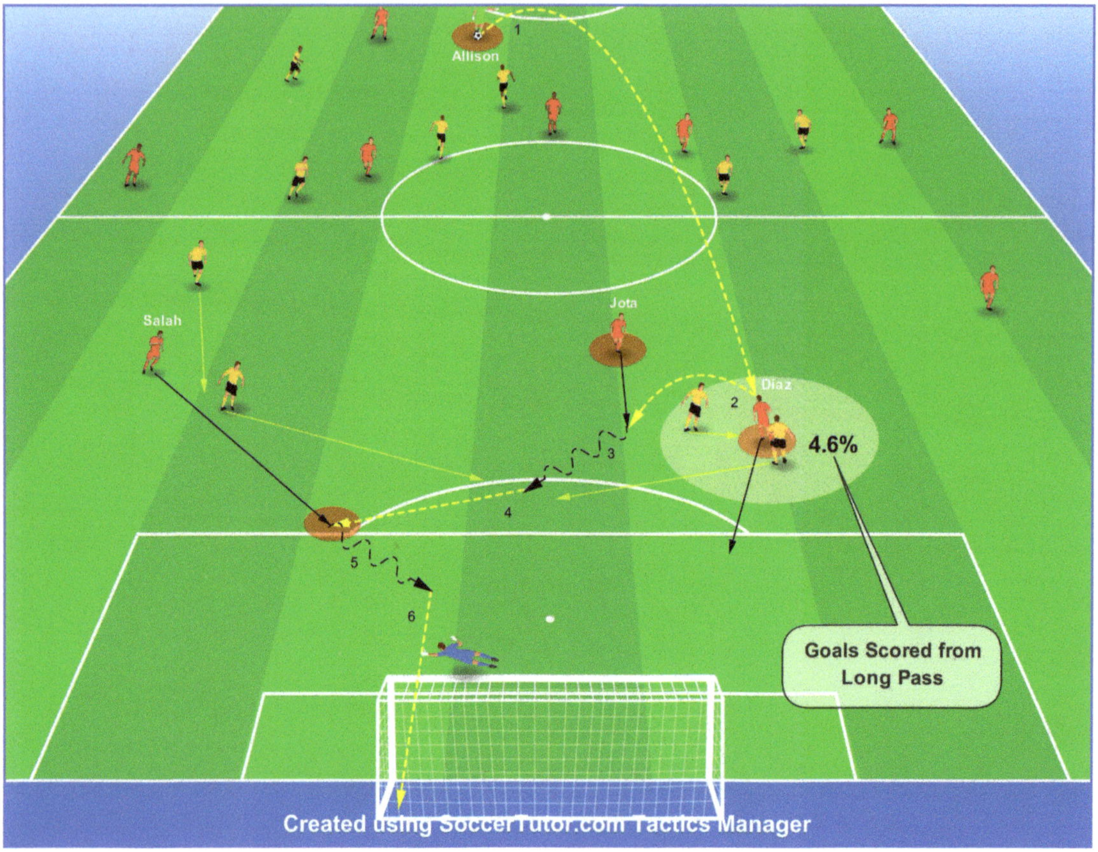

Description
This is a very typical Liverpool phase of play with the long pass from the GK. In this example, **Allison** directs his pass towards the left winger **Díaz**, who challenges for the ball. The second ball is won by the centre forward **Jota**, who dribbles forward and passes for the run of winger **Salah** on the right. **Salah** arrives at speed, bursts past the defender and scores at the near post.

Key Aspects
1. By using the GK outside of his box, Liverpool have 1 more outfield player to build up play. This helps them get an equal 3v3 situation high up the pitch.

2. This phase of play is repeated often by Liverpool. As **Salah** has a lot of speed, he waits for the ball to arrive in this zone and attacks the space. The Liverpool players know that they should quickly move the ball into this area.

3. The individual quality of **Salah** does the rest as he is an exceptional finisher 1v1 with the GK.

TRAINING SESSION 9A

Through Lines / Centre — 40 Goals

FOR PLAY THROUGH LINES & ATTACK THROUGH CENTRE (13.1% OF GOALS)

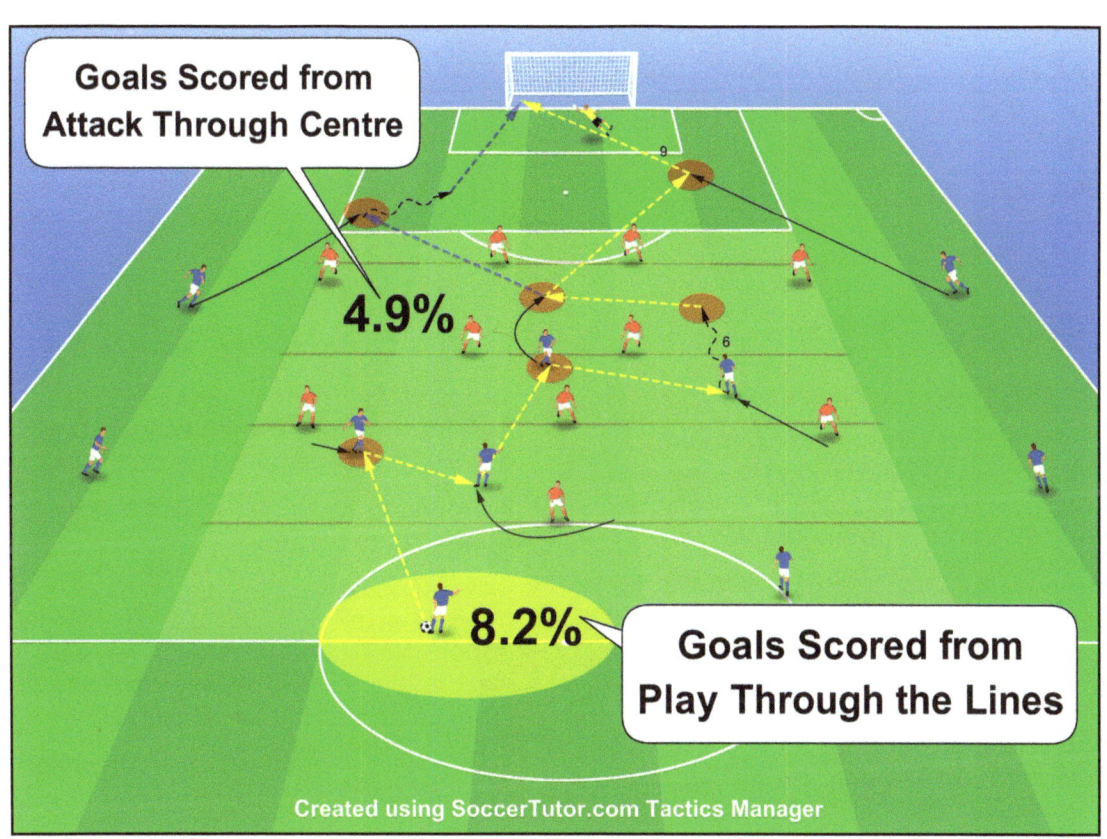

Goals Scored from Attack Through Centre — 4.9%

Goals Scored from Play Through the Lines — 8.2%

Training Session 9A: **Play Through Lines & Attack Through Centre (13.1% of Goals)**

SESSION FOR THIS TACTICAL SITUATION (4 PRACTICES)

1. Play Through the Lines and Attack Through the Centre Pattern of Play

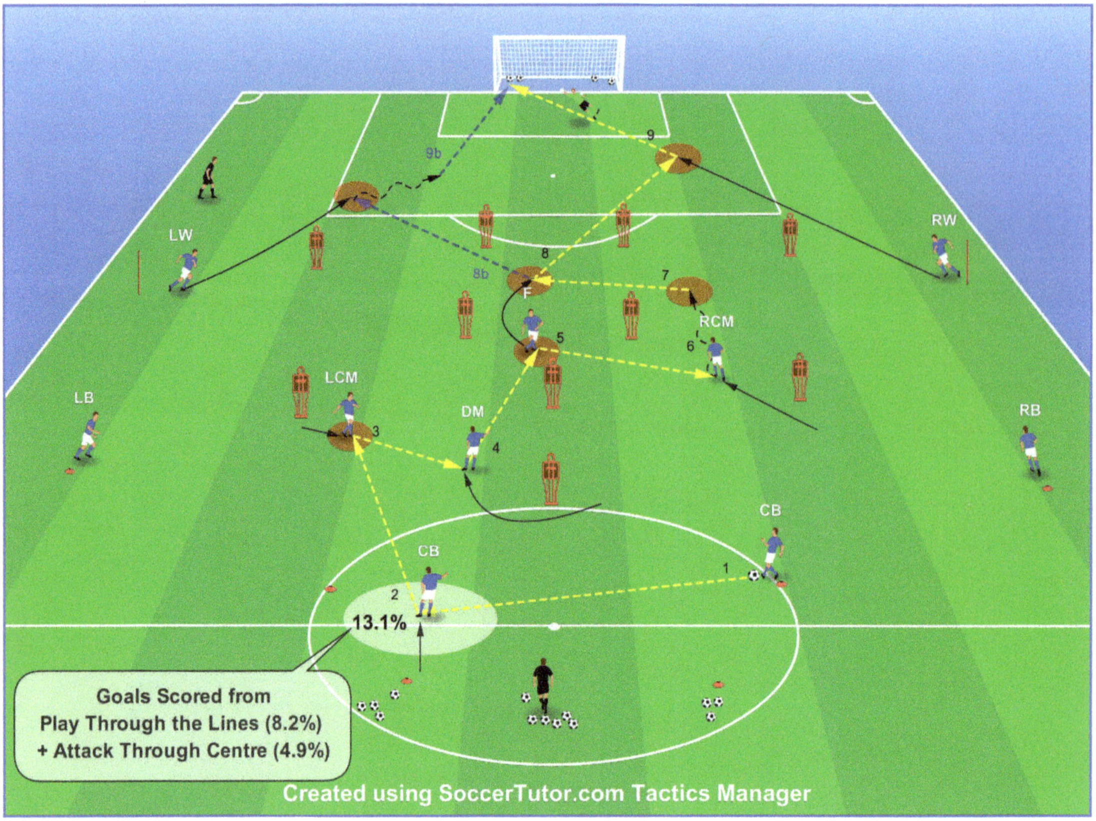

Description

- The players can use many different variations to play through the lines and attack through the centre. The diagram displays a good example.

- The first centre back passes to the other centre back **(CB)** to start. He passes forward to the left central midfielder **(LCM)**, who lays the ball back to the defensive midfielder **(DM)**. The **DM** passes to the deep forward **(F)**, who passes back to the right central midfielder **(RCM)**. The **RCM** dribbles forward and plays back to **F**.

- The forward **(F)** either plays a through pass for the run of the left winger **(LW)** or the right winger **(RW)** inside the box.

- From there, the winger who receives tries to score past the GK.

- Players should get their heads up, so they see all the positioning and passing options available. If possible, always use mannequins instead of cones to make it more game realistic for visibility.

- You can increase the difficulty by playing at a higher speed.

Training Session 9A: **Play Through Lines & Attack Through Centre (13.1% of Goals)**

PROGRESSION

2. Play Through the Lines (Zones) and in Behind in a Dynamic Functional Practice

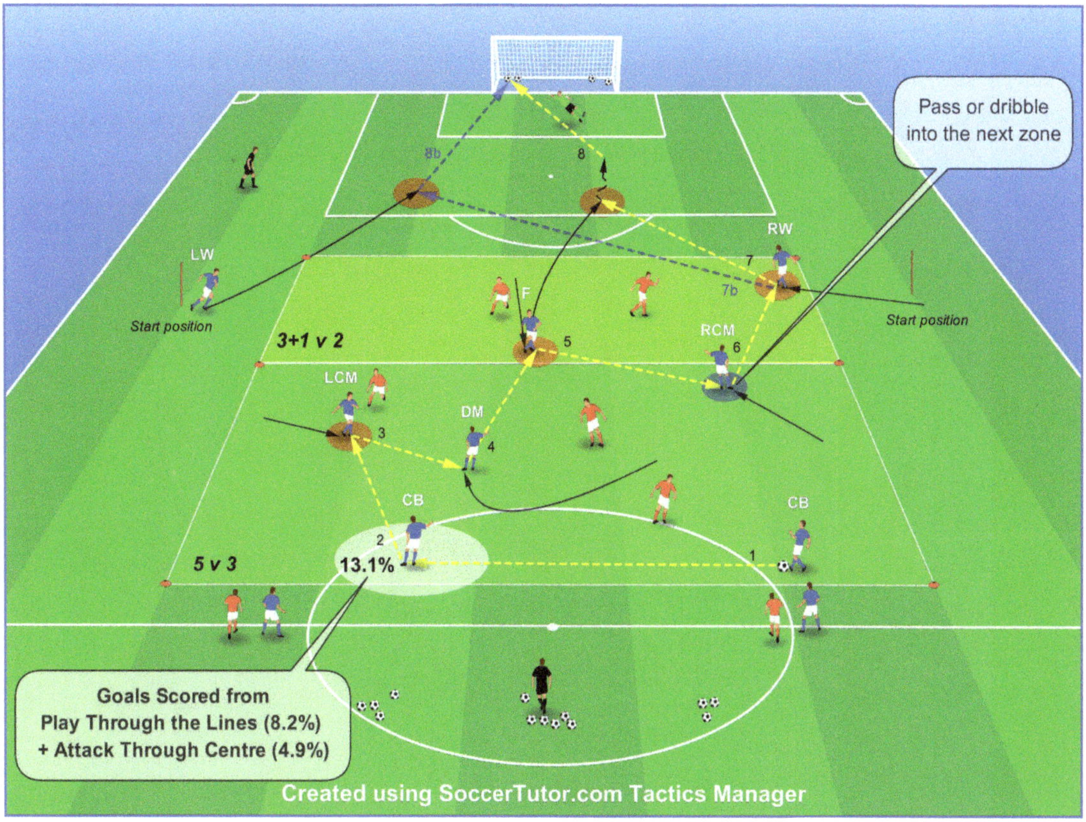

Description

- We start in the first zone with a 5 v 3 situation. The blues must complete 3 passes before playing into the second zone.

- They can pass to the forward **(F)** or either winger **(LW or RW)**, who can move inside the second zone to receive. Alternatively, 1 blue player is allowed to dribble into the second zone.

- From the second zone, the aim is to play the ball in behind and into the box.

- In the diagram example, **RW** moves inside the second zone to receive the right central midfielder's **(RCM)** pass. He can then either play in behind for **F** or **LW**, as shown.

- The red defenders are not allowed to leave their zones at any time.

- Once the phase is finished, restart from a blue centre back **(CB)**. After a set number of repetitions, switch the team roles, so the reds become the attacking team, and the blues defend.

- The players waiting outside can rotate in throughout to give players rest.

Training Session 9A: Play Through Lines & Attack Through Centre (13.1% of Goals)

PROGRESSION

3. Attack Through the Centre and Play in Behind in a 5v5 (+2) +GKs Small Sided Game

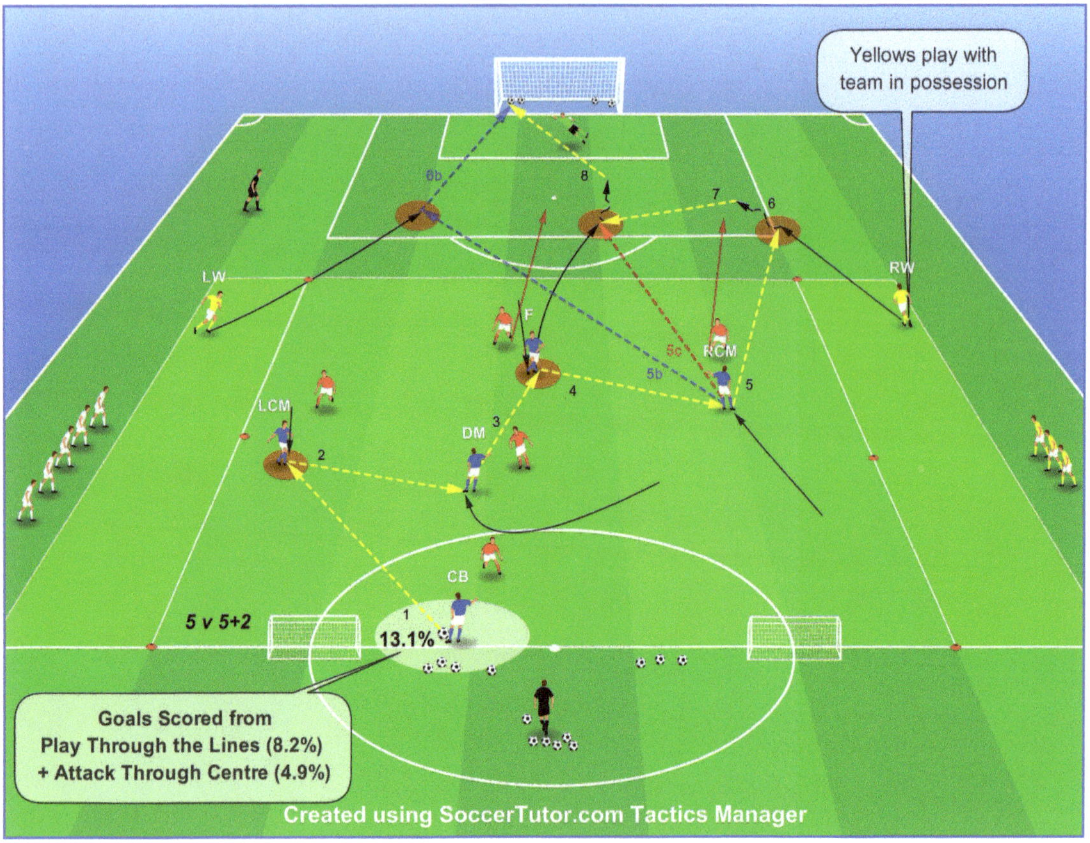

Description

- We play short 4-5 minute games with 4 teams of 5 players involved. After each game, rotate the teams. Keep a total score to determine the winning team.

- The practice starts with the blue team and their aim is to attack through the centre and score.

- They can use the yellow wide players who play with the team in possession and operate in their own side zones, where no other players can enter.

- The blues must complete 3 passes before being able to play in behind and into the box to score.

- In the diagram example, the player in possession **(RCM)** has 3 options to play in behind for the forward **(F)** or either of the wingers **(LW or RW)**.

- The defending players (reds) must stay in the central zone at all times.

- After the phase is finished, restart with the red team attacking with the same aims.

Training Session 9A: **Play Through Lines & Attack Through Centre (13.1% of Goals)**

PROGRESSION

4. Complete 5 Passes and Attack Through the Centre in a Multi-Zone Two-Direction Small Sided Game

- Minimum of 5 passes
- Teams can attack either goal

Yellows play with team in possession

5 v 5 +4

13.1%

Goals Scored from
Play Through the Lines (8.2%)
+ Attack Through Centre (4.9%)

Description

- The Coach starts by passing the ball into the central zone. The team in possession (blues) must complete 5 passes with the help of 4 Jokers (5v5 +4 situation), who are positioned within their own outside yellow zones.

- Once 5 passes are completed, the blue players can attack either goal, as this is a two-direction game. For the attack, you can use 2 of the Jokers who make forward runs, as shown in the diagram example.

- In addition, there is a blue forward in the green zone who joins the attack opposed by a red defender who moves to defend the goal.

- The pass can be played in behind to any of the 3 attacking players mentioned, who combine to try and score a goal.

- When the attack ends, whether the ball goes wide, a goal is scored, or the GK produces a save, the phase is over and we restart with a new ball from the Coach to the red team, who now become the attacking team.

TRAINING SESSION 9B

Wide Attacks — 21 Goals

FOR ATTACKING OUT WIDE / CROSSING (6.9% OF GOALS)

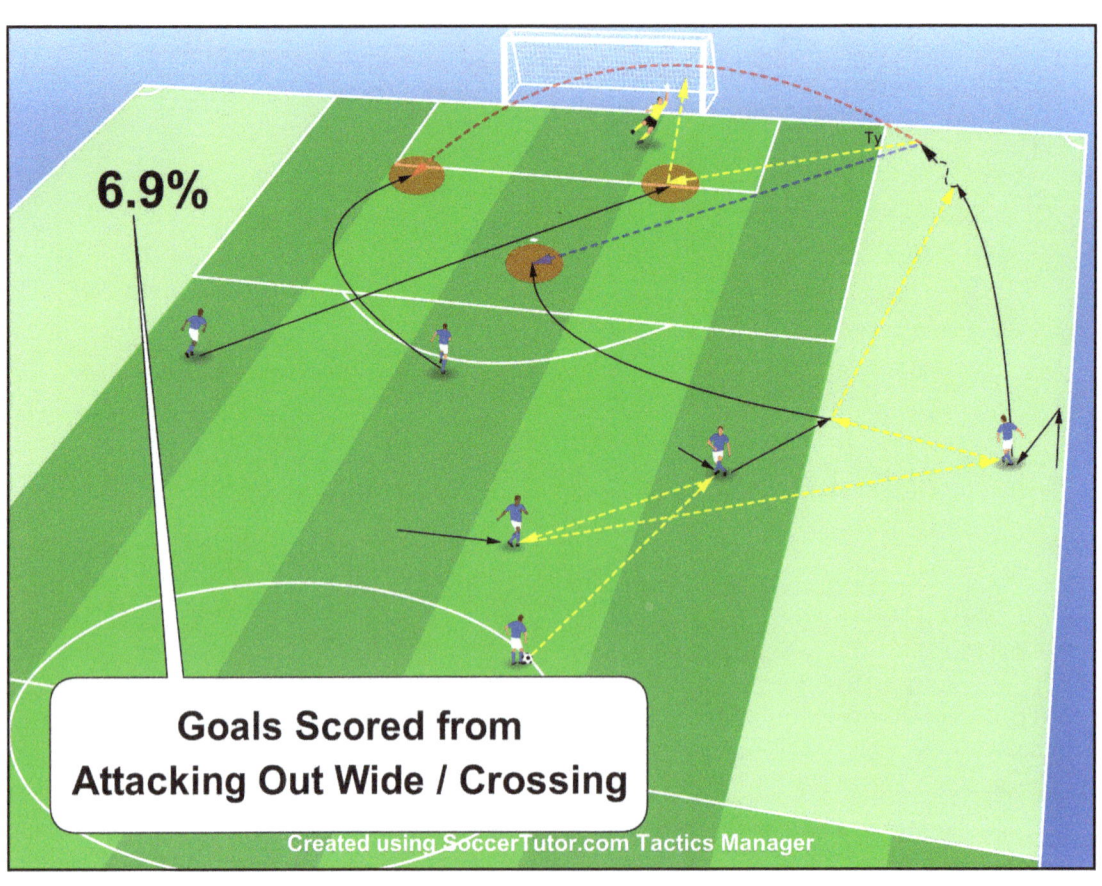

Goals Scored from Attacking Out Wide / Crossing

Training Session 9B: Attacking Wide / Crossing (6.9% of Goals)

SESSION FOR THIS TACTICAL SITUATION (4 PRACTICES)

1. Quick Combination Play Out Wide, One-Two, Overlap Run, Cross, and Finish

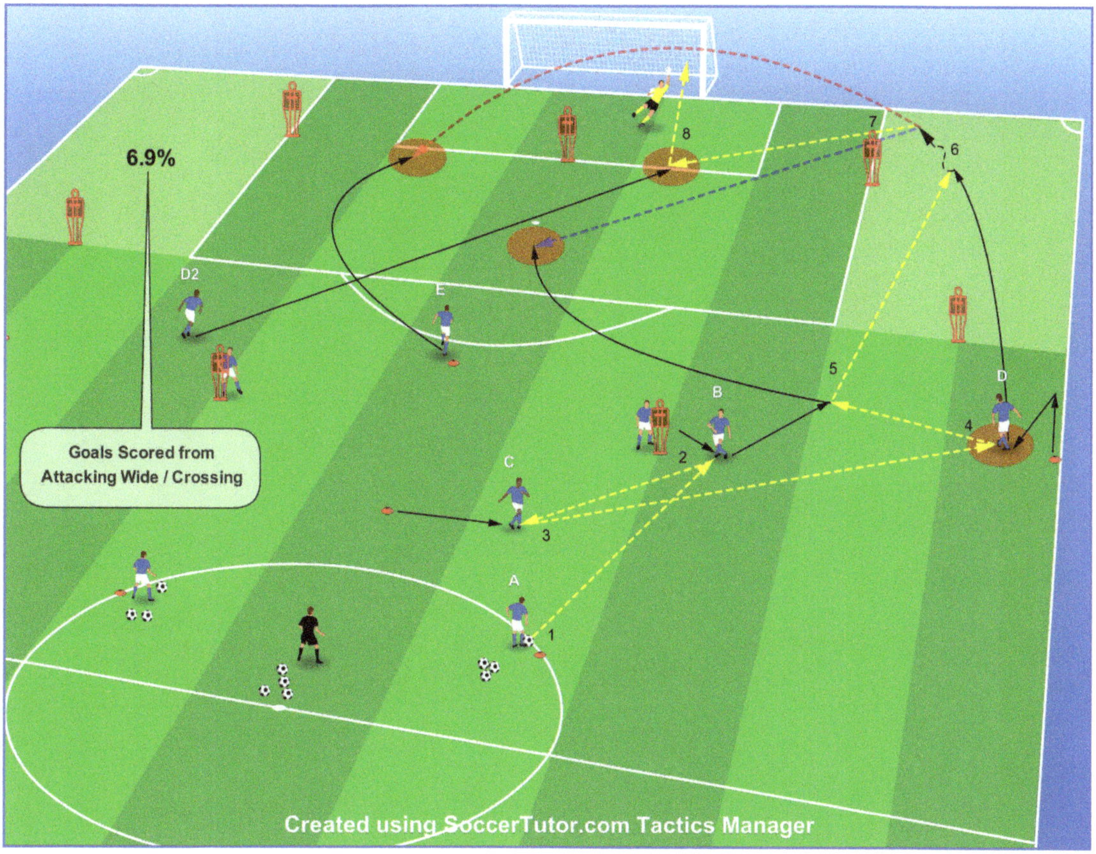

Description

- **A** passes forward to **B**.
- **B** passes back to **C**, who moves across off his cone.
- **C** passes out wide to the winger (**D**).
- **D** plays a one-two with **B**, who has moved forward.
- **D** receives the return pass high up the flank near the byline and crosses the ball into the box for a teammate to score.
- The type of cross can vary, as shown.
- Player **B**, the forward (**E**), and the opposite winger (**D1**) all make runs into the box, to the penalty spot, far post, and near post respectively.
- The players rotate positions:
  A → B → C → D → E → A.
- After the phase is complete, repeat the same sequence with a new ball from the left side.

Training Session 9B: **Attacking Wide / Crossing (6.9% of Goals)**

PROGRESSION

2. Quick Combination Play, 2 v 1 Out Wide with One-Two and Overlap Run, Cross, and Finish vs Defender

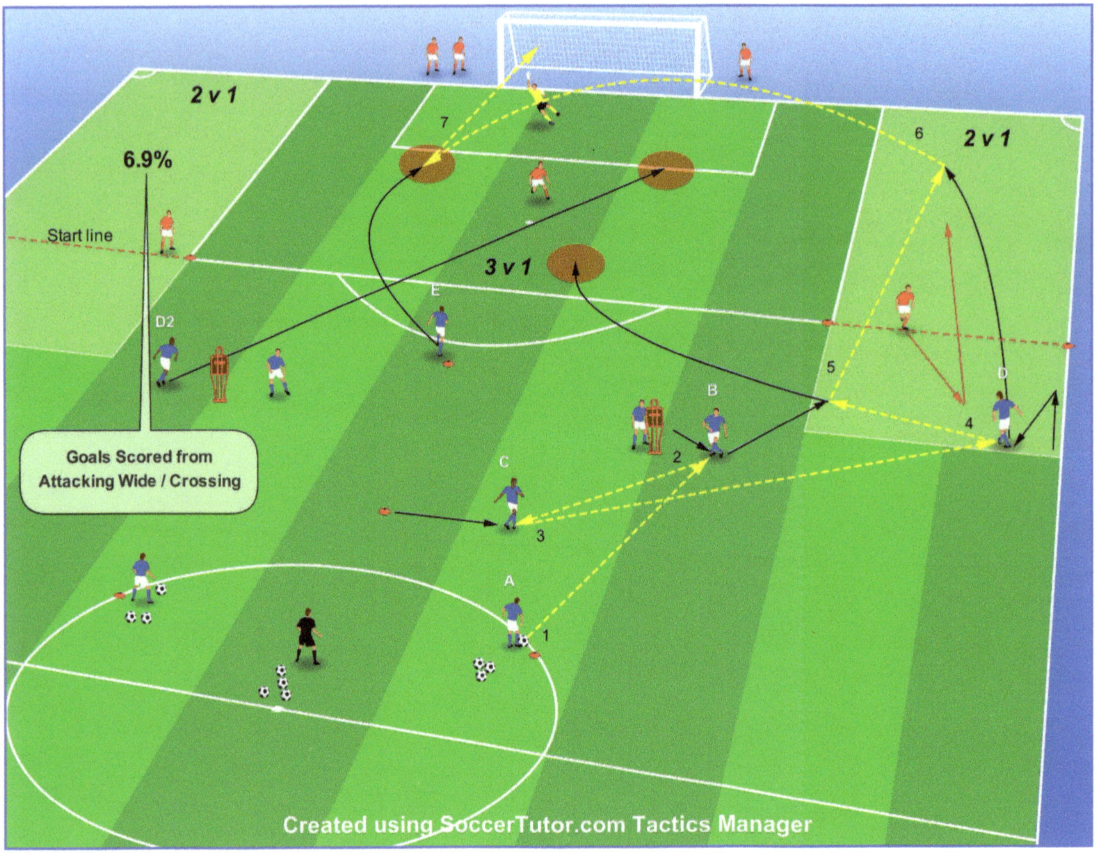

Description

- The initial combination is exactly the same as the previous practice
- In this progression, we now have a red defender in the highlighted wide zone. He first tries to intercept **D's** pass to **B**, and then moves back to try and stop the cross into the box.
- The same 3 blue players **(B, E & D2)** make runs into the box to try and score, but this time there is a red defender trying to defend the goal.

- The players rotate positions:
  A → B → C → D → E → A
- After the phase is complete, repeat from the left with a new ball.
- Rotate the defenders with the 3 resting outside often. You can also switch the player roles (attackers ←→ defenders).

Training Session 9B: Attacking Wide / Crossing (6.9% of Goals)

PROGRESSION

3. Crossing and Finishing in a Multi-Zone 6v6 (+1) +GKs Conditioned Small Sided Game

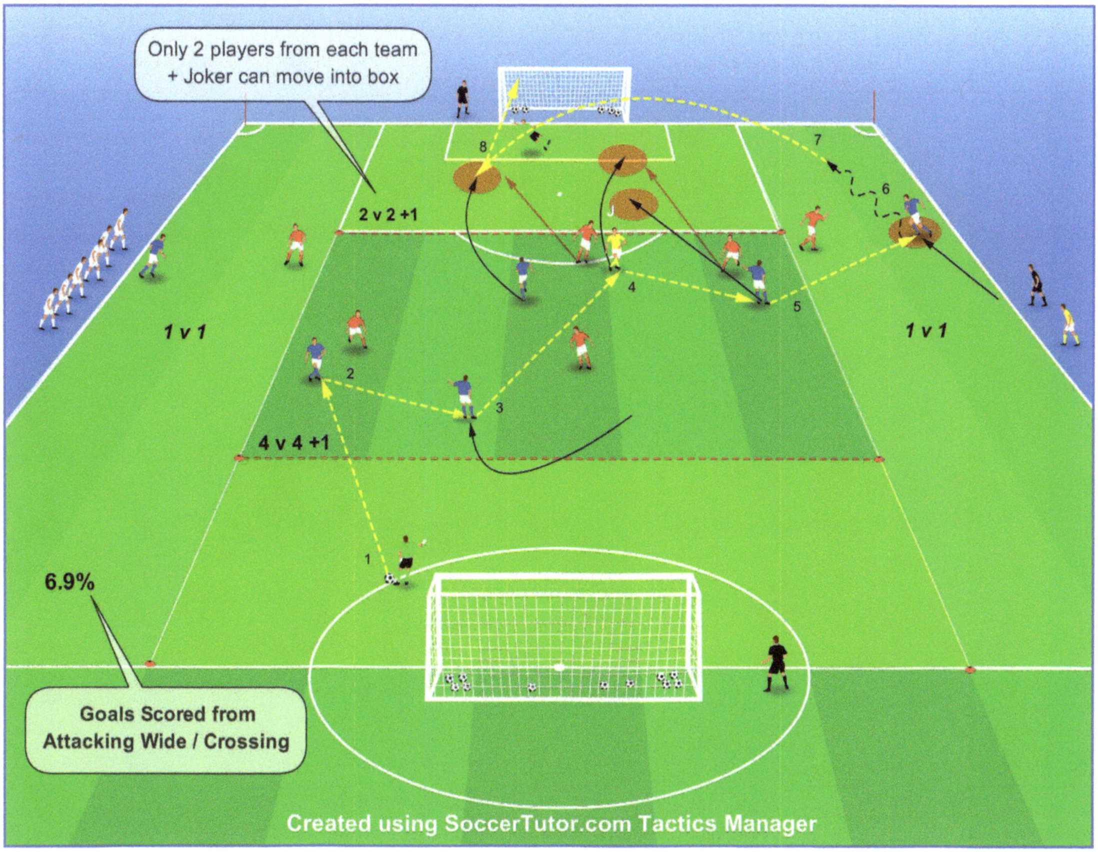

Description

- For this 6v6 (+1) +GKs game, we mark out 5 zones in half a pitch. The yellow Joker plays with the team in possession.
- The game starts with the GK's pass into the central zone where there is a 4v4 (+1) situation.
- To score a goal, the ball first must be moved from the central zone into a wide zone (1v1), and then into the box.
- Only 2 players from each team + the Joker can move into the box.
- This creates a 3v2 (2v2 +1) situation to finish the attack.
- There is a third team (whites) outside resting because the teams rotate. There is also a Joker outside who rotates.
- The games are 3-5 minutes. The team that scores the most goals after a set number of games wins.
- Every time there is a goal, the GK starts the game with the team that conceded the last goal becoming the new attacking team.

Training Session 9B: Attacking Wide / Crossing (6.9% of Goals)

PROGRESSION

4. Crossing and Finishing in a Multi-Zone 8v8 (+2) +GKs Conditioned Small Sided Game

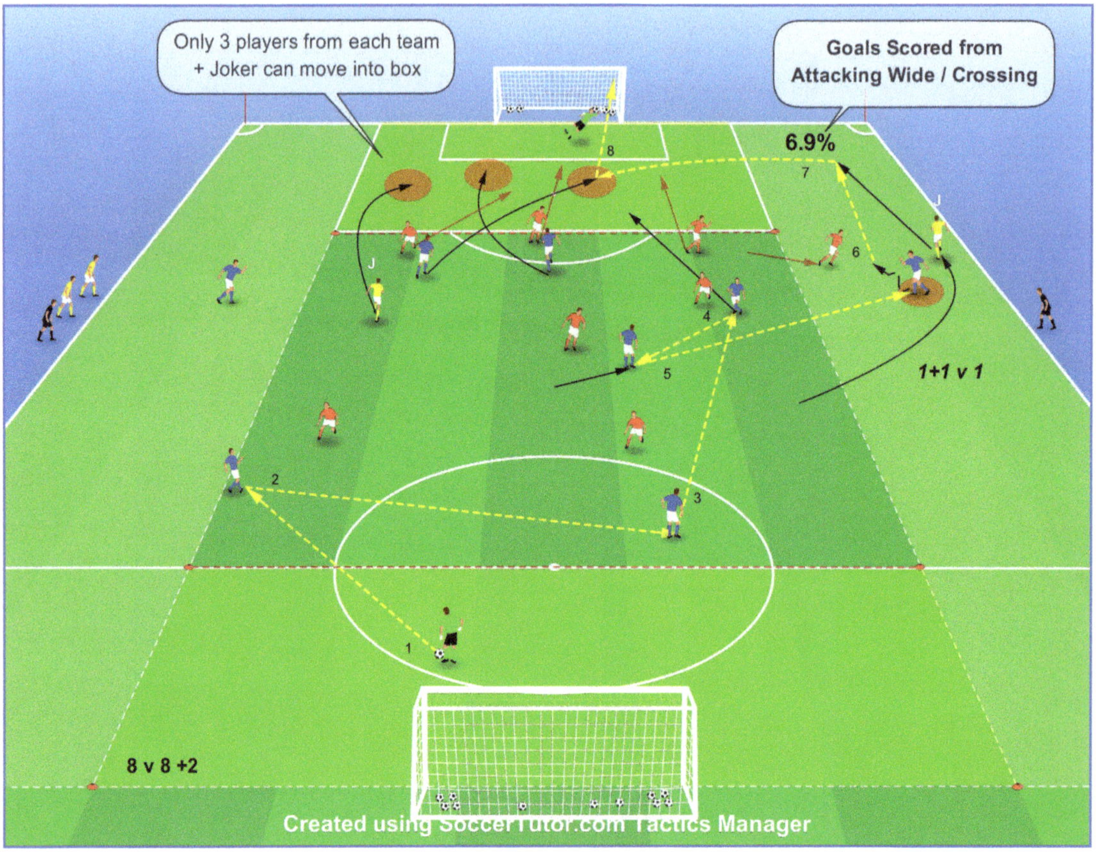

Description

- In this progression of the previous practice, we increase the size of the playing area and now have an 8v8 (+2) +GKs game.

- To score a goal, the ball first must be moved from the central zone into a wide zone, and then into the box.

- In the wide zones, one of the Jokers can join to create a 2v1 (1v1 +1) situation. In the diagram example, the Joker makes an overlap run and crosses into the box.

- Only 3 players from each team + the Joker can move into the box. This creates a 4v3 (3v3 +1) situation to finish the attack.

- There are 2 Jokers outside who rotate in to make sure all the Jokers get enough rest because they have to make a lot of runs into the wide zones.

- Every time there is a goal, the GK starts the game with the team that conceded the last goal becoming the new attacking team.

TRAINING SESSION 9C

Switch + Long Passes
35 Goals

FOR SWITCH OF PLAY & LONG PASSES (11.5% OF GOALS)

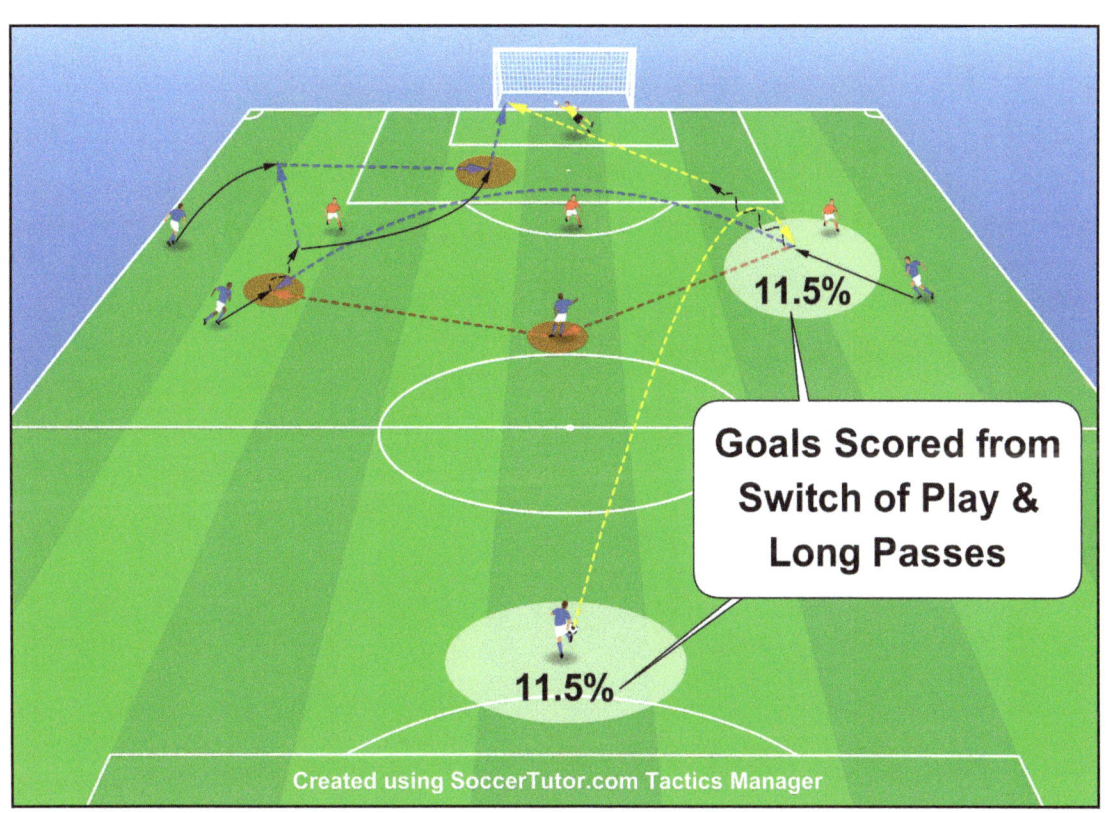

Goals Scored from Switch of Play & Long Passes

Training Session 9C: Switch of Play & Long Passes (11.5% of Goals)

SESSION FOR THIS TACTICAL SITUATION (4 PRACTICES)

1. Long Passes and Switches of Play in a Functional Practice with Cut Back and Finish

Description

- The practice begins with a long pass from deep. Each repetition starts from a different cone (**A1** → **A2** → **A3** → **A4**) to practice different angles. These players rotate after each pass, as shown in the diagram.

- The long pass is aimed towards **Player B1** or **B2**. He controls the ball and then switches play to the other **Player B** (B2 in diagram example), who moves forward off their cone to receive.

- **B2** then switches play again to **C1**, who moves off his cone to receive inside the box.

- To finish the attack, **C1** cuts the ball back for the forward (**D**) to time his run and try to score.

- The practice is then repeated starting from **Position A3**. Players **B**, **C** and **D** rotate with the resting players. Rotate the player roles after a set number of repetitions.

Training Session 9C: Switch of Play & Long Passes (11.5% of Goals)

PROGRESSION

2. Long Pass into the Receiving Zone and Attacking Combination Play to Finish in the Final Third

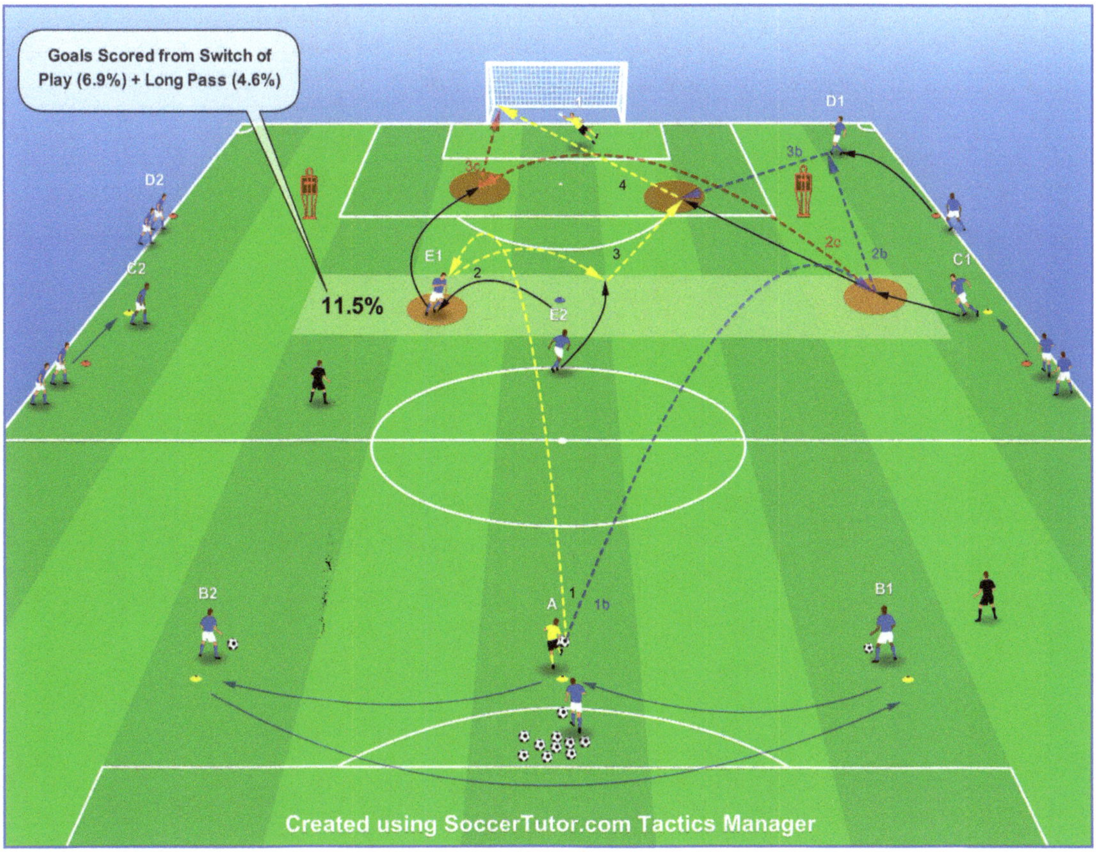

Description

- The practice begins with a long pass from deep. From **Position B**, the passes are hit diagonally to **C1** or **C2**. From **Position A** (diagram example), the pass can be hit towards the left, right, or centre.

- If the long pass is played wide towards **C**, they control the ball and have 2 options. The first option is to pass for the forward run of **D** off their cone near to the byline, move to receive the cut back in the box, and shoot **(blue arrows)**.

- The second option is for **C** to deliver a cross into the box for the run of the forward **(E)** to score **(red arrows)**.

- If the long pass is played into the centre, **E1** and **E2** combine with **C1** or **C2** to try and score a goal. In the diagram example **(yellow arrows)**, **E2** plays a through pass for the run of **C1**.

- Players **C** and **D** rotate with the resting players. Players **A** and **B** rotate after each pass, as shown in the diagram. Rotate the player roles after a set number of repetitions.

Training Session 9C: Switch of Play & Long Passes (11.5% of Goals)

PROGRESSION

3. Long Passes into Opposition's Half and Second Ball Attacks Across (6v3 +GK) with 2v1 Zones

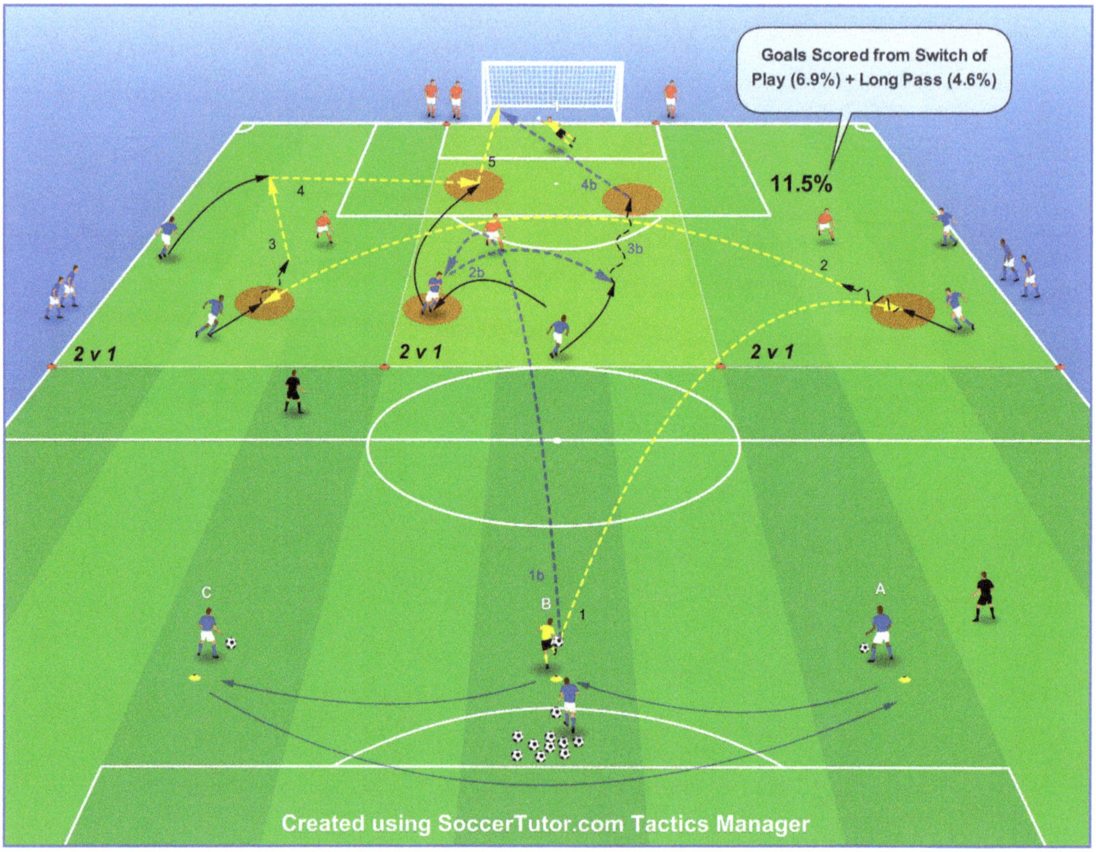

Description

- The practice begins with a long pass from deep. Each repetition starts from a different cone (**A → B → C**) to practice different angles. These players rotate after each pass, as shown in the diagram.

- The long pass can be played into any of the 3 zones where there are 2v1 situations.

- If the ball is played into a wide zone, the 2 blue players attack out wide themselves or switch play **(yellow arrows)**.

- They cross into the box for one of the central zone blue players to finish.

- If the long pass is played into the central zone, the 2 blue players combine and try to score a goal attacking through the centre **(blue arrows)**.

- Once the phase is complete, even if the reds win the ball, the practice is then repeated starting from **Position C**.

- The red defenders rotate with the resting players after 1-2 repetitions.

Training Session 9C: Switch of Play & Long Passes (11.5% of Goals)

PROGRESSION

4. Switching Play from Zone to Zone and Creating 2v1 Situations for the Second Ball in a Conditioned Game

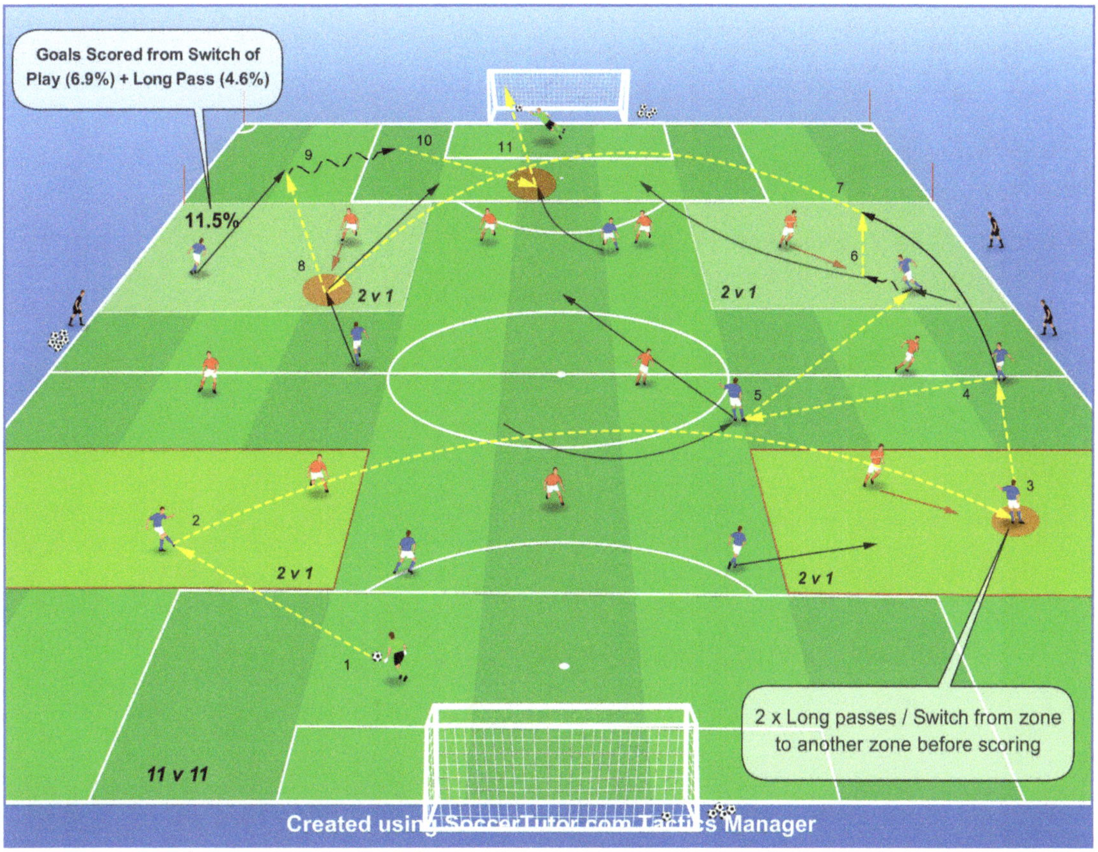

Description

- To complete the session, we play an 11v11 conditioned game on a full pitch. There are 4 zones marked out as shown. At any time, there can only be a maximum of 2 attacking players (blues) and 1 defending player (red) within any of these zones.

- The game starts from the GK and the team in possession (blues) must complete 2 long passes/switches of play from zone to zone before they are allowed to score a goal.

- If the defending team (reds) win the ball, they have to complete 2 zone to zone passes themselves before they are allowed to score a goal.

- If the ball goes out of play or the GK saves a shot, the game refreshes and the team in possession has to complete 2 zone to zone passes before they are allowed to score a goal.

TACTICAL EXAMPLES

10. ATTACKING COMBINATION PLAY IN FINAL THIRD (19.0% OF GOALS)

19.0%

Goals Scored from Attacking Combination Play in Final Third

10. Attacking Combination Play in Final Third = 19.0% of All Goals Scored

Viktoria Plzen 2-4 FC Barcelona (Ferrán 44') - 01/11/2022

Example 1 (FC Barcelona): Attacking Combination Play in Final Third **CENTRE** = 43 of 304 Goals (14.1%)

Description

The centre back **Alonso** passes to central midfielder **Pablo Torre**, who passes inside to defensive midfielder **Kessié**.

Kessié drives forward with the ball and then plays back into the centre for right winger **Raphinha**, who plays a precise lob pass over the top of the defence for the run of the advanced left back **J. Alba** into the box.

J. Alba passes across the 6-yard box for the left winger **Ferrán Torres** to score with a simple close range finish.

Key Aspects

1. As **Kessié** ends up with his back to goal, he passes back to **Raphinha**, who is in position to see the whole picture of the game. Barcelona lose metres initially but they gain visibility of the options.

2. Also, **Raphinha** understands that an open pass is better than an inside pass. It is the best solution for scoring a goal.

3. With **J. Alba** arriving from deep, he surprises the crowded defence. He has been adept at this over many years.

10. Attacking Combination Play in Final Third = 19.0% of All Goals Scored

Napoli 3-0 Rangers (Simeone 11') - ²⁶/10/2022

Example 2 (Napoli): Attacking Combination Play in Final Third <u>WIDE</u> = 15 of 304 Goals Scored (4.9%)

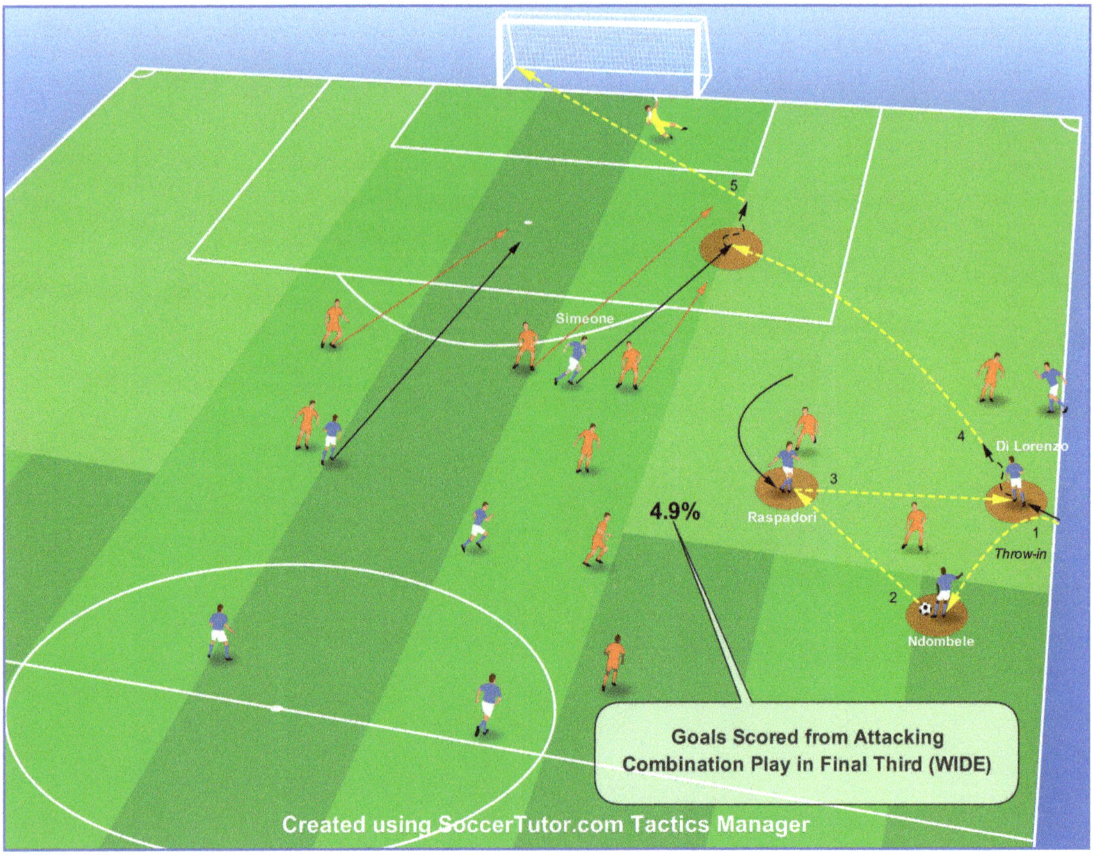

Description

The right back **Di Lorenzo** starts the phase with a throw-in back to central midfielder **Ndombele**. The left winger **Raspadori** (who is out of position on the right) drops back to receive **Ndombele's** pass and move the ball to **Di Lorenzo** next to the sideline. **Di Lorenzo** takes a touch and then delivers an excellent pass into the box for the run of the centre forward **Simeone** in behind the defensive line. **Simeone** takes a good first touch to control the pass and then finishes with a powerful shot into the far corner.

Key Aspects

1. Napoli create a 4v3 numerical advantage in the wide area, which enables them to find a free player with available time and space (**Di Lorenzo**) to play forward.

2. The left winger **Raspadori** (out of position) is able to provide an extra player to create this advantage. His movement and angle enables the ball to be moved to the free player **Di Lorenzo**, who can then look up and play a pass in behind for the well timed **Simeone** run.

TRAINING SESSION 10A

Centre Combo
43 Goals

FOR ATTACKING COMBINATION PLAY IN FINAL THIRD CENTRE (14.1% OF GOALS)

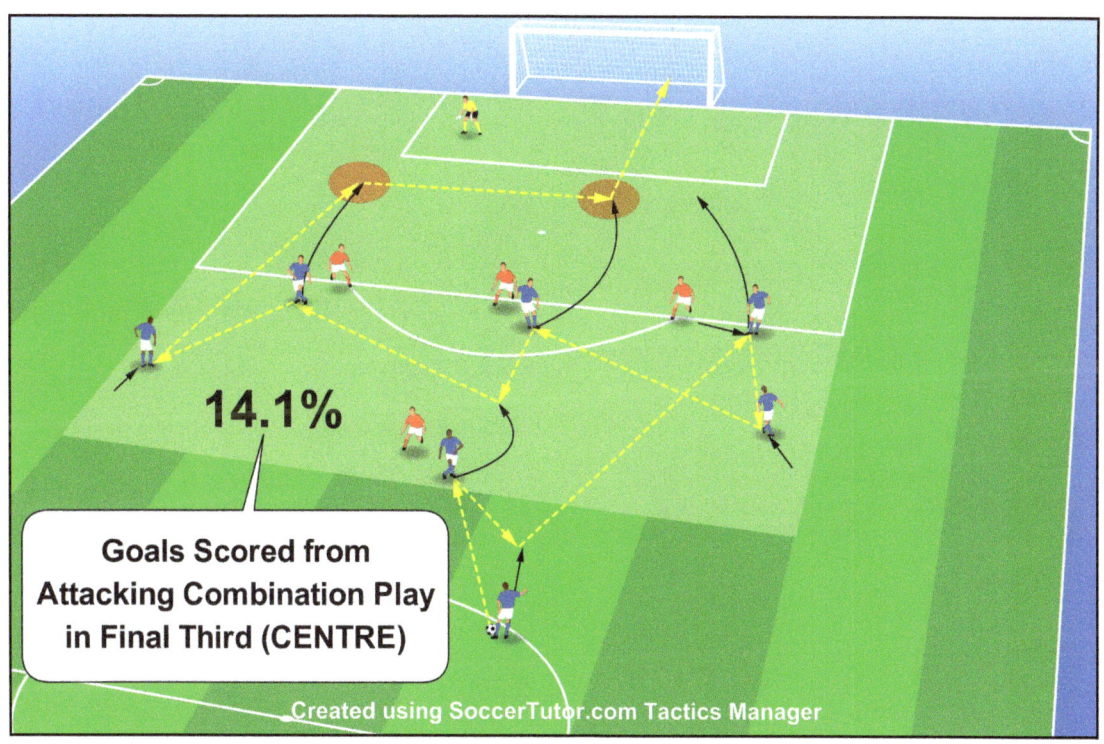

14.1%

Goals Scored from Attacking Combination Play in Final Third (CENTRE)

Training Session 10A: Attacking Combination Play in Final Third <u>CENTRE</u> (14.1% of Goals)

SESSION FOR THIS TACTICAL SITUATION (4 PRACTICES)
1. Attacking Combination Play Around the Box, Through Pass, and Finish

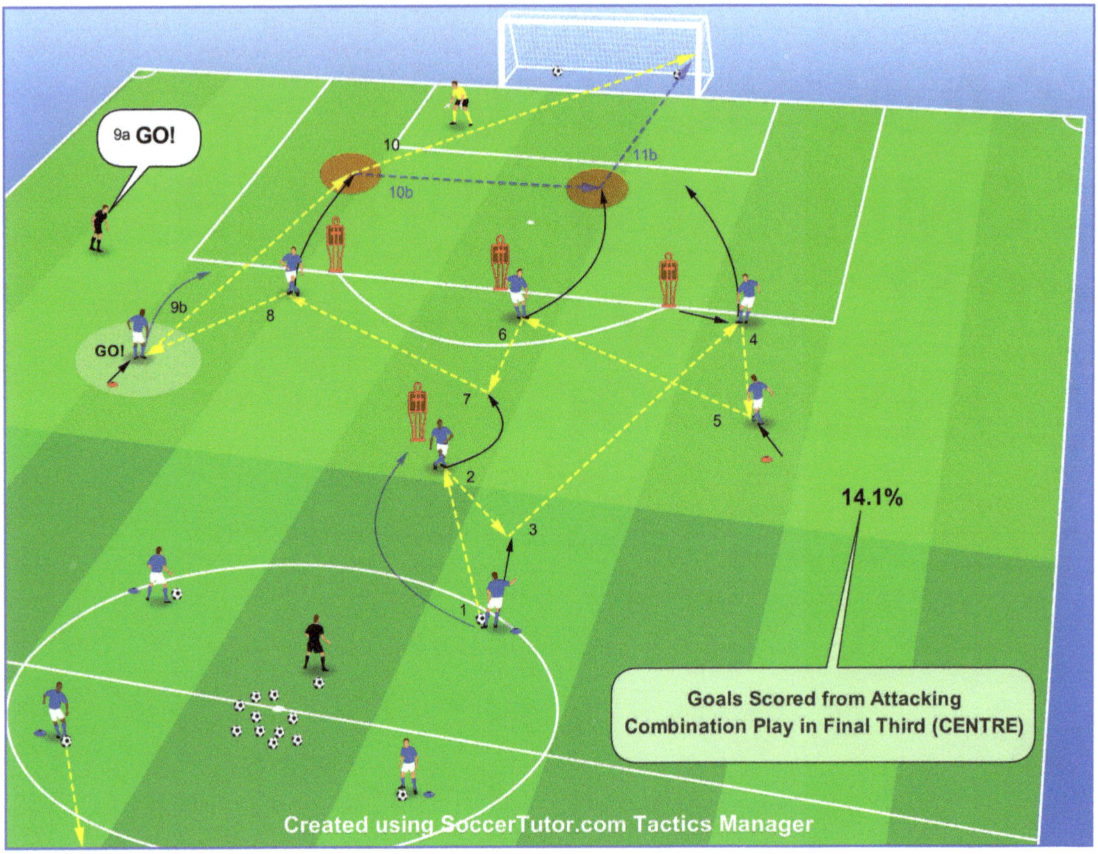

Description

- The players start in the positions shown and there are 4 mannequins set out.
- The sequence starts from the left or right. The players combine with speed and precision. They are free to pass forwards, backwards, to the right, or the left.
- When the Coach calls out **"GO!"**, the player in possession has to pass into the box (assist) for the run of a teammate, who receives and tries to score.
- The players can rotate positions and then restart with a new ball from the other side.
- You can have 2 groups working in either half of the pitch, as shown.

Training Session 10A: **Attacking Combination Play in Final Third CENTRE (14.1% of Goals)**

PROGRESSION

2. Combination Play and Passing in Behind Defensive Line (Edge of Box) in a Functional 6v3 +GK Practice

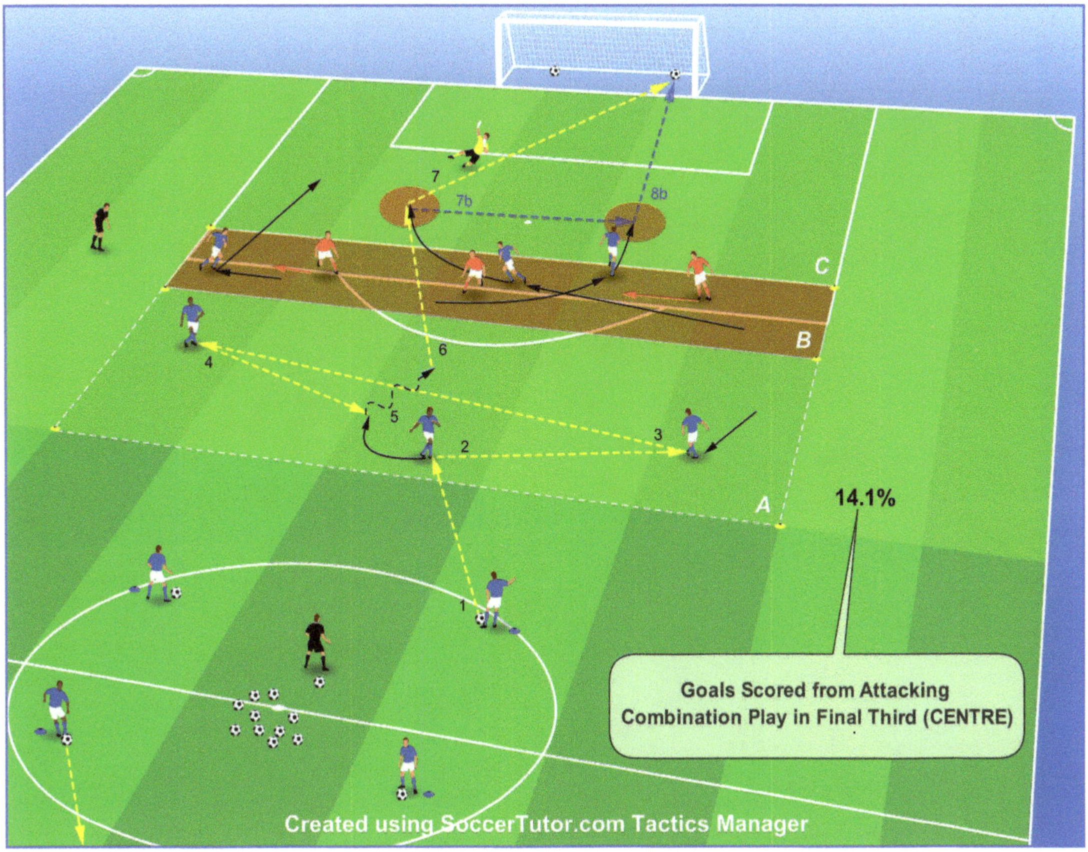

Description

- The sequence starts from the left or right outside blue player, who pass the ball into **Zone A**.

- The players in **Zone A** must complete 3 passes before finding the right moment to play a through pass into **Zone C**.

- **Zone B** starts with a 3v3 situation. The blue attacking players make runs into the box **(Zone C)** to receive and the red defenders move horizontally, trying to intercept the through passes.

- When a blue player receives in **Zone C**, he can either shoot himself **(7)** or pass for a teammate to score **(7b-8b)** as the other 2 players also move forward. The red defenders cannot enter **Zone C**.

- The deep player who plays the first pass moves into **Zone A**, the player who plays the through pass moves into **Zone C**, and the player who shoots moves to the start position.

- The practice continues with a new ball from the left outside player.

Training Session 10A: Attacking Combination Play in Final Third CENTRE (14.1% of Goals)

PROGRESSION
3. Attacking Combination Play Through the Centre in a 4v4 (+1) +GK 3-Zone Functional Game

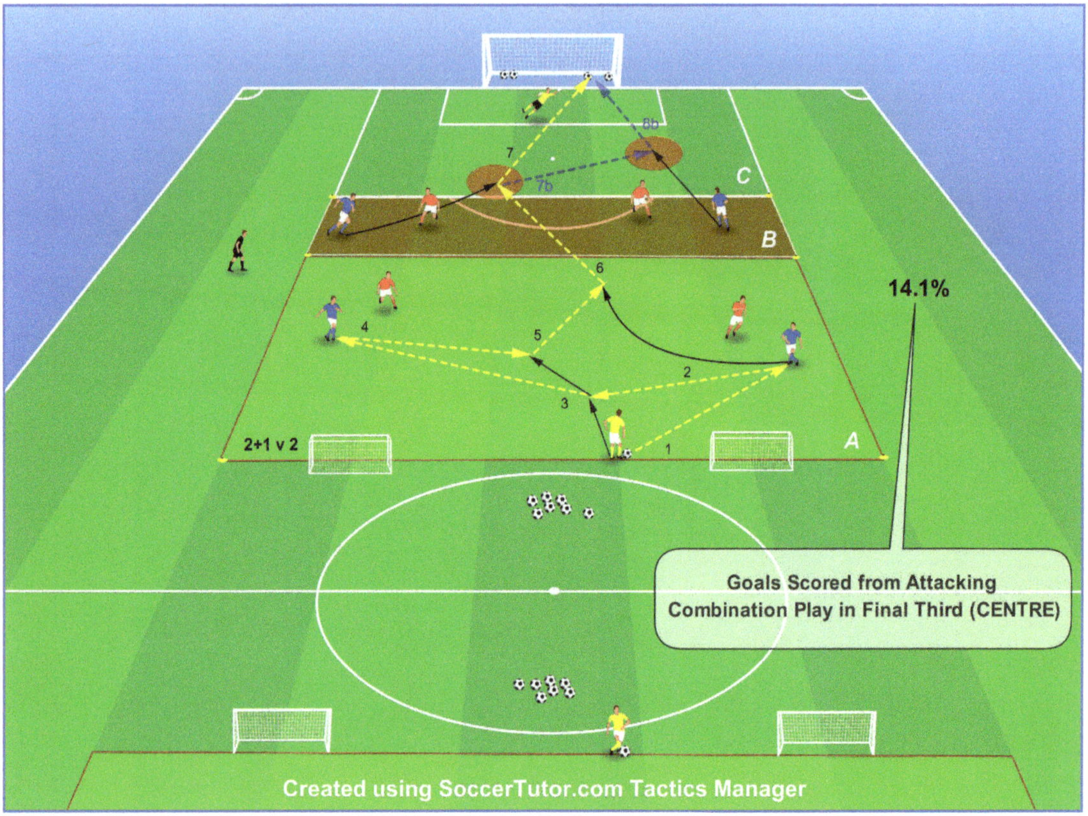

Goals Scored from Attacking Combination Play in Final Third (CENTRE)

Description

- We start with a 2 (+1) v 2 situation in **Zone A**, which is effectively 3v1 as the Joker plays with the team in possession.
- There is a 2v2 situation in **Zone B**.
- The blue team attack the large goal with GK. The reds defend, try to win the ball, and then counter attack to score in the 2 small goals.
- The players in **Zone A** must complete 3 passes before finding the right moment to play a through pass into **Zone C**.
- The 2 blue attacking players in **Zone B** make runs into the box **(Zone C)** to receive and the 2 red defenders move horizontally, trying to intercept the through passes.
- Restart from the yellow Joker.
- After a set period of time, switch the team roles so the reds become the attacking team.
- You can have another group working in the other half of the pitch, as shown. A competition can be made with a league, or a semi-final and final.

Training Session 10A: **Attacking Combination Play in Final Third CENTRE (14.1% of Goals)**

PROGRESSION

4. Attacking Combination Play Through the Centre in a Two-Direction 8v8 (+2) +GKs 5-Zone Game

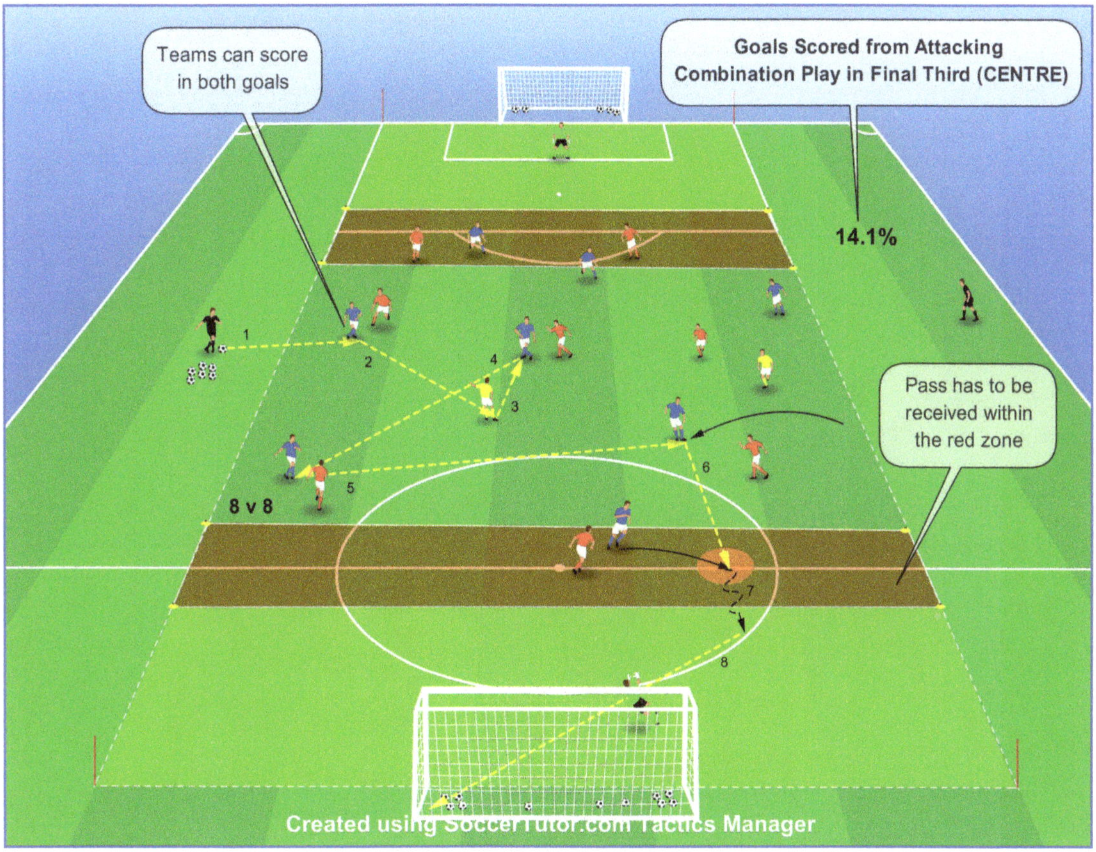

Description

- The Coach starts by passing the ball into the central zone. The team in possession (blues) can attack either goal with the help of the 2 Jokers. There is no offside rule applied.

- To score, you must pass to a player within the red receiving zone. From that point, that player must try to score a goal on their own without help from their teammates.

- The defending players (reds) are not allowed to move into the end zones, so they must try to make a decisive defensive action within the red zone.

- If the blue player cannot score a goal after receiving in the red zone, he has to pass back into the central zone. The blues can change the direction of the play to attack the other goal, or they can attack the same goal again.

- If the ball goes out of play, restart with a new ball from the Coach and with the team that was defending now in possession.

TRAINING SESSION 10B

Wide Combo — 15 Goals

FOR ATTACKING COMBINATION PLAY IN FINAL THIRD WIDE (4.9%% OF GOALS)

4.9%

Goals Scored from Attacking Combination Play in Final Third (WIDE)

Training Session 10B: Attacking Combination Play in Final Third <u>WIDE</u> (4.9% of Goals)

SESSION FOR THIS TACTICAL SITUATION (4 PRACTICES)

1. Attacking Combination Play Out Wide with Give & Go, Cross, and Finish

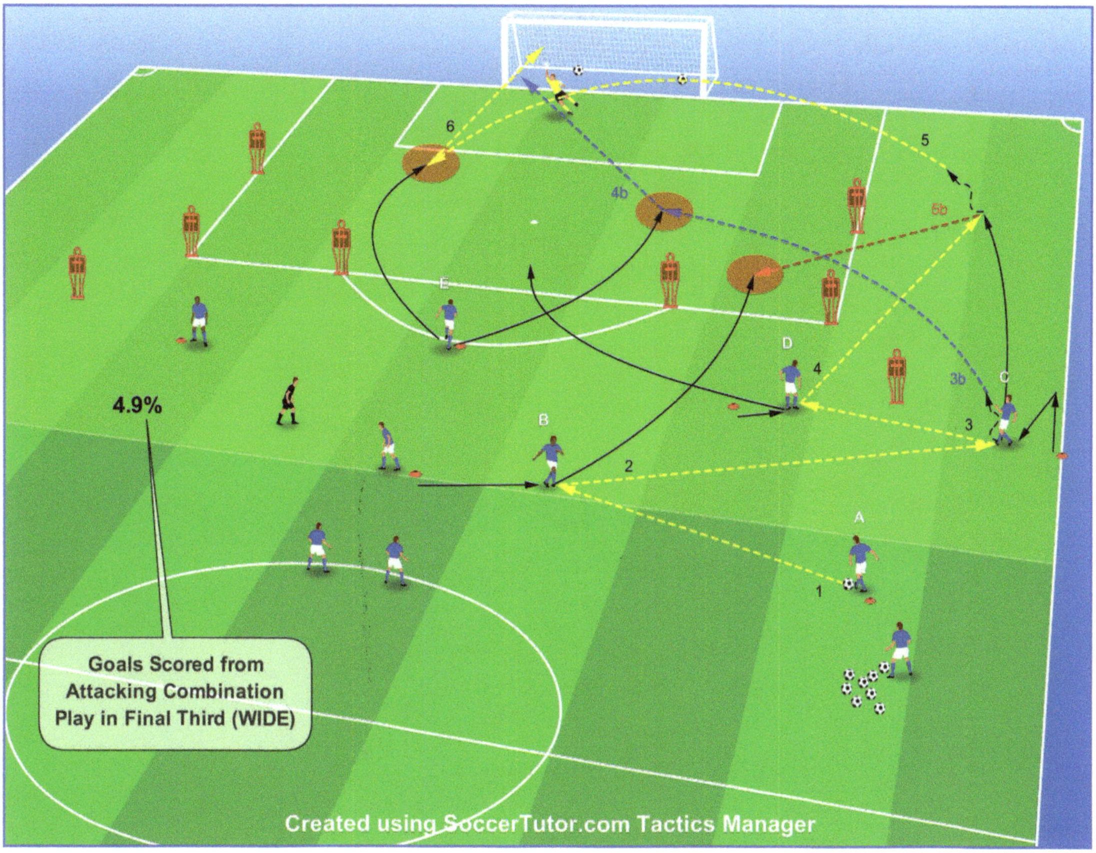

Goals Scored from Attacking Combination Play in Final Third (WIDE) — 4.9%

Description

- The players start in the positions shown and there are 4 mannequins set out on each side.

- **A** starts with a diagonal pass to **B** in the centre. **B** passes out wide to **C**, who checks off his cone before receiving.

- From there, **C** either plays a give and go with **D** and receives the return high up the flank **(3-4)**, or passes into the box for the run of the forward **E** - **(3b)**, who tries to score.

- For the give and go, **C** controls the pass and has 2 options:

  5 - Aerial cross for **E** at the back post.
  5b - Cut back or low cross for oncoming runners **B** or **D** to shoot.

- The players can rotate positions and the sequence is repeated starting with Player A on the left side.

- You can have 2 groups working in either half of the pitch.

Training Session 10B: Attacking Combination Play in Final Third WIDE (4.9% of Goals)

PROGRESSION

2. Attacking Combination Play Out Wide in a 4v3 +GK Functional Practice

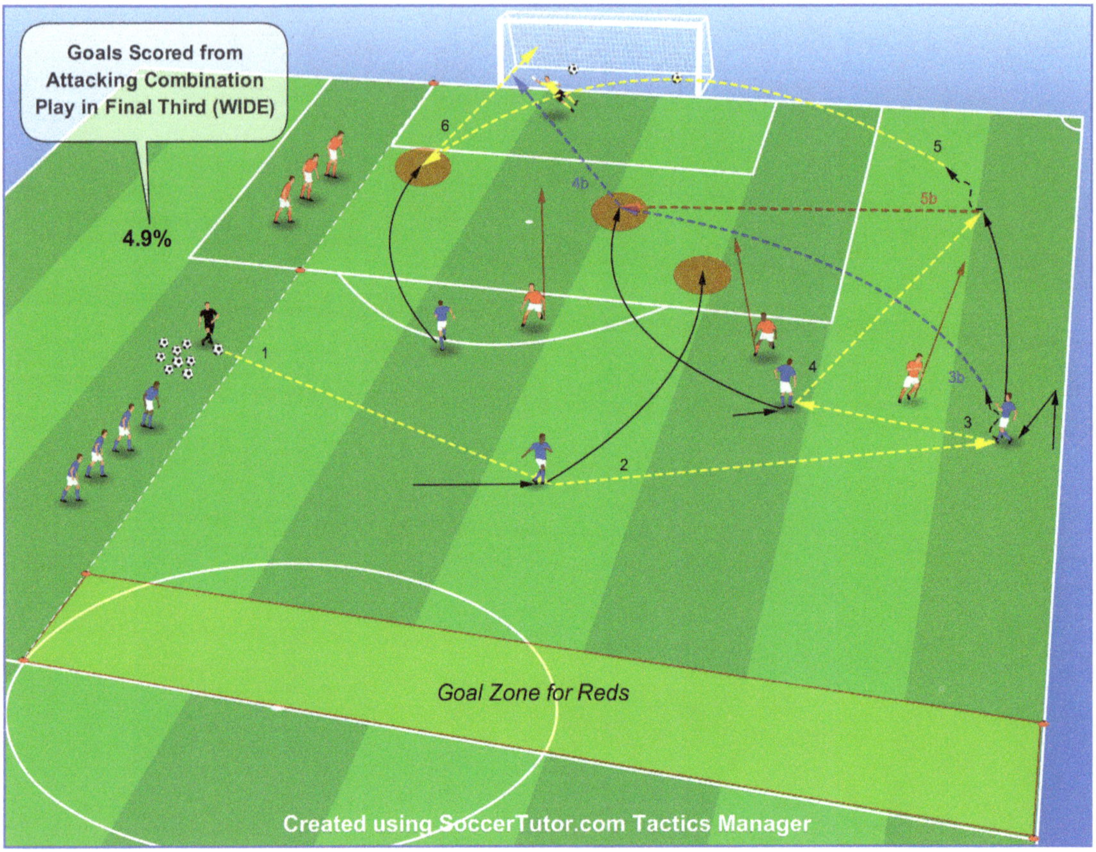

Goals Scored from Attacking Combination Play in Final Third (WIDE)

4.9%

Goal Zone for Reds

Created using SoccerTutor.com Tactics Manager

Description

- Mark out the size of area shown with a "Goal Zone" for the red team to score. The Coach starts the practice, and the blues play 4v3 +GK for their attack.

- A goal is only valid if the attack is focused down the right flank.

- If the reds win the ball, they score if any player successfully receives a pass within the "Goal Zone."

- As soon as a phase ends, the players rotate with the outside resting players.

- Halfway through the practice, move the cones and start working on attacking combination play on the left side of the pitch.

©SOCCERTUTOR.COM — COACH YOUR TEAM TO SCORE MORE GOALS

Training Session 10B: Attacking Combination Play in Final Third <u>WIDE</u> (4.9% of Goals)

PROGRESSION

3. Attacking Combination Play Out Wide in a 6v6 (+1) +GKs Game with Vertically Split Zones

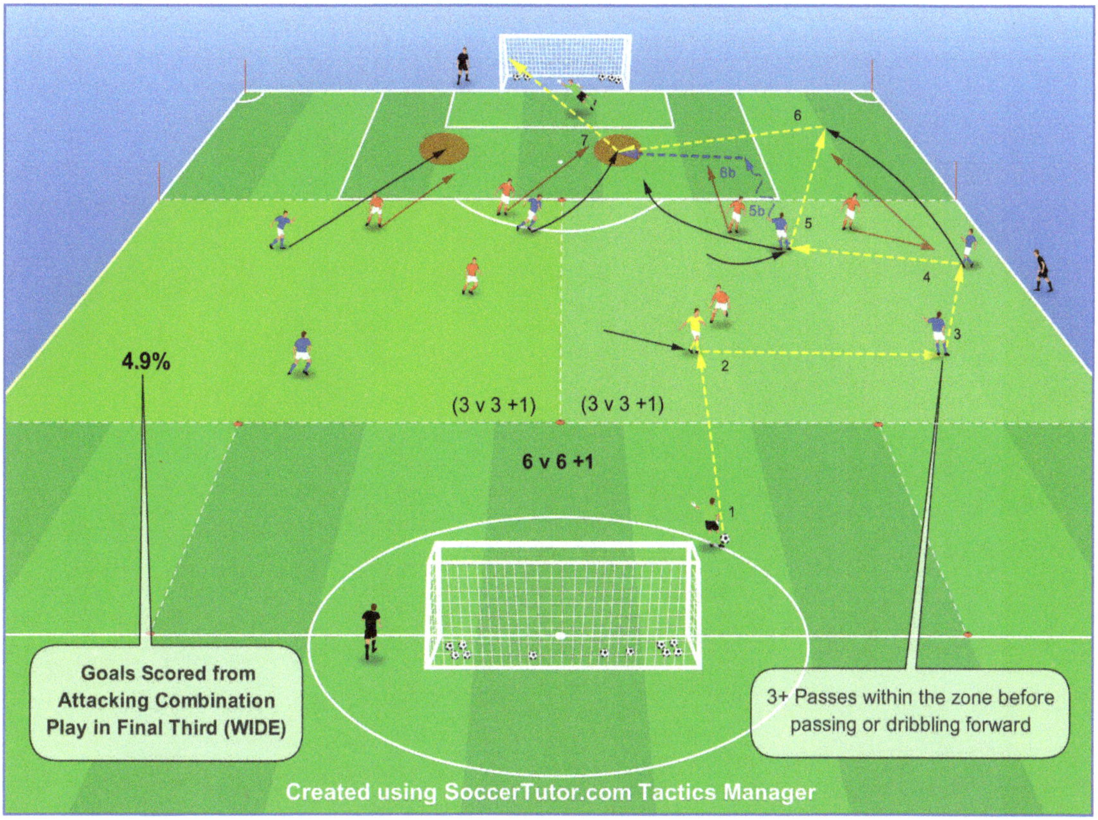

Goals Scored from Attacking Combination Play in Final Third (WIDE)

3+ Passes within the zone before passing or dribbling forward

(3 v 3 +1)   (3 v 3 +1)

6 v 6 +1

Description

- Using half a pitch, we have 2 penalty areas (boxes) and 2 central zones which are split horizontally. There is a 3v3 situation in both halves + 1 Joker who can move across both zones.

- The GK starts the game with a pass into one of the central zones.

- The blue team must attack down that side using attacking combination play in the final third.

- Players can either play a through pass in behind or try to dribble in behind.

- Once a player gets in behind, players from both central zones can move into the box to attack/defend.

- In the diagram we show 2 options:

  5 - Play a through pass for the wide player to deliver a cross into the box.

  5b - Dribble in between defenders and into the box.

- If the reds win the ball at any time, they counter attack and try to score.

- Whenever the phase ends, restart from the red team's GK with the team roles reversed.

Training Session 10B: Attacking Combination Play in Final Third WIDE (4.9% of Goals)

PROGRESSION

4. Attacking Combination Play Out Wide in a Conditioned Multi-Zone Game

Description

- To complete the practice, we play a conditioned 11v11 game on a full pitch. The blue attacking team are in a 4-3-3 formation and the red defending team are in a 4-4-2 formation - you can adjust to best suit your training.

- In the 2 low zones, only 2 blue players and 1 red player are allowed in there at a time.

- In the 2 high zones, only 3 blue players and 2 red players are allowed in there at a time.

- The GK starts the practice, and the blues build up play.

- To score a goal, the ball must be played through either of the high zones (attacking combination play in the final third - wide).

- Once the ball is played in behind, players make runs into the box to attack/defend.

- If the reds win the ball at any time, they counter attack and try to score.

- Whenever the phase ends, restart from the red team's GK with the team roles reversed.

TACTICAL EXAMPLES

11. COUNTER ATTACKS (20.7% OF GOALS)

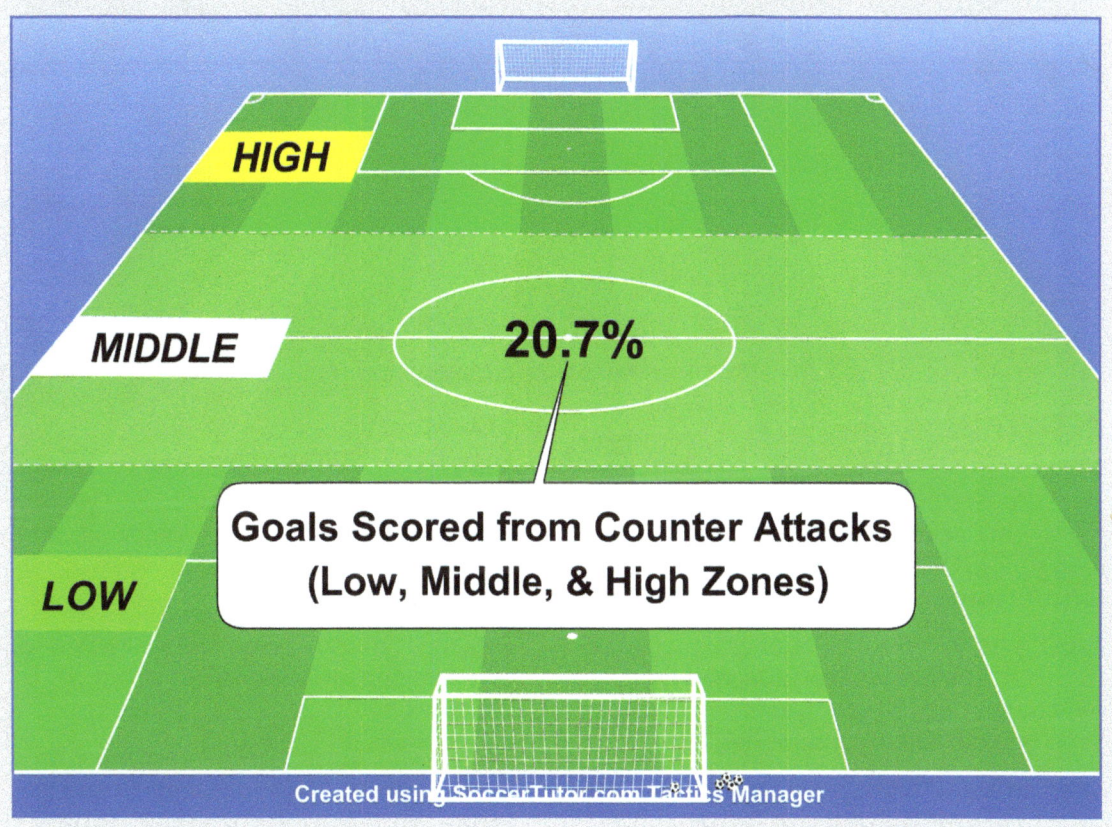

11. Counter Attacks = 20.7% of All Goals Scored

Rangers 1-7 Liverpool (Salah 81') - 12/10/2022

Goal Example 1 (Liverpool): Counter Attack from Low Zone = 14 of 304 Goals Scored (4.6%)

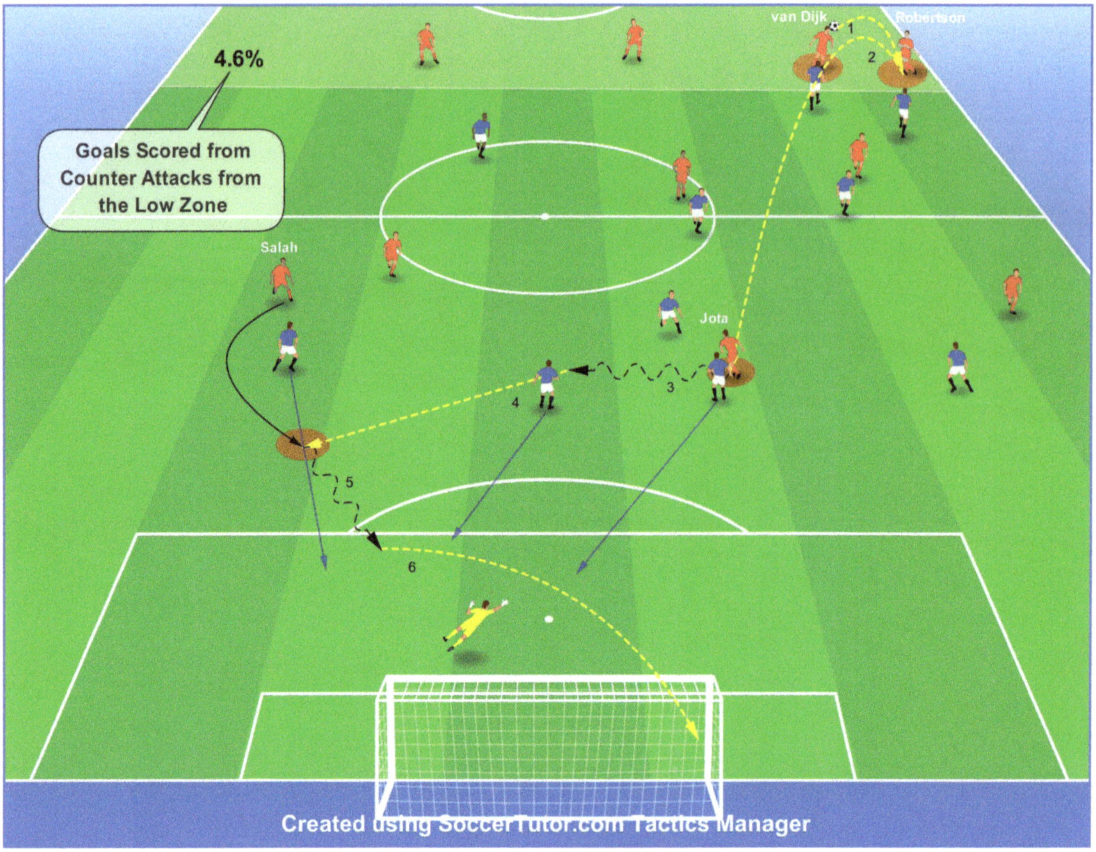

Description

With the ball up in the air, the centre back **van Dijk** wins the header and directs it to the left back **Robertson**, who sends a long pass up the pitch towards the centre forward **Jota**.

Jota fights with the defender and manages to control the ball, drive inside, and then pass to the right winger **Salah**, who makes a run beyond his direct opponent.

Salah arrives at high speed, receives, enters the box and curls a shot into the far corner.

Key Aspects

1. The Liverpool defenders know that their forwards fight for all the balls, and win many of them. From there, quick passes create chances in the final third.

2. Once the defender loses his duel with **Jota**, he is quickly able to move away and take him and another defender out of the game.

3. Once again, **Salah's** perfect driving with the ball, vision, and shot demonstrate his technical excellence in these situations.

11. Counter Attacks = 20.7% of All Goals Scored

AC Milan 4-0 RB Salzburg (Messias 90+1') - 02/11/2022

Goal Example 2 (AC Milan): **Counter Attack from Middle Zone =** 34 of 304 Goals Scored (11.2%)

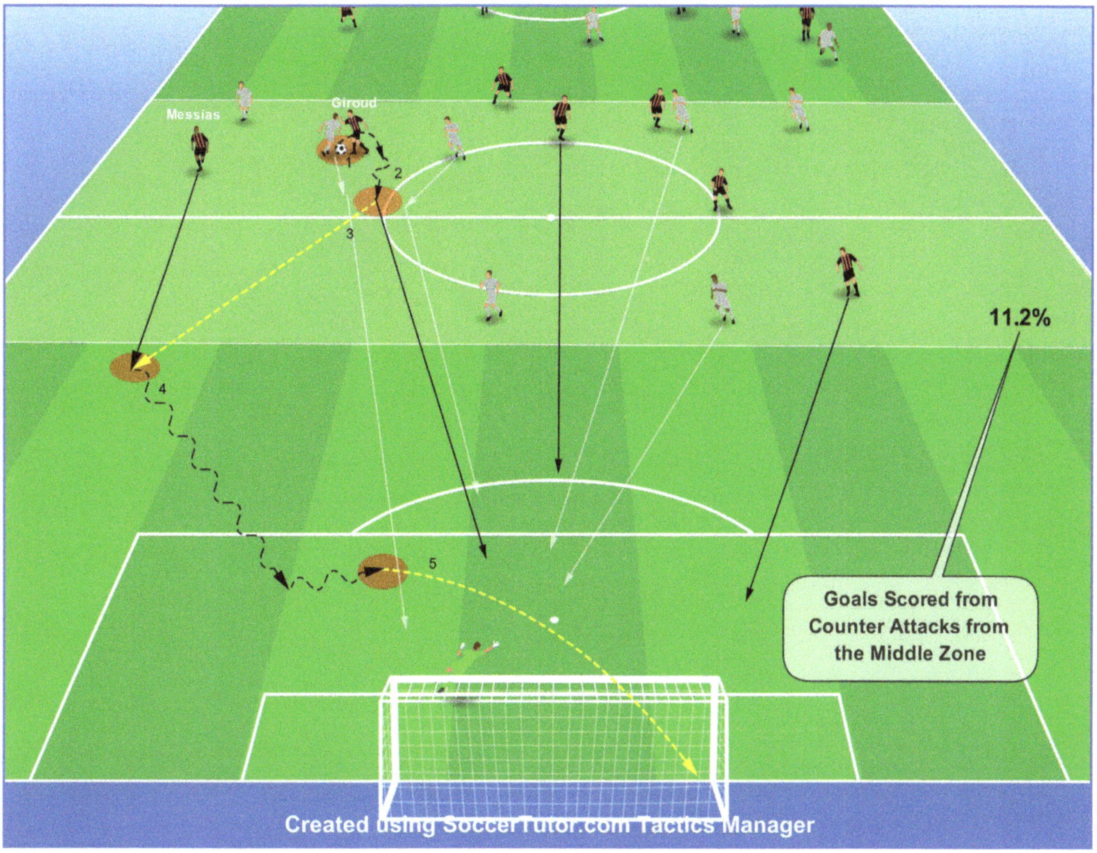

Description

The centre forward **Giroud** wins the ball in his own half, turns away from his direct opponent, and dribbles the ball forward. From there, he plays a pass out to the right for the run of the winger **Messias**. **Messias** carries the ball into the box, stops, cuts inside the defender, and then curls the ball into the far corner with his left foot.

Key Aspects

1. The centre forward **Giroud** produces a strong defensive action, then protects the ball, turns with a perfect pivot move, and completes his involvement by producing a pass to release **Messias** into a lot of free space.

2. The winger **Messias** is very fast and agile. First he runs and takes advantage of the empty space, then he carries the ball safely. Finally, he finishes the attack with good dribbling skills and a good finish.

11. Counter Attacks = 20.7% of All Goals Scored

Manchester City 3-1 Sevilla (Mahrez 83') - 02/11/2022

Goal Example 3 (Manchester City)
High Press + Counter = 15 of 304 Goals Scored (4.9%)

Description
The Sevilla centre back tries to carry the ball forward. Manchester City's centre forward **Álvarez** is alert and smart - he presses and steals the ball. He carries the ball forward and then opens up the play to release the left winger **Mahrez**, who controls the pass and shoots into the top corner.

Key Aspects
1. Pep Guardiola's team consistently take risks and press high up the pitch.
2. City press man to man, often leaving a numerical disadvantage in their own half.
3. This makes it difficult for Sevilla's defence play out, which causes the error. There were no passing lanes available into midfield, so **Álvarez** was able to win the ball.
4. The Manchester City forwards are like "Pit bulls", they bite, intimidate, scare, and finally, they steal the ball. The defenders have a lack of time to think and execute their actions.

TRAINING SESSION 11A

Low + Middle Counter — 48 Goals

FOR COUNTER ATTACKS FROM LOW OR MIDDLE ZONE (15.8% OF GOALS)

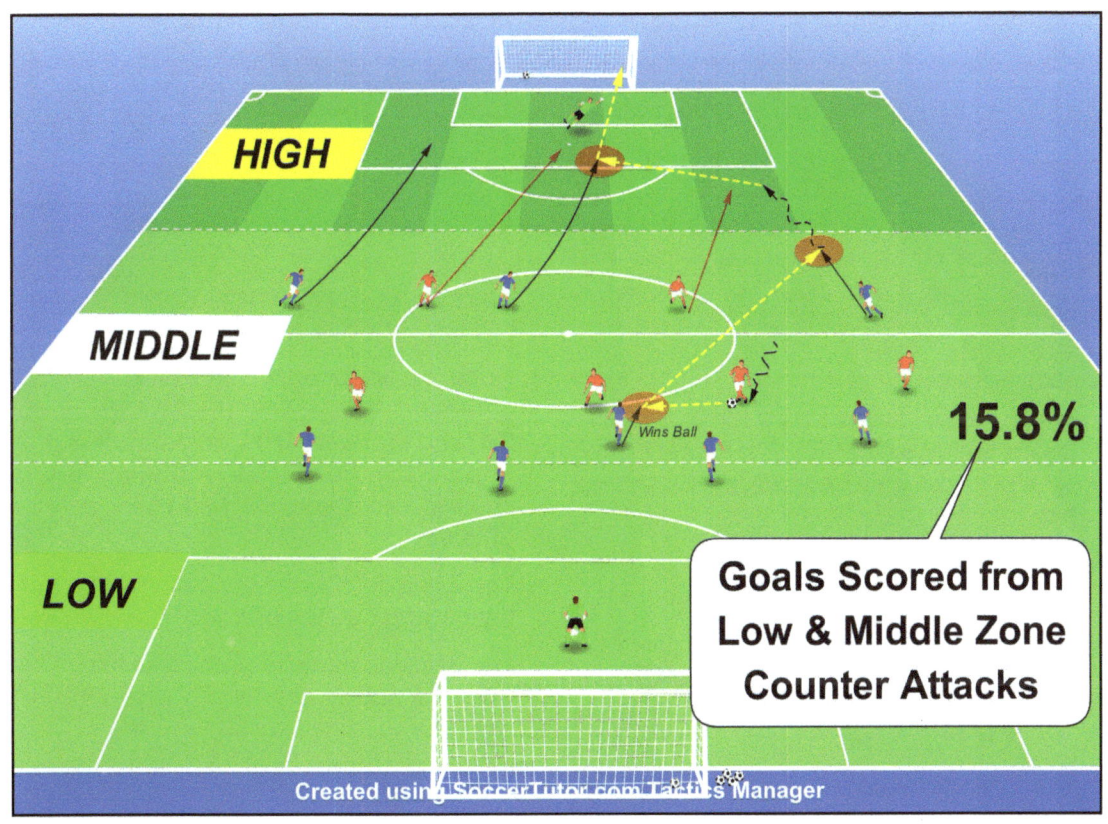

Training Session 11A: Counter Attacks from Low or Middle Zone (15.8% of Goals Scored)

SESSION FOR THIS TACTICAL SITUATION (4 PRACTICES)

1. Defending a Free Kick + Fast Counter Attack from the Low Zone

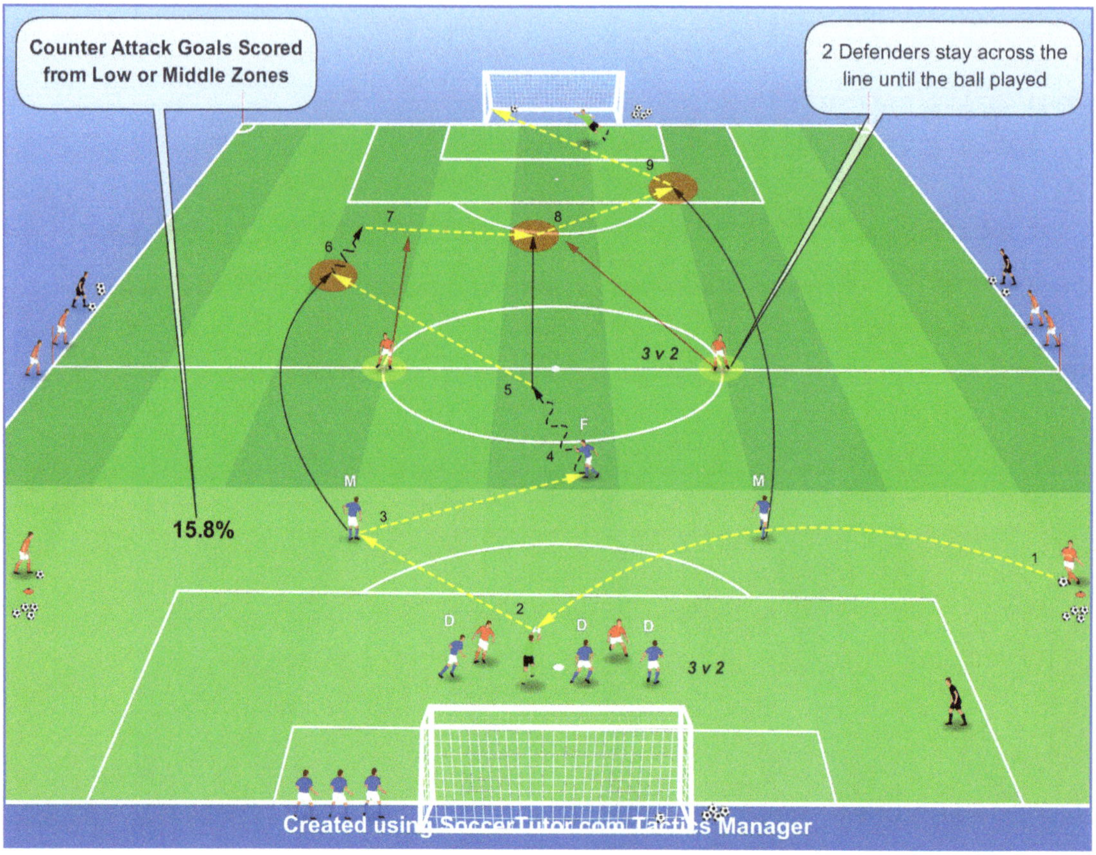

Description

- The practice starts with a wide red player taking a free kick. There are 2 red attackers vs 3 blue defenders + GK in the box.

- If the defenders **(D)** clear the ball or the GK catches it, the counter attack begins.

- Only once the ball leaves the box can the 2 blue midfielders **(M)** move. These 2 + the forward **(F)** launch a fast counter attack to try and score (3v2).

- The 2 red defenders defend their goal.

- Once the phase ends, the 3 blue defenders **(D)** become the 2 midfielders **(M)** and 1 forward **(F)**. The defenders are replaced by the outside resting players and the 2 attackers **(M, M & F)** move outside.

- The 2 red defenders also switch with 2 of the resting outside players.

- The practice restarts with a free kick from the opposite side.

Training Session 11A: Counter Attacks from Low or Middle Zone (15.8% of Goals Scored)

PROGRESSION

2. Win the Ball and Launch a Fast Counter Attack in a Dynamic 4 (+1) v 3 +GKs Functional Game

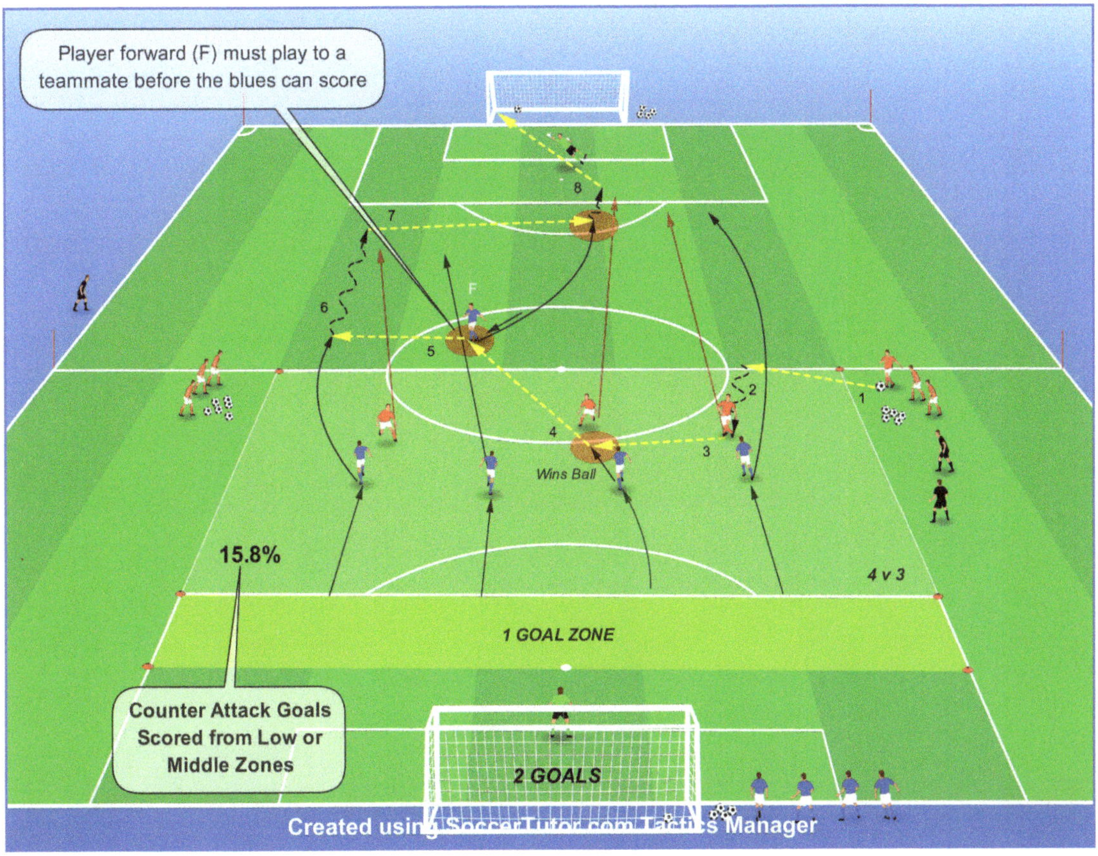

Description

- On a full pitch, mark out a "1 Goal Zone" in the position shown.
- The ball is played in, and the reds start with a 3v4 situation, trying to receive a pass within the "1 Goal Zone" to score 1 goal, and then score in the goal (2 goals).
- The 4 blue players start from the edge of the box and move forward together to try and win the ball from the reds.
- If they win the ball, they start a counter attack by passing to the forward (F).
- All 4 blue players join the counter attack to try and score. The 3 red players sprint back to defend the goal.
- When the phase is complete, 4 new blue players and 3 new red players enter to play with a new ball.
- Change the team roles halfway through and make it a competition for which team scores the most goals.

Training Session 11A: Counter Attacks from Low or Middle Zone (15.8% of Goals Scored)

PROGRESSION
3. Win the Ball in the Defensive Half and Launch a Counter Attack in a 2-Zone 8v6 +GKs Transition Game

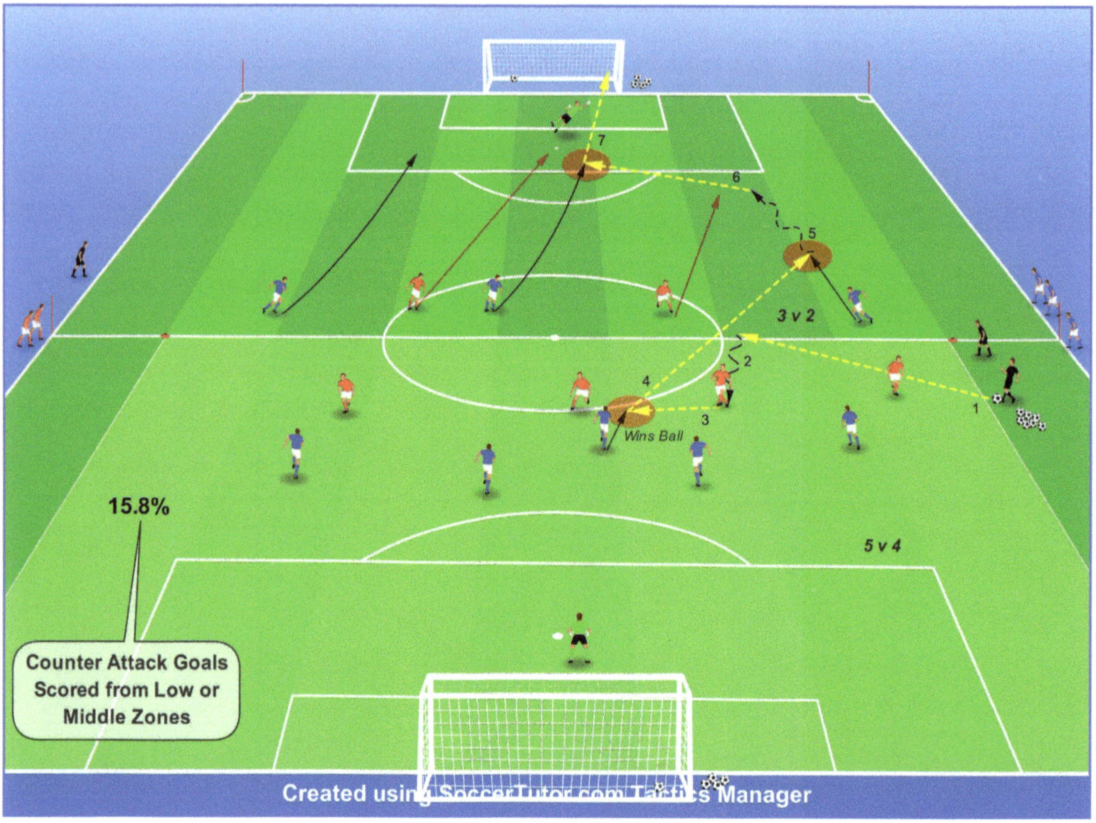

Description

- Mark out an area in one half with reduced width, as shown. The Coach starts the practice, and the reds attack the blues in a 4v5 +GK situation.

- The reds try to score a goal.

- The blue players try to win the ball, and then pass to a teammate in the attacking half (starting a counter attack).

- 3 blue attackers and 2 red defenders (3v2) are waiting near the halfway line for a forward pass to be played.

- Once a blue attacker receives, they try to finish their attack with their 3v2 advantage.

- The 2 red defenders work together to defend their goal.

- After each phase, the 3 blue forwards and the 2 red defenders are changed for the players resting outside.

- The game then restarts with the Coach passing a new ball to the 4 red players again.

Training Session 11A: Counter Attacks from Low or Middle Zone (15.8% of Goals Scored)

PROGRESSION

4. Win the Ball in the Defensive Half and Launch a Counter Attack in a 7 v 7 (+2) +GKs Conditioned Game

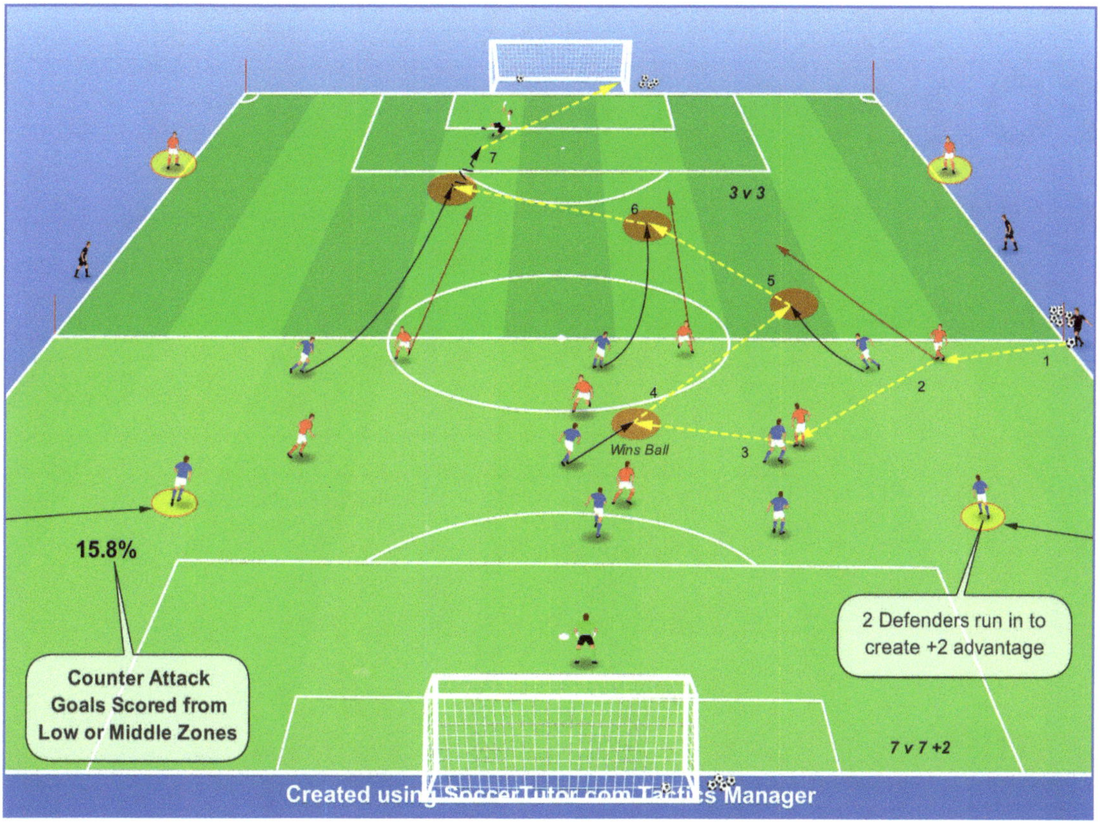

Description

- The pitch is split into 2 halves as shown. The Coach starts the practice, and the reds attack the blues in an initial 7v7 +GK situation. However, 2 blue defenders run in to create a +2 advantage. This means there are more chances for the defending team to win the ball from the attacking team, so there are more counter attacks.

- The reds try to score a goal. The blue players try to win the ball, and then pass to a teammate in the attacking half (starting a counter attack).

- Once a blue attacker receives, they try to score with the help of 2 teammates. 3 red players can also move back to defend, creating a 3v3 counter situation.

- 2 blue defenders must leave the pitch. They can be different to the 2 players who entered, so it's not the same 2 every time.

- All goals in this game (blues or reds) count as 1 goal.

- The game then restarts with the Coach passing a new ball to the red team at the other end with the team roles reversed.

TRAINING SESSION 11B

High Counter
15 Goals

FOR HIGH PRESS + COUNTER (4.9% OF GOALS)

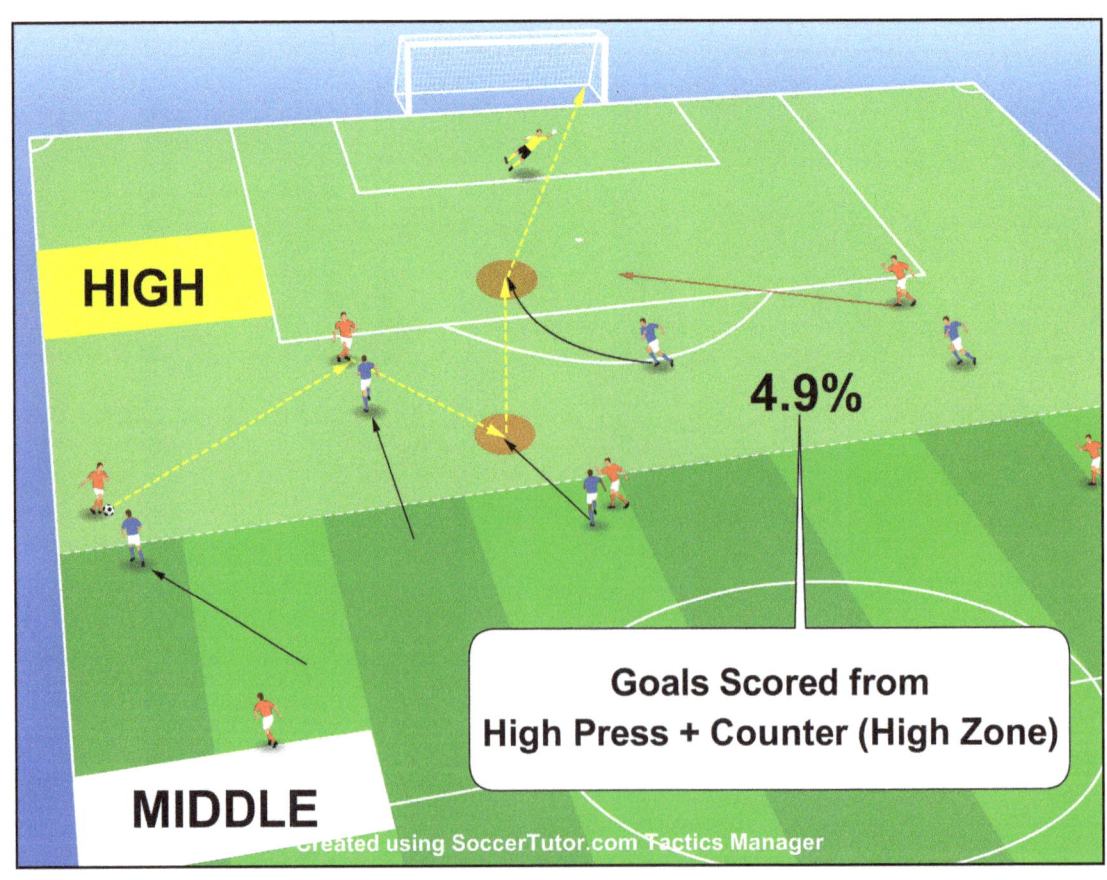

Goals Scored from High Press + Counter (High Zone)

Training Session 11B: **High Press + Counter (4.9% of Goals Scored)**

SESSION FOR THIS TACTICAL SITUATION (4 PRACTICES)

1. 3v1 Pressing High Up the Pitch + Fast Transition to Attack and Score

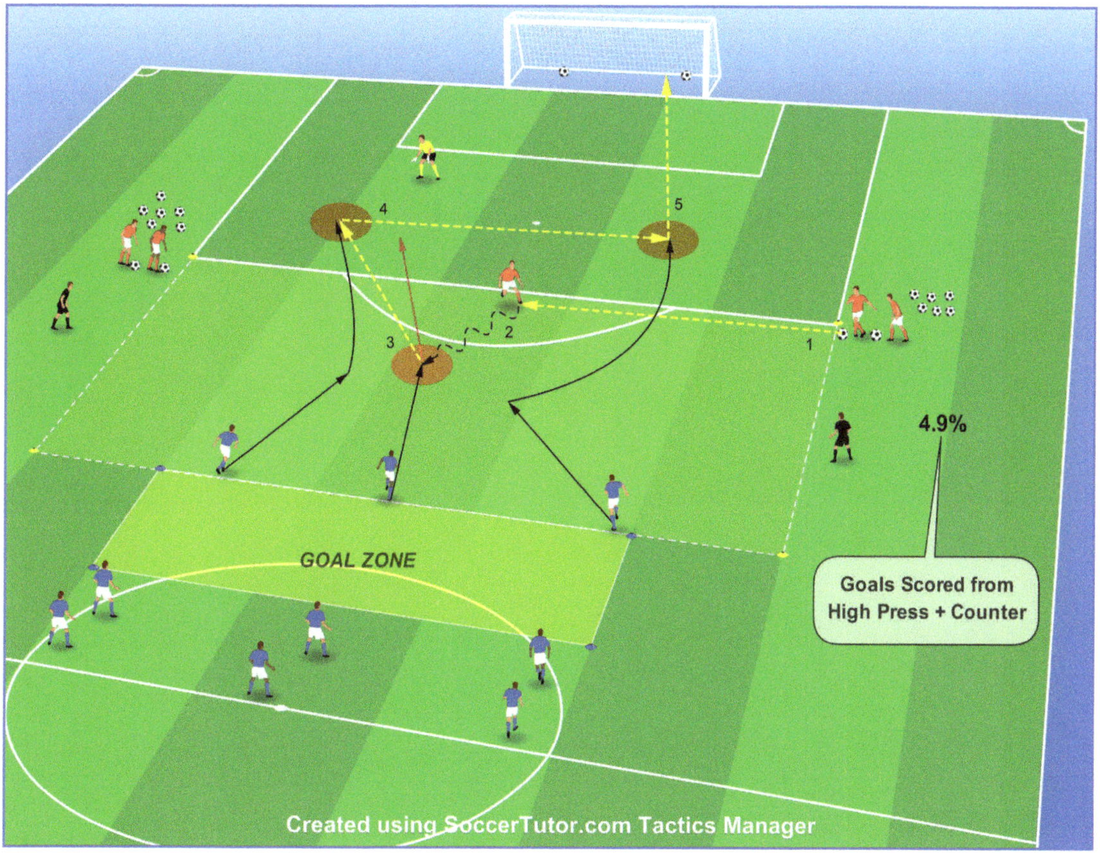

Description

- We mark out a zone the same size as the box + a "Goal Zone" for the red player.
- The practice starts with an outside red player passing to the red player inside the penalty arc. He receives and tries to dribble the ball into the "Goal Zone" to score.
- The 3 blue players move forward together to press the red player and try to win the ball. Once they win the ball, they quickly counter attack to score.
- No offside rule is applied.
- All of the players rotate out and are replaced by the outside resting players.
- The practice restarts with a new ball from the left side.

Training Session 11B: **High Press + Counter (4.9% of Goals Scored)**

PROGRESSION
2. 4v2 Pressing High Up the Pitch + Fast Transition to Attack and Score

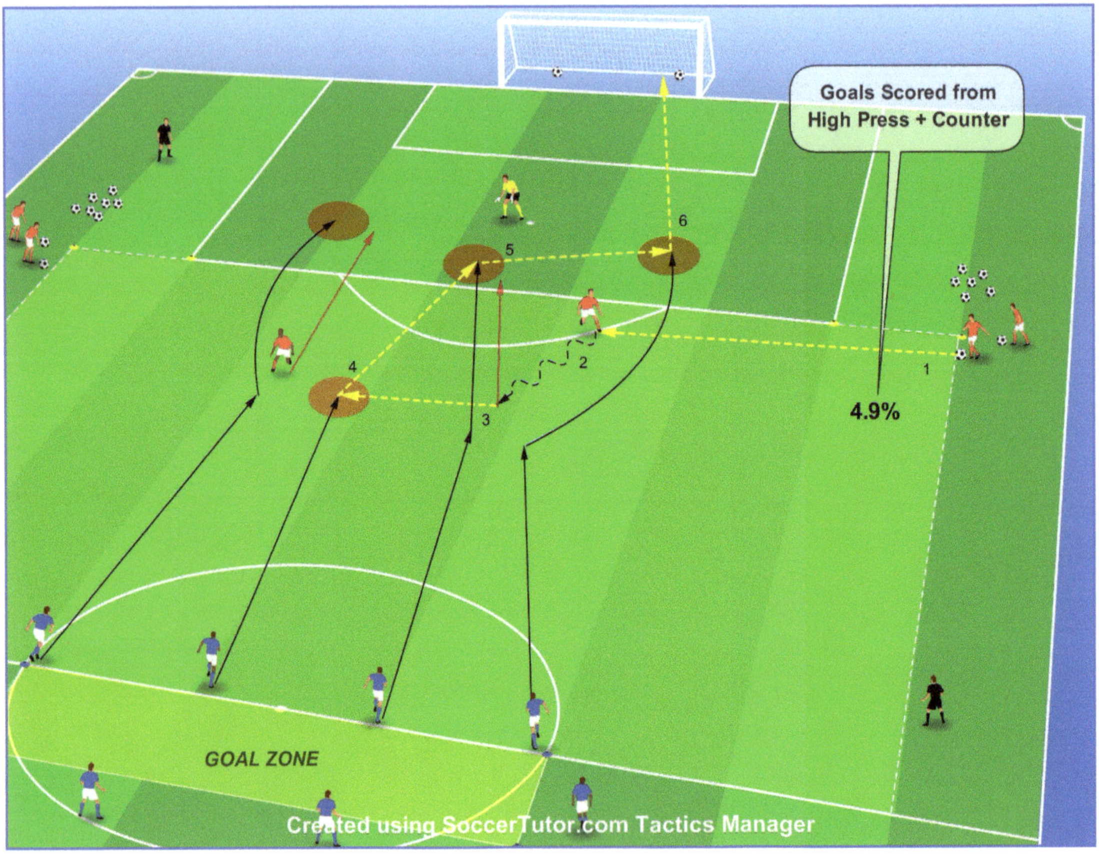

Description

- In this progression of the previous practice, we now mark out a larger playing area and add more players.
- The practice is now 4v2 instead of 3v1.
- The practice starts with an outside red player passing inside to one of the 2 red players.
- A red player receives, and they dribble the ball into the "Goal Zone" or receive a pass inside it to score.
- The 4 blue players move forward together to press the 2 red players and try to win the ball. Once they win the ball, they quickly counter attack to score.
- No offside rule is applied.
- All of the players rotate out and are replaced by the outside resting players.
- The practice restarts with a new ball from the left side.

148

©SOCCERTUTOR.COM COACH YOUR TEAM TO SCORE MORE GOALS

Training Session 11B: **High Press + Counter (4.9% of Goals Scored)**

PROGRESSION

3. 5v5 Pressing High Up the Pitch + Fast Transition to Attack and Score

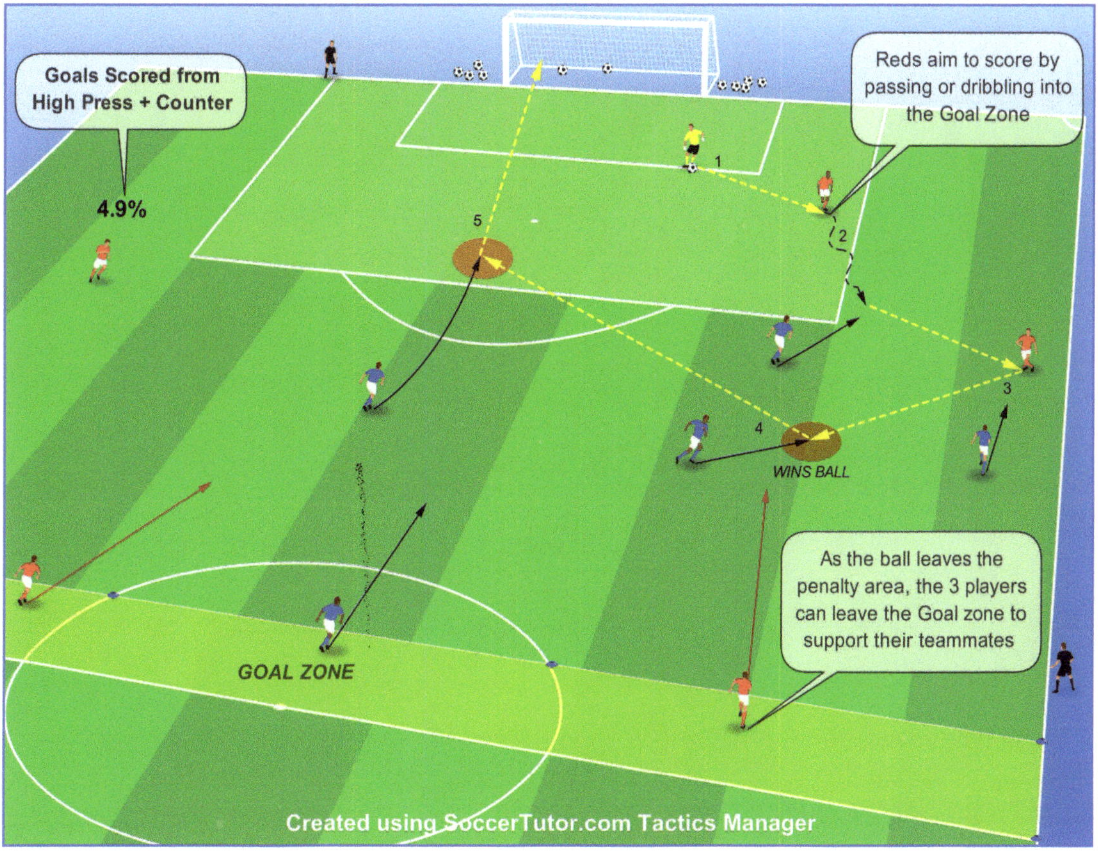

Description

- In this progression of the previous practice, we now play in the full half pitch and add more players. The practice is now 5v5 instead of 4v2.
- The practice starts with a short goal kick to the red player in the box. The reds aim to dribble the ball into the "Goal Zone" or receive a pass inside it to score.
- As soon as the ball leaves the box, the 3 players that start inside the "Goal Zone" can leave to support their teammates.
- The 5 blue players press the reds together and try to win the ball.
- Once they win the ball, they quickly counter attack to score.
- No offside rule is applied.
- The practice always restarts with a new goal kick.
- Change the team roles halfway through and challenge the teams to see who can score the most goals.

Training Session 11B: **High Press + Counter (4.9% of Goals Scored)**

PROGRESSION

4. High Press + Counter in a Dynamic 2-Zone Conditioned Transition Game

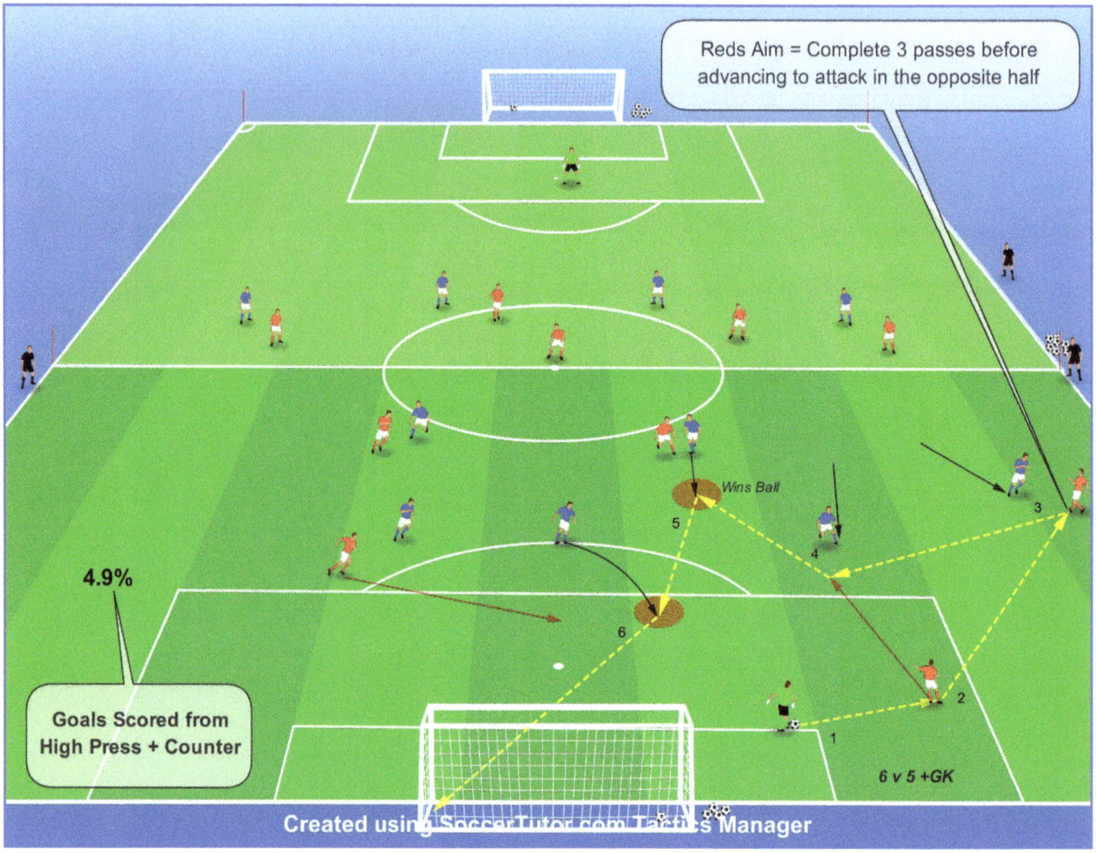

Description

- The game to complete the session starts with a goal kick for the red team. The blue team apply high pressing in a 6v5 (+GK) situation within the half.

- The reds have to complete at least 3 passes before they can play to their teammates in the other half. This rule gives the advantage to the high pressing team. If the reds do play into the other half successfully, it turns into a normal game with the reds trying to score in the goal at the other end.

- The blues try to win the ball within the low half and then score quickly on the counter attack, as shown in the diagram example.

- The practice always restarts with a new goal kick with the team roles reversed (blues building up vs high pressing reds).

COMBINED SESSION

Using the Data to Create Training Sessions for Goal Scoring Efficiency

Using the Data to Create Training Sessions for Goal Scoring Efficiency

USING THE DATA TO CREATE TRAINING SESSIONS FOR GOAL SCORING EFFICIENCY

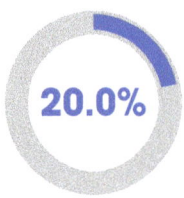

Type of Assist = Cut Backs
61 GOALS

Assist = Side of Box
56 GOALS

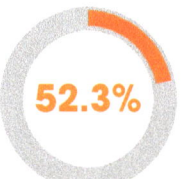

Goal = Front Centre of Box
159 GOALS

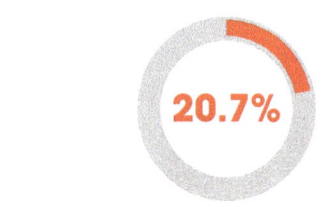

Tactic = Counter Attacks
63 GOALS

The above statistics have been taken from our data analysis and show the leading percentage winners for the 4 main topics covered in this book:

1. **Type of Assist**
2. **Pitch Zone of Assist**
3. **Pitch Zone Goal Was Scored**
4. **Tactical Aspect**

On the following pages, we have incorporated all of these factors to create a session that makes creating chances and scoring goals as efficient as possible. One practice from each of these 4 topics has been used to create the session.

This works as an example to show you how you can create data-driven sessions yourself.

NOTE: Build-up Play/Attacks was technically the highest percentage for "Tactical Aspect" but includes many sub-categories within it: Play Through Lines, Switch of Play, Attack Wide/Crossing, Attack Through Centre, and Long Pass.

Using the Data to Create Training Sessions for Goal Scoring Efficiency

COMBINED TRAINING SESSION (4 PRACTICES)

1. Pass to Winger Out Wide for 1v1 and Cut Back for Oncoming Runners to Score

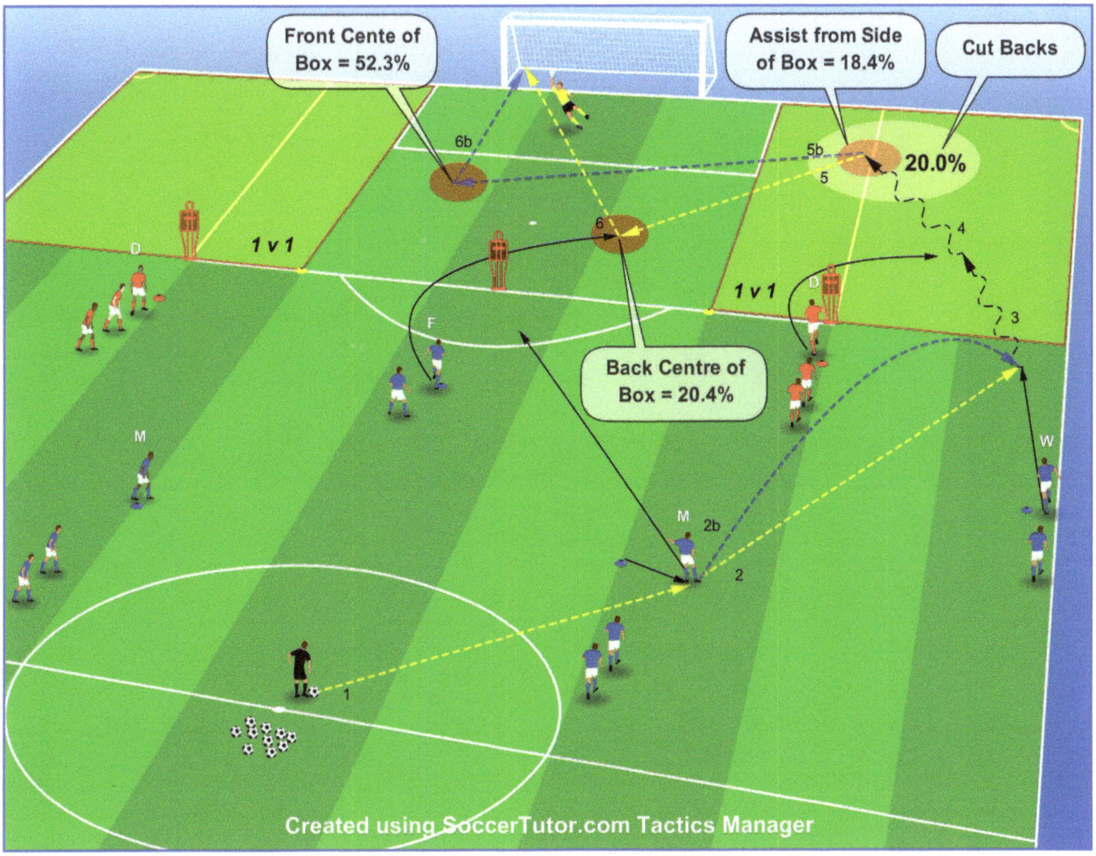

Description

- The Coach starts the practice with a pass to the blue midfielder **(M)**, who then passes out wide and in front of the winger **(W)** so they can run onto the ball.

- The red defender **(D)** runs around the mannequin and takes up a defensive position within the corner area.

- The winger **(W)** moves forward with the ball into the corner area and starts a 1v1 action.

- The winger's **(W)** aim is to beat the defender and then play a cut back pass for either the forward **(F)** or the midfielder **(M)**, who make runs to the near and far post areas respectively to score.

- After finishing the phase, the 3 participating players return to their starting positions. Alternatively, they can rotate positions.

- When the phase ends, the practice continues with the next players waiting on the other side.

153

©SOCCERTUTOR.COM — COACH YOUR TEAM TO SCORE MORE GOALS

Using the Data to Create Training Sessions for Goal Scoring Efficiency

2. Wide Combination, Wing Play into Side of Box, and Cut Back for Finish in a 2v2 Situation

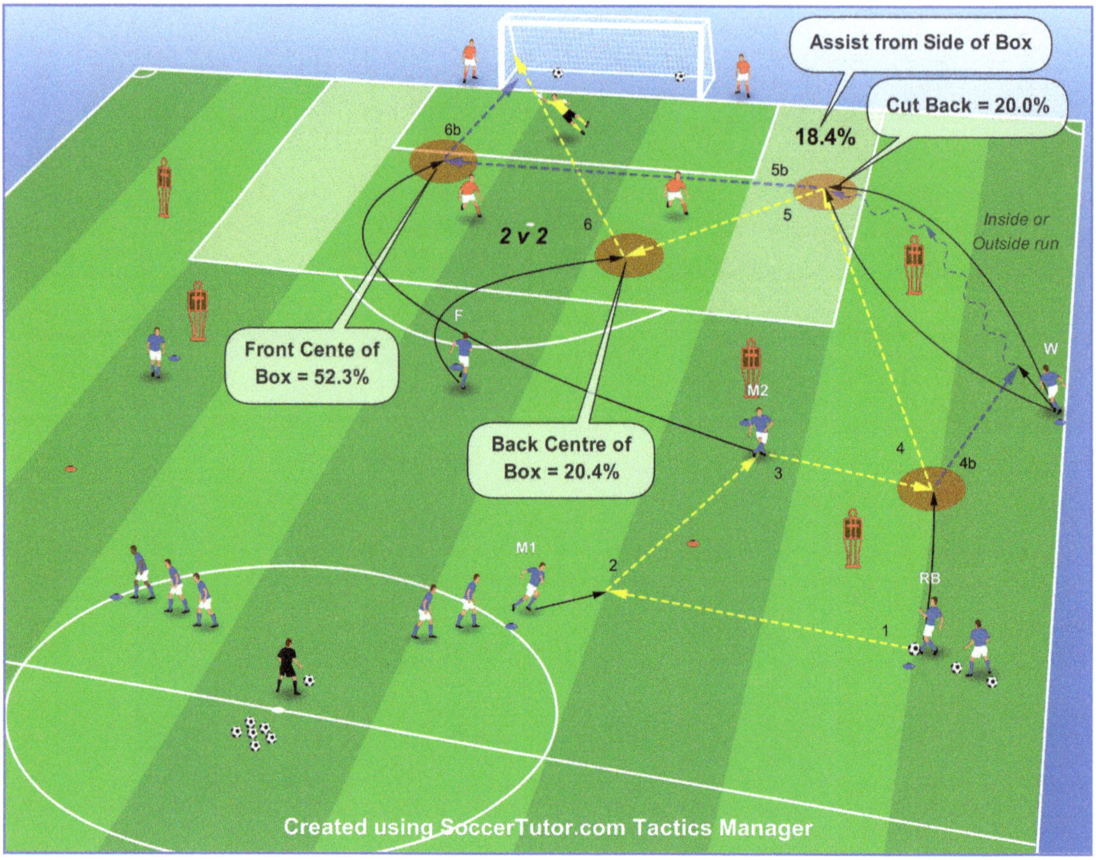

Description

- There are 5 blue players involved in the combination **(RB, M1, M2, W & F)** and 2 red defenders in the box, as shown.

- The right back **(RB)** passes inside to the first midfielder **(M1)**, who passes forward to the second midfielder **(M2)**. He passes wide for the forward run of the right back **(RB)** to receive.

- The right back either plays a through pass for the winger's **(W)** run in behind or plays a short pass to the winger **(W)** who then dribbles past the mannequin and into the side of the box.

- When inside the side of the box area, the winger **(W)** looks up to find a teammate **(M2 or forward F)** with a cut back **(5)** or a low cross across the box **(5b)**. The 2 red defenders try to block or intercept.

- After the phase is finished, the same sequence is repeated from the left side and 2 new red defenders rotate in.

- The players all rotate positional roles throughout the practice.

Using the Data to Create Training Sessions for Goal Scoring Efficiency

3. Score in the Front Centre of the Box in a Multi-Zone 4v4 (+3) +GKs SSG with Wide Crossing Zones

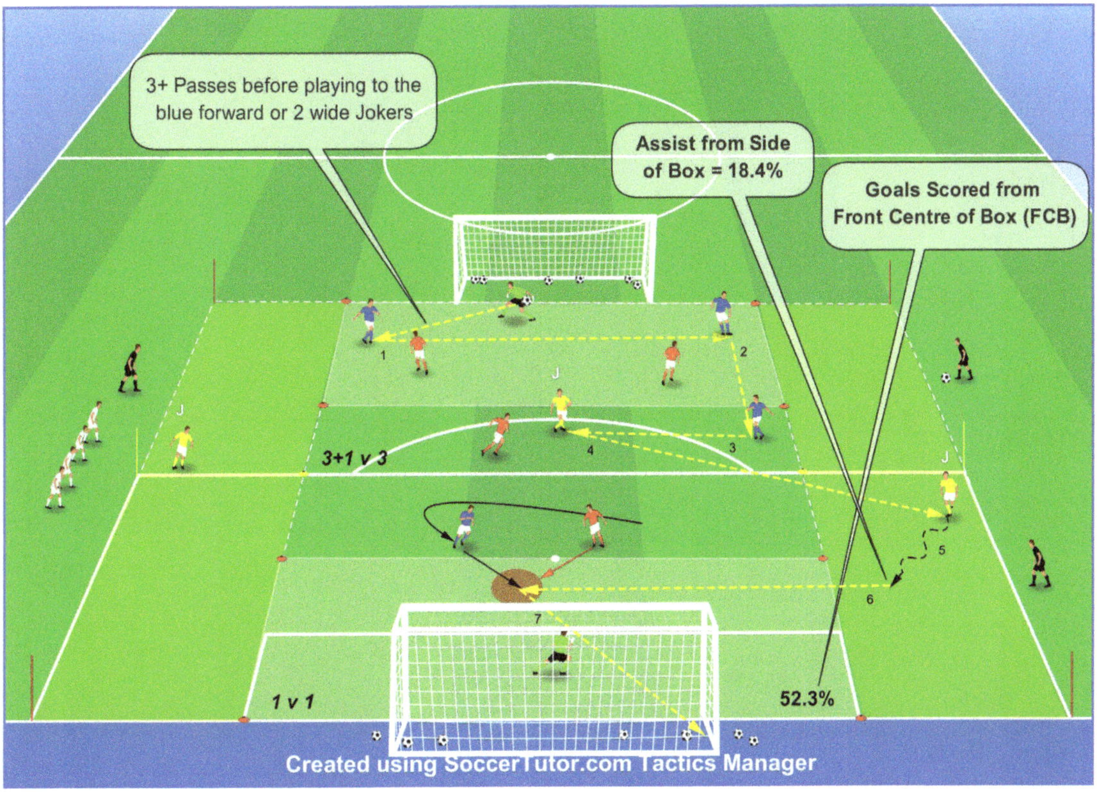

Description

- The GK starts the practice with a 3 (+1) v 3 situation played only within the central part of the defensive half. The blues must complete 3 passes before passing to the blue forward or a wide Joker.

- If the reds win the ball, they then have to complete 3 passes before passing forward and trying to score.

- The 2 wide Jokers play only within the wide crossing zones and no blue or red players are allowed to enter these zones.

- The aim is to feed the blue forward who has a 1v1 situation against the red defender within the front centre of the box, trying to score a goal. They start outside as shown and move into the front centre of the box to attack/defend the crosses.

- When the forward receives from a wide player, he tries to score. However, if he is unable to find a good opportunity to shoot, he can pass back out to a wide player and the practice continues.

- There is a third team outside (whites) resting because the teams rotate. Each game is 3-5 minutes. The team that scores the most goals after a set number of games wins.

Using the Data to Create Training Sessions for Goal Scoring Efficiency

4. Win the Ball in the Defensive Half and Launch a Counter Attack in a 2-Zone 8v6 +GKs Transition Game

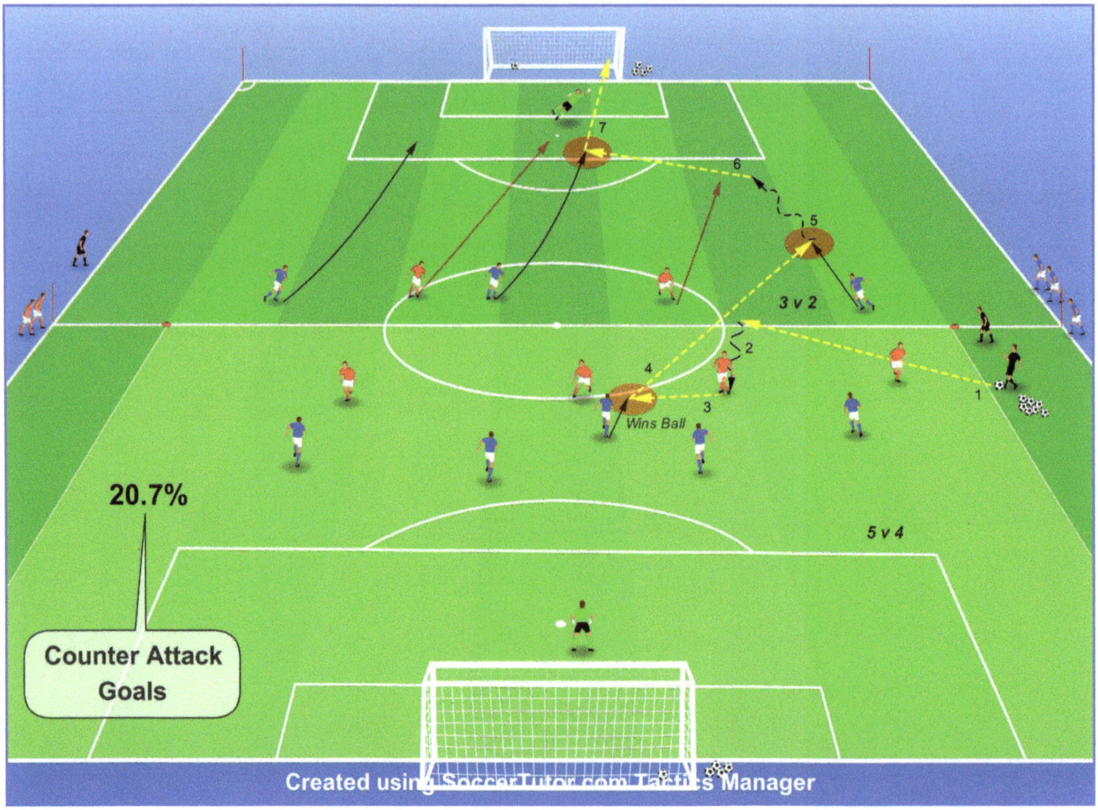

Description

- Mark out an area in one half with reduced width, as shown. The Coach starts the practice, and the reds attack the blues in a 4v5 +GK situation.
- The reds try to score a goal.
- The blue players try to win the ball, and then pass to a teammate in the attacking half (starting a counter attack).
- 3 blue attackers and 2 red defenders (3v2) are waiting near the halfway line for a forward pass to be played.
- Once a blue attacker receives, they try to finish their attack with their 3v2 advantage.
- The 2 red defenders work together to defend their goal.
- After each phase, the 3 blue forwards and the 2 red defenders are changed for the players resting outside.
- The game then restarts with the Coach passing a new ball to the 4 red players again.

Free Trial

Football Coaching Specialists Since 2001

Tactics Manager
Create your own Practices, Tactics & Plan Sessions!

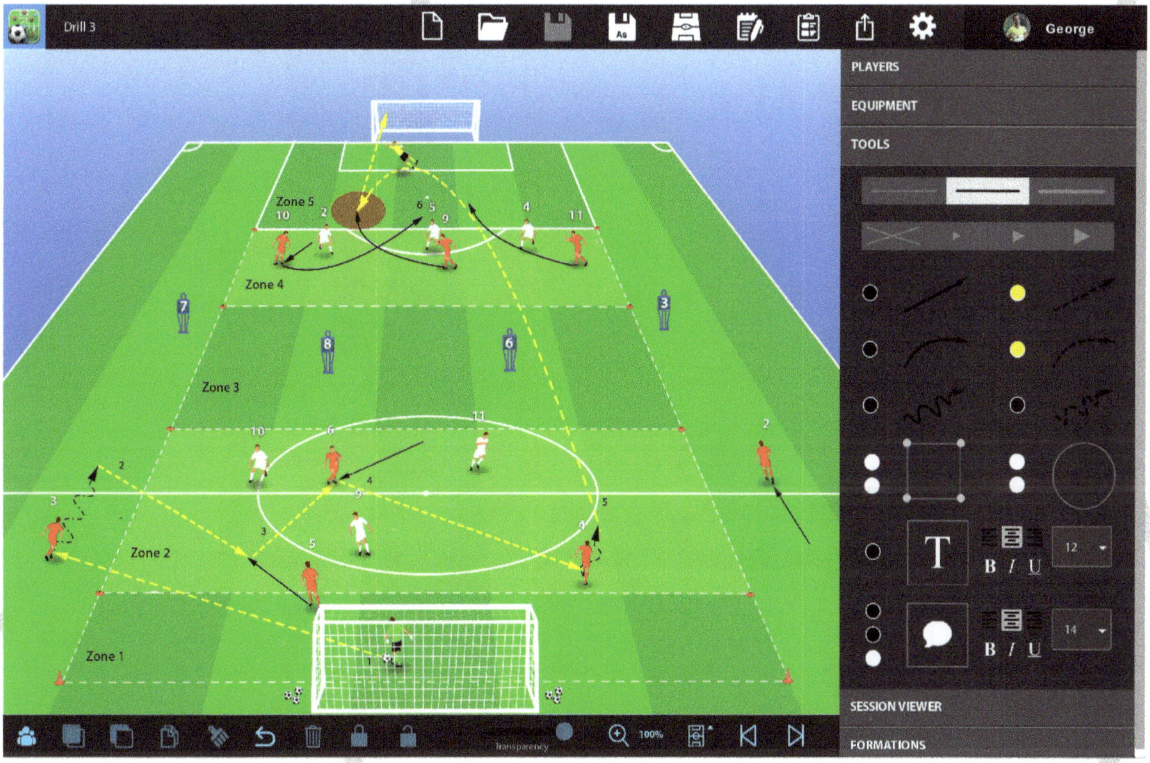

Tactics Manager App

SoccerTutor.com

Football Coaching Specialists Since 2001

Coaching Books Available in Full Colour Print and eBook!
PC | Mac | iPhone | iPad | Android Phone / Tablet | Chromebook

FREE Coach Viewer **APP**

SoccerTutor.com

Football Coaching Specialists Since 2001

Jürgen Klopp
102 Passing, Counter-pressing Possession Games, Speed & Warm-ups Direct from Klopp's Training Sessions

Vol. 1

Jürgen Klopp
80 Attacking Combinations, Finishing, Positional Patterns of Play, Transition & SSGs Direct from Klopp's Training Sessions

Vol. 2

Coaching Books Available in Full Colour Print and eBook!
PC | Mac | iPhone | iPad | Android Phone / Tablet | Chromebook

 **FREE** Coach Viewer **APP**

SoccerTutor.com

www.ingramcontent.com/pod-product-compliance
Lightning Source LLC
Chambersburg PA
CBHW061209230426

43665CB00028B/2958